BERT HARDY: My Life

BERT HARDY: My Life

1944: A

1939: B

1944: C

1941: D

BERT HARDY : My Life

1943: E

1950: F

1946: I

1942: H

1942: G

GORDON FRASER · London

List of illustrations preceding the text

First published in 1985 by
The Gordon Fraser Gallery Ltd, London and Bedford
Copyright © Bert Hardy 1985

1950: J

1951: K

All rights reserved. No part of this publication may be
reproduced or transmitted in any form or by any means
electronic or mechanical, including photocopying, recording or
any information storage and retrieval system, without permission
in writing from the publishers.

BRITISH LIBRARY CATALOGUING IN PUBLICATION DATA
Hardy, Bert
    Bert Hardy: my life
    1. Hardy, Bert   2. Photographers – England – Biography
    I. Title
    770'.92'4   TR140.H2/

    ISBN 0–86092–083–6
    ISBN 0–86092–086–0 Pbk

Type set in Monophoto Apollo by
August Filmsetting, Haydock, St Helens
Illustrations originated by
Westerham Press, Westerham, Kent
Printed by Fletcher and Son, Norwich
Designed by Peter Guy

Contents

1944: L

1950: M

1951: N

A nice young lady called Sheila who worked for *Picture Post* wasn't impressed by the big photographer. Later on she developed a great liking for this picture of the Hercules bicycle factory, and for the photographer.

To Sheila

Acknowledgements

1950: O

1950: P

I would like to give my special thanks to
Charlie Keeble for doing such a first-class job
on my prints, and also to John Parfitt for his fine repro
work on the book. 'Uncle' Simon Kingston was involved
at all stages: without his humour and his help the book
would have suffered (though my wine cellar would be
fuller).

Copyright photographs from *Picture Post* are
reproduced by courtesy of the BBC Hulton Picture
Library, and my thanks go to David Lee and his staff.
Picture Post text and covers are by courtesy of
Syndication International and IPC Magazines Ltd.

I would like to thank the Arts Council of Great Britain
for the subsidy which assisted the publication of this
book.

My Life

1952: Q

1942: R

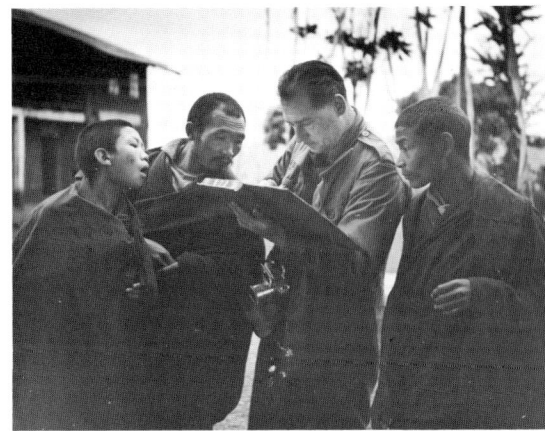

1951: S

1: Childhood

My mum with myself
at a few months old.

My mum used to give birth more or less every other year. I was born on 19 May 1913, the first of seven children: Alice (Lally), Sid, Lily, Charlie, Harry (who was known as Ginger), and the baby of the family Dolly, who was born when I was seventeen.

Up until the time I was eight, we lived in just one room with a scullery on the top floor of the Priory Buildings, near Blackfriars in London. There were four floors altogether, with two flats on each floor and a gas-lit stone staircase running up the centre of each of the Priory Buildings' two halves. Behind the Buildings was a yard where they used to smoke haddocks. I loved to see the haddocks strung from long poles after they had been smoked.

My earliest memory, though, is of lying in my cot, high up in the Buildings. I must have been two or three at the time – I still didn't have any brothers or sisters – and my mum and dad had gone out to the pub for the evening. I was lying with my head back, looking up out of the window behind me at the moon with clouds racing past it. I could see a face in the moon, and I was lying in my cot making faces at it, when all of a sudden *it* pulled a face back at *me*. I was terrified. I threw the covers over my head and waited in fear for my parents to come home. I never pulled faces at the moon again.

When there were more of us, we all used to sleep in one big double bed, arranged like sardines, with some at the top and some at the bottom, our feet meeting in the middle. The bed was also the only place to play in the day-time; but our games were as real as we could make them: once when Sid, Lally and I were playing cowboys and Indians, Sid seized the axe we used for chopping wood (to fuel the little stove in the

Above left: My dad (wearing the cap) standing in his workshop. I took this when I was sixteen, on a cheap plate camera. Little did I know then that photography would become my career.

Above right: The Priory Buildings. Our first flat, a single room and scullery, is at the third window from the right on the top floor. The street used to be called Friar Street.

Right: I'm on the right, with my older cousin.

fireplace), and split my head open in an attempt to scalp me, which luckily proved only partly successful. Cowboys don't always win.

When we moved for the first time, we migrated as far as the other half of the Buildings, to a flat with two rooms and a scullery on the first floor.

The new flat was directly above my Uncle Fred and Aunt Maud, and Jack's, the Italian Barber Shop. We were never very well off. I was named Albert after my dad, but everyone used to call him 'Seagull'. It was a nickname he earned one Friday night.

He was a good old boozer, my dad, and especially so on Fridays. He worked all his life for a surgical goods company off Fenchurch Street, as a carpenter making splints, stretcher handles, and crutches. Although he never earned very much he was lucky to have that job, because when the First World War came along, it was classified as emergency war work, and he wasn't called up. He always got paid on a Friday, and naturally his first thought was to celebrate. My mum's main worry each week was how much money would be left out of his wages when he got back.

It was after midnight one Friday, and my mum was waiting anxiously for him to return. Meanwhile my father, having spent the evening in the pub with his mates, was staggering back across Blackfriars Bridge (which he always called

'Seagull' Hardy in his local pub, *The Crown* in Blackfriars Road.

'the Bender'), wondering how to explain where his money had gone, when he had an idea.

When he got home, my mum called him a few horrible names. Then she asked him where her money was. Looking almost pleased with himself, my dad said: 'It's all right m'dear. You know how careful I am with your money. Well, just as I was coming back across the Bender, I thought I'd better check my wage packet to make sure I hadn't lost it. But as soon as I got it out of my inside pocket, a bloody great seagull comes swooping down and swipes it out of my hand.'

Nobody believed him, of course, but the nickname stuck with him to the end of his life.

My mum, Blanche, was a very hard-working woman. She had to be with seven kids to bring up. She often had to go out to work to make ends meet. At one time, she used to work in the evenings as a charlady at a big private house near the Tottenham Court Road. As the eldest child, I had to look after my brothers and sisters while she was away. At about 8.30 we would go and wait for her by the bus stop at the Obelisk (now St George's Circus) – a line of us, with the youngest in a push-chair. It was very miserable and it always seemed to be raining. At last a number 1 Tilling Stevens bus (a strange bus which was partly electric and partly petrol-driven) would arrive, and my mum would get off and we would rush up to her, happy once more. Sometimes, if she

could afford it, she would buy us a penn'orth of sweets between us as we walked home.

Her dad was an ex-drayman, whose wife had left him. She lived in a smart little house at Crystal Palace, but he lived in poverty, not far from us, and I used to take him money from my parents to help him get by.

My father's parents also lived close by, at Smyrks Road, off the Old Kent Road. I was given a penny every Saturday to take a number 36 tram over there and fetch their shopping for them, but I preferred to walk and keep the penny; if I did catch the tram, I sat on the semi-circular wooden bench at the front on top and stared intently out of the window whenever the conductor came round for the fares.

This grandfather was a master painter, of doors, not canvases, who could use a comb to produce wood-graining and other effects. An uncle of mine (who because of a deformity was unable to go out to work) lived in the house and did boot repairs or 'snobbing' in a wooden hut in the back yard. They also had a lodger called Frank, a tall thin man who worked in the railway goods yard in the Old Kent Road. Being a bachelor, he was better off than many people, and was the proud possessor of a magnificent radio receiving set: a clutter of bits and pieces, not in a cabinet. It was the first radio I ever heard, and I was sometimes allowed to listen as he tuned in to different stations around the world.

My mum,
Blanche.

On these Saturdays I spent the whole morning doing the shopping, buying everything from a loaf of bread to a penny packet of hay for the rabbits. They gave me my lunch, and afterwards my uncle would come in from his shed, and we all sat round for the ritual reading of the newspaper. I couldn't read yet, and I don't think my grandmother could read either. My grandfather would get out an old cracked magnifying glass and read aloud all the murders and gory stories while we listened, spellbound. In the end, though, my mum said I was always to come home before they started reading the paper, because I started having nightmares about murder, and woke up screaming in the night.

On another visit to Smyrks Road, I saw a bucket in the scullery with a heavy stone resting on top of it. Something about the stone intrigued me. Why was it there? How I ever lifted it off, I don't know; it was huge. Underneath, lying in water, was a litter of kittens which had been put in there to drown. I got a whack round the ear'ole when they found out that I'd had a look.

Because the family was so hard up most of the time, I started doing little jobs for money very early on. On Saturday mornings I helped my Uncle Fred on his greengrocer's horse-and-cart. We set out at about seven o'clock in the morning, and it took us about an hour to get to the Herne Hill and Crystal Palace area where he worked that day. I used to go to the door of each house and take the order, then run back to the cart where my uncle would weigh it out. Then I carried the order to the door, and collected the money.

I was paid sixpence for a full day's work. Usually we dropped in on my mum's mother in her smart little house at Crystal Palace. She had a curtain of glass beads over her front door which sparkled different colours in the sun, and tinkled in the wind.

One day while we were going round from house to house, I suddenly had a desperate urge to go to the lavatory. 'Just a few more houses', Fred said every time I told him. 'Wait until we get to your grandma's, then you can go.'

We went to a few more houses, then a few more, but we never seemed any nearer the glass bead curtain; never closer to grandma's. At last I couldn't wait any longer: I did it in my trousers. I struggled on bravely of course: what else could I do? But I can still remember the total humiliation I felt when, as I approached two ladies who were chatting by their front door, one of them wrinkled up her nose to the other and said: 'What's that terrible smell?'

I was allowed to keep a penny or two out of the sixpence I earned, and I used the money to buy sweets. I loved sweets, but I had to learn to ration myself to make them last, so I hid them in a drawer in our flat at Priory Buildings and took them out one at a time. My mother found out where I kept them, and pinched them to give to my sister; or perhaps my sister took them herself: in any case they slowly disappeared. It was a terrible job to keep anything for yourself, because we were all so much on top of each other. In the Priory Buildings, property changed hands more often than

its owners intended. Even the best Christmas present I ever had was pinched.

One Christmas Eve I went out shopping with my mum and my Aunt Maud at the street market called the Cut, at the back of Waterloo Station, quite near where I lived. The place was very crowded, with everybody pushing and shoving and buying things. And there was a toyshop which was open at the front like a bazaar, with toys hanging up and people clustering round. Among all the bustle and confusion, my Aunt Maud pushed her way to the front, pulled out a scooter, and passed it to me without the shopkeeper noticing.

It was a marvellous scooter, the most terrific scooter you can imagine, with spoked wheels, rubber tyres, and a little seat for somebody to sit on just in front of you as you scooted along. As soon as I got it, I jumped on and scooted like mad all the way back to the Buildings, about two or three minutes away, rushed upstairs with it, and hid it under the bed.

Aunt Maud was married to my Uncle Fred, the one with the greengrocer's cart. They had two children, both from previous marriages: Dollie from Aunt Maud's first marriage, and Fred from Uncle Fred's first marriage. Fred was a ginger-haired kid of about my age, and something told me that Aunt Maud hadn't pinched the scooter for me, but for her Fred.

When I heard her and my mum coming back up the stairs, I stationed myself in front of the cupboard as if the scooter was in it. My Aunt Maud came straight in and said 'I want that scooter. Where's that scooter?' and tried to pull me away from the cupboard. I resisted with all my strength. Eventually she gave up: I was allowed to keep the scooter as a Christmas present, and so could retrieve it from its safe place under the bed. In the end, as I suppose was inevitable, somebody pinched it from me.

I was always on the look-out for odd bits of work. Once I sold ice creams with a man who had filled a home-made barrow with home-made ice cream, operating from the now disused haddock-smoking yard at the back of the Buildings. Despite working really hard all day, we didn't manage to sell all the ice cream, but the result wasn't too bad: we had quite a job trying to eat up everything that was left over when we finally got back. I ended up very tired and very full, but happy.

In fact I was always tired at this time because I was paid sixpence a week for lighting the gas lights on the landings of Priory Buildings each evening, and turning them off again last thing at night. The procedure for lighting them was to unlock the cupboard just inside the front entrance of the Buildings, turn on the gas, and then rush up the four flights of steps with a lighted taper as quickly as possible, because the gas was running all the time. I enjoyed this, because I was fit and fast, but I was not allowed to turn them off before midnight, so I had to try to sit up and keep awake until then every night.

One evening I found a large sack of chestnuts behind the door by the gas cupboard. I showed them excitedly to a friend but he said that they were horse chestnuts. I had hoped they were ordinary chestnuts, which I could sell, but not to be put off, I took them along to a greengrocer I knew who had a horse and cart. 'What are they?' he asked. 'They're horse chestnuts', I said, 'and if they're *horse* chestnuts they must be all right for horses.' Whereupon he gave me sixpence for the sack and fed them to his horse, which survived, as far as I know.

All the kids in the district used to make a bit of money every year on Derby Day, when all the coaches and chara-bancs passed through the Elephant and Castle on their way back from Epsom. There were no traffic lights then: just a policeman holding up the traffic and directing it, and great queues formed. There were dozens and dozens of coaches, and as they went creeping slowly past, we used to stand by the road and shout 'Throw out your mouldies', which meant throw out your odd coppers. And if they'd had a decent day, race-goers threw their small change out of the windows, and we'd dive in amongst the traffic, fighting each other to pick up coins.

When I was about eight or nine, I worked for a short time at Price's the greengrocer's shop, nearby in Lancaster Street. One of my jobs was to take the potatoes out of their sacks behind the shop and shake them in a sieve to get the mud off; then carrying the sieve on my head – I wore a cap with a handkerchief underneath to keep the wire of the sieve from sticking into me – I would bring it into the shop and empty the potatoes into a bin. Through handling potatoes so much, I began to get a lot of large warts on my hands. I didn't know what to do about them, but when I showed them to my teacher, she said that I should go along to St Thomas's Hospital, not far away, and have them seen to.

So I went to St Thomas's, where a doctor saw me, and gave me a card with the time of an appointment for the following week. I suppose I still could not read very well, because when I went back to the hospital the following week, I had to show the card to the porter to find out where to go, and he told me to go and sit on a bench in the waiting room.

It was a very long wooden bench that could seat at least twenty people side by side, and I went up and sat down right next to an old man. He looked at me curiously, a little dirty boy, and asked:

'What you here for?'

'I dunno', I said. 'I've got these warts.'

'Show us your card', he said. So I showed him my card.

'Oh, you're going to such-and-such Theatre', he said.

'Am I?' I said, astounded. 'What am I going to see?'

He explained that I was not going to a theatre with actors and actresses, but to an operating theatre. I was not much the wiser, and asked him what that meant. He explained again:

'It means they're going to cut your warts off.'

The penny dropped. I suddenly had visions of surgeons with big knives doing terrible things to me. 'They're bloody well not!' I said. And I scarpered.

A week or two later, I was walking through the market in the Cut one Sunday morning, when I passed a stall covered with little tiny boxes, with a man shouting 'Cure all your corns, bunions and warts! Buy my special ointment!' So I bought a box for sixpence, and used it as instructed, and my warts disappeared.

Soon afterwards I stopped working for Price's and started working for Hammond's. Hammond's was a grocery shop just across the road from Priory Buildings. I was paid 7s 6d a week. From Mondays to Fridays I worked from seven-thirty in the morning until nine o'clock, when I had to go to school. The shop was on a corner with a door at the corner and windows on either side. Each of the windows had four heavy wooden shutters, and my first job each day was to unscrew the metal bar that held them in place, lift the shutters down, and carry them through to the back yard. I used to carry two each trip to save time.

At nine o'clock I used to go to school like any other child, until lunchtime. Then I went back to Hammond's to help out with the lunchtime rush. Lots of people who worked in the neighbourhood came into the shop to buy ham, bread and biscuits for their lunch, and Mr Hammond, who for no clear reason was also known as Mr Black (we never knew what to call him), would be behind the counter slicing ham and serving customers. If I had time, I went home across the road for ten minutes and had my own lunch. Then it was back to school until 4.30, when I went home, had my dinner, and then went back to Hammond's from 5.30 until towards midnight.

The shop only closed when there were no more customers, and there were always more customers – people coming home late from work and so on. Usually we closed at about ten o'clock. Then we had a variety of other jobs to do: cleaning up; weighing out sugar and putting it in bags; and unpacking eggs.

Eggs came in great flat crates about eight feet long and three feet wide, but only three or four inches deep. Inside the eggs were packed in straw. We used to break open the cases and take out the eggs and inspect them. To make sure they weren't bad, we used to have to hold them up individually against a lighted candle and check that the light passed through them. Then they were sorted into different compartments by size.

Saturdays were very busy: I started at eight in the morning, and finished at twelve at night; but on Sundays we had a half day, starting at nine and finishing at about three o'clock.

I was working in all about sixty hours each week on top of my school work, which naturally began to suffer. I was always a bit behind with my reading – to this day I find it difficult to say the alphabet through from start to finish; my arithmetic wasn't too bad – it couldn't be – all cockneys are good at adding up money; and I still haven't a clue about history. But I always felt an interest in art, and a strong desire to draw. I wanted to express myself.

When I was very young, our teacher told us that all the wonderful patterns on cups and china were made by painting on the colours and then firing them in a special kind of oven. The fact that the colours had to be of a special kind, and so did the oven, passed me by. I went straight home – my mum and dad must have been out – and got out my paint box and painted up all our plain old cups and saucers, and put them in the little oven in the fireplace. I probably got a clip round the ear.

I was always quite good at making things. When we lived in the other part of Priory Buildings, we were over Jack's barber shop. My brothers and I used to go and have our hair cut there. Even though it was so close, we still had to sit around waiting for ages, listening to people talking about racing.

Then Jack got himself a radio. It was the very early days of radio, and he had one that really boomed out. When the shop shut at night, he and his family used to listen to dance music, and I used to lie on my bed upstairs enjoying the music too as it came through the floor.

My dad hated it: he used to come stumbling home late at night and curse those bastards downstairs with their bloody noise. But I really liked it.

At last I decided that we ought to have a radio. I had already built a cat's whisker set, but now I got a kit. There were valves and bits and pieces and a little chart to help you put it together. I made it up and bought a wooden cabinet to put it in, and to my joy, when I connected it to the batteries, it worked.

At school, my greatest sense of achievement came when class six went for a country walk and collected wild flowers and leaves and bits of plants. We were all given a large piece of card, and we had to dry out what we had collected, stick it on the card, and label it. I really enjoyed doing it, and felt pretty pleased with myself when I got top prize for it.

I suppose the teachers did their best under difficult circumstances, although sometimes they could behave strangely themselves. In classes 2, 3 and 4, we were taught by Miss Cook and Miss Phillips. One day at the end of classes, Miss Cook announced that she wanted all of us boys to stand up and turn our backs to her, because she wanted to pull up her stockings. If anyone dared to turn round, she would beat them and keep them in after school.

Johnny Sweet was a bit of a lad, and Johnny Sweet dared to turn round. It was almost as if she wanted somebody to turn round so she could beat them and keep them in after school. I managed to resist the temptation.

Our other lady teacher, Miss Phillips, was an older woman who took a liking to me. I made her a wooden case for her pencils, and in return she bought a penknife which she said was mine. But I was never allowed to have that penknife: she kept it for sharpening pencils, and whenever she sharpened a pencil, she would say that she was using my penknife to sharpen it.

In the higher classes, 5, 6 and 7, we had men teachers. I didn't get as far as class seven because I was so behind with the work. One of these teachers took us on a so-called educa-

My youngest sister, Dolly: I have used the window to provide natural side-lighting.

tional trip to Trafalgar Square, where I took my very first photograph.

We were wandering round looking at Nelson's column and the famous lions, when the teacher was suddenly seized by the desire to go somewhere. Obviously he must have thought I was the most trustworthy boy, because he gave me his Box Brownie to hold while he went off; although he perhaps had his doubts, because he took the precaution of jamming a piece of cardboard underneath the lever so that I couldn't accidentally release the shutter.

As soon as the teacher was out of sight, one of my mates dared me to take a picture of him in front of the fountains. That was enough for me: I pulled the cardboard out, got my mate in the viewfinder, and clicked the shutter. When the teacher came back, I handed him back his camera apologetically: 'Sorry Sir', I said, 'but the bit of cardboard fell out and the shutter accidentally clicked.'

I have never seen the results of this, my first photographic effort.

Apart from day trips, we used to have a proper holiday once a year. Our parents used to pay in so much each week, and we were all packed off to the country, to stay on a farm if

The usual means of travel in my early days. As we grew older, we progressed to faster things like lorries.

we were lucky, but more usually to stay in an ordinary house, for which the lady of the house would get about ten shillings a week. I went to Westbury-on-Severn several times: sometimes with my brother Sid, and once with another boy whose name I can't remember.

On that holiday I was sent with this other boy each morning to fetch the milk from a farmhouse just down the road. We took a jug for the milk and some money to pay for it, and the farmer's wife used to take our money and give us our change, then go and fill our jug for us.

The boy I was with noticed how she kept the change in a jar on the dresser. I was against it, but he thought it was an easy touch. Next day, while the farmer's wife was in the dairy filling our jug for us, he nipped in through the door and pinched all the money out of the jar.

I was terrified: it was obvious that the farmer's wife would know that we had taken it, so I made him hide the money under a pile of sand in the road. We waited a day or two, and when nobody said anything, or came after us, we went and recovered the money and shared it out.

It's something I'm not particularly proud of, but then I suppose that my moral sense wasn't particularly highly developed at that age: why should it be? I had been to a Sunday

School at St Alphage's Catholic Church in Lancaster Street, and even won books of an uplifting nature for memorising biblical texts; but I stopped going there after the priest came down to the lavatory when I was having a pee with some other boys one Sunday, and made indecent suggestions.

It was all a question of the struggle for survival. As kids, our thoughts continually revolved around how we could make a few pence here or there. I remember at one time my friend Bobby Messenger and I always used to go scrounging across Blackfriars Bridge as soon as we came out of school. We'd hang around the riverside, seeing what wood we could find, or breaking in and out of warehouses, or persuading blokes to give us old crates.

Our usual means of transport was jumping on the backs of carts. You had to grab hold of the tailboard of any cart or lorry which was going slowly enough, and the next minute your feet would be flying through the air. The art for the more advanced was then to keep hold of the tailboard, and get your feet on the ground running fast enough to vault up and over it into the back of the lorry. Once when Bobby and I were doing this, I managed all right, but Bobby's hands gave way and he fell with sickening force on his chin in the road.

I had to leap quickly out of the lorry and help him from

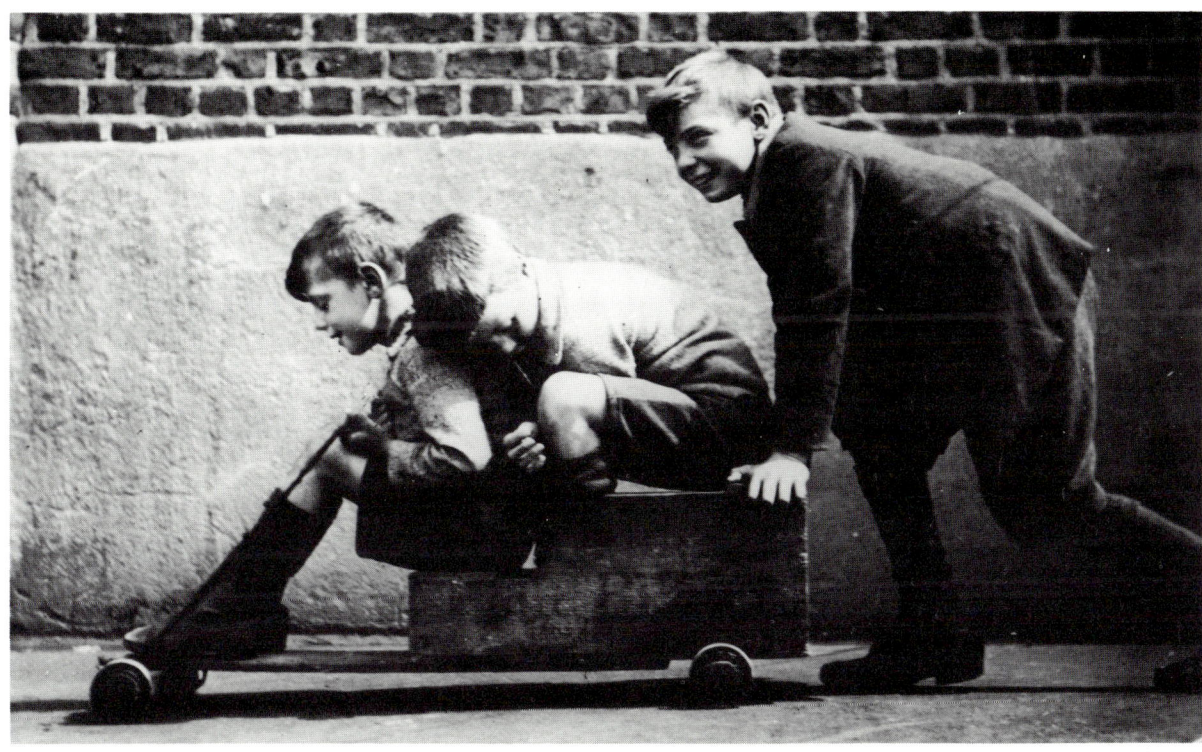

One of the carts I made, being driven by Charlie, Ginger and Sid.

the road. There was blood everywhere, and Bobby had a great big gash under his chin which must have taken some explaining to his parents. I took him to St Thomas's Hospital where he was given a record number of stitches.

It was with Bobby that I had my closest ever brush with the law. We had heard from a friend who was a night watchman that the road was being dug up in Piccadilly. In those days road surfaces were made of wooden blocks soaked in tar which were laid down fitted close together, and then covered with a further layer of tar and fine stones. When roads were dug up, some old tarry blocks were usually thrown out, and they were good for putting on the fire (there were no smokeless zones then), provided you didn't mind the stones they fired around the room.

Bobby and I made ourselves a cart out of an old Tate & Lyle sugar box, a plank, and four ball-bearing wheels, and in the evenings we took this cart up to Piccadilly and filled it with old tarry blocks which the night watchman had put out for us. Then we would tow it home and give some blocks to our parents and sell some to neighbours for burning.

To get back to Blackfriars, we went down Villiers Street (which led off the Strand) and across the Hungerford railway and pedestrian bridge. To get up onto the Bridge, we had to go up some steps, but luckily, each evening when we got there, there was a policeman on duty at the bottom of the steps, and we used to grab one end of the cart while he grabbed the other and gave us a hand up.

One evening when we arrived at Piccadilly, the night watchman was not there, but we found a pile of what looked like old tarry blocks and loaded up the cart. All went well until we got to the steps up to the Hungerford Bridge at the bottom of Villiers Street. There was a different policeman on duty, with a big moustache and a rather self-important air. We stopped and looked at him and then at our cart, then asked, 'Is it all right if we go up here, Sir?' – meaning, Give us a hand up, mate. But PC Jackson (that was his name) was suspicious. Looking at our cart, he asked: 'Where did you get that lot?' We told him where they came from, and how the night watchman usually put them aside for us, and how we used them for burning on the fire at home, but he wasn't satisfied. When we told him we were thirteen, he said that we could go to borstal until we were sixteen if we weren't careful. Then he said that we had to go with him back to Piccadilly to check whether we had been telling the truth. It sounded bad.

Bobby and I walked ahead of him, pulling our cart up Villiers Street. We knew that he wouldn't believe us if the night watchman still wasn't there, and we seemed to hear the doors of the borstal closing behind us. By the time we got to the Strand, we were in such a state that we ran for it. Without letting go of the trolley, we ran as fast as we could along the Strand, weaving in and out of the traffic, with PC Jackson hot in pursuit. We didn't get very far before we felt his big fat hands on our collars. This time there was no hesitation: he took us straight to Bow Street Police Station.

We had to empty our pockets at the Station Sergeant's desk. What came out of them was nobody's business: bits of string, cigarette cards, penknives, our joint collection of keys, and tuppence each. All of these things naturally made the police very suspicious, especially the keys, although in fact we used to fix caps to them then tie them on a bit of string and bang them against the wall as we walked along, to

A portrait of my dad, once more making use of side-lighting.

make a loud noise and give people a bit of a fright. Then we were put in the cells.

I still remember looking through the barred door at the sergeant's desk and the pairs of handcuffs hanging on the wall behind him.

At about ten o'clock in the evening, our fathers arrived, and we were taken to Vine Street Police Station, which was nearer the scene of the crime. The night watchman had been found, and the contractor, and it had been established that some of the tarry blocks we had taken were not old ones, but off-cuts of new ones, so we were charged with theft.

We were finally allowed to go at about two in the morning. My father gave me a clip round the ear'ole, and we walked home over Waterloo Bridge, stopping at a coffee stall on the way back for a cup of tea.

Our case was heard not long afterwards at a magistrates' court in Soho. There was me and my father and Bobby Messenger and his father. My father was shaking like a leaf. Bobby's dad, who had been gassed in the First World War and had a tendency to pass out under strain, keeled over and crashed to the floor. The magistrates, two ladies in big flowery hats, and a man, were glaring at us as if we were hardened criminals.

In the end, though, we were let off with a warning because we had good character references from Friar Street School. Only then were the contents of our pockets given back to us (we had felt sure that PC Jackson had pinched our tuppences).

The year after that I was fourteen, and it was time to leave school and find a proper job. I had seen a notice up saying LAD WANTED at a firm called Elephant Motors in the Borough Road. I'd had my eye on it for some time, and the same afternoon I finished school I went along there and asked to see the foreman.

The interview went very well at first. He asked me how old I was, and I told him; he asked me was I good with my hands, and I said yes, but then he asked:

'What's your mathematics like?'

'Do you mean sums, Sir?' I replied brightly.

'Yes.'

'Oh', I said, 'they're very good.'

So he said:

'What's thirteen times thirteen?'

If there was a thirteen times table, I'd never got as far as learning it. Numbers revolved in my mind, but no answer came out. I was stuck, and I didn't get the job.

I went home feeling very sorry for myself. If I had got it, I'd probably be an engineer or a mechanic or something like that now, but that evening my Aunt Maud, who went out charring somewhere in the Strand, mentioned that she had seen a sign saying BOY WANTED in a house in Craven Street, parallel to Villiers Street, off the Strand. There was a brass plate up outside the house, engraved with the name of the company advertising the job: the Central Photographic Service.

2: Central Photographic Service and Cycling

The following morning, I went along to Craven Street, and got the job. I would now be earning ten shillings a week; I carried on working at Hammond's grocery shop for some time after starting at Central Photo Service to bring in a bit more money.

The firm operated from the basement of the house in Craven Street, and the rest of the building was occupied by the architectural practice run by the boss, Mr Duke, and his partner Mr Lazenby. The staff consisted of a Scottish girl and myself, although we did take on extra people in the summer, and the basement itself was a gloomy and depressing place.

My job was to go round the chemists' shops in the West End collecting films for processing, and delivering ones which had been processed. I went round twice a day, walking or jumping on the backs of carts to save my bus fares. In between my rounds, the Scottish girl taught me how to develop and print, and also some other interesting activities you can get up to in the darkroom. I was a quick learner.

Conditions were primitive to say the least. There were four large developing tanks each about four feet deep, and the films were clipped to metal rods suspended over these: six films to a rod, and four rods to a tank.

Usually we were so rushed that we put up to ten films on a rod, and as we lowered the films into the tank, one or two sometimes dropped off, and sank to the bottom of the developing fluid. When the films had been fixed and washed, we used to count the total to see how many we had lost, then take a broom handle with a piece of flat wood nailed to the end and fish the missing films from the bottom of the developing tank by scraping them up the side. These films were often hopelessly overdeveloped by then, and badly scratched, so the only thing to do was to scrap them and send fogged film back to the chemist in their place. The customers never complained, of course: they always thought that something had gone wrong with their cameras, and took them in to be repaired.

The luckier films were dried hanging from the mantelshelf in front of an electric fire, and the prints were glazed with a foul-smelling solution of ox-gall, which we mixed up ourselves, and spread on glass. The photos were then placed face down on the glaze, and squeegeed to remove the excess moisture, and then dried by leaning the sheet of glass against a chair in front of the electric fire.

Again, this primitive process was not very efficient, and when photographs stuck to the glass, we had to soak them in water to get them off, and start all over again. Later on, the governor bought us a terribly advanced German glazing machine; it was electrically driven and gas heated – you had to light a burner in the middle of the drum – but the only difference was that when the photographs stuck on the drum, you couldn't put the whole thing in water like a sheet of glass to soak them off; you had to spend ages dabbing at them with a damp cloth.

Apart from the usual 'happy snaps', an astonishing number of people sent in naughty pictures. There were one or two chemists in Soho from whom we expected that sort of thing: pictures of prostitutes for their clients, and we adjusted our rates accordingly. But there was also a chemist's at the top of Northumberland Avenue from which we quite regularly collected films sent in by a famous surgeon.

The surgeon's pictures were always beautifully taken on a quarter-plate camera on roll film, six pictures in a roll. All the pictures were of popsies: beautiful creatures with nothing on doing the most terrible things, but always wearing marvellous hats. And the last picture on each roll of the film was always of the surgeon himself: a stout gentleman with no clothes on, and the tiniest little withered thing between his legs.

I don't suppose he appreciated what an opportunity for blackmail he gave. Instead, we charged him double and printed up copies for ourselves.

After a while I had accumulated quite a collection of photographs of this type, and I used to carry them around in a grubby envelope in the inside pocket of my jacket. Some of the chemists I used to collect from liked to look through them, and in the evenings I used to pass them around among my mates and we'd have a laugh.

We were still not too well off at this time, and my clothes always had holes in them. One night, when I took my jacket off and hung it on the back of the chair before going to bed at home, the envelope must have fallen through a hole in the lining of my pocket. The next day when I was on my rounds, one of the chemists (who used to entertain me with stories of his amorous exploits while I pinched bottles of perfume from his shelves) said that he would like to look at my pictures.

I felt in my pocket and found they were gone.

My first thought was that they must have fallen out of my pocket at home, in which case my mum would have found them, and I would be in terrible trouble. I leapt on my bike (I was using a cycle to go round by that stage) and raced straight home to Priory Buildings.

My mum looked at me oddly when I got home. Breathlessly, I said:

'Mum! I'm going to be in terrible trouble – I had a packet of pictures to deliver to the Law Courts in the Strand this morning. There's some sort of case on there. I don't know what was in the pictures, but I've lost them, and now I'm for it.'

She looked slightly relieved:

'Are you sure you didn't know what was in them?' she asked.

'No', I said. 'No idea.'

'Promise you won't look at them.'

'I promise.'

And she took them out from inside her blouse where she had hidden them for safe keeping, and gave them back to me, as she thought, to deliver.

As soon as I had learned developing and printing, I began to do work on my own account at home. My brothers and sisters collected films from people at the firms where they worked, and I developed them at Central Photo Service, then rolled them up, still wet, in thick newspaper, and brought them home. At home, I washed them and hung them up to dry in the scullery, then printed them up in a print box I'd made for myself. By undercutting other people's prices, I kept busy and made a bit of money on the side.

It wasn't long before developing other people's pictures made me think that I ought to be taking a few pictures myself. Besides, I'd heard that Fleet Street photographers could earn £5 a week.

Each evening when I was walking home from CPS, I passed a pawn shop on the corner of the Cut, opposite the Old Vic Theatre. There were always a lot of old plate cameras on display in the window, and my first camera was one of these. I bought it for ten shillings.

I hadn't a clue how to take pictures, not a clue. I didn't know what a stop was; I worked out speeds and apertures by common sense; focusing was straightforward – you simply had to adjust the lens and look at the image on a sheet of ground glass at the back of the camera. I bought a lot of out-of-date plates from a shop in Holborn where you could get a dozen for 6d, and began working by trial and error.

Bath-time at the Priory Buildings.

One of my earliest successful pictures, taken with flash powder, is one of my sisters with Harry being given a bath by my mum in front of the fire at Priory Buildings. I still remember how embarrassed I felt when Dolly was born – I was old enough to be knocking around with girls at the time – and when I found out that my mum was pregnant; I remember that when the midwife was delivering Dolly, I was in the next room of our two-room flat, scrubbing the floor.

My first commercially successful picture was of King George V and Queen Mary driving down the Blackfriars Road in an open carriage. It was a beautiful day and the streets were lined with people. I stood beside a sandbin, using my sister Lally's head as a tripod, and focused on the tram-lines in the middle of the road to get the right distance.

Just as the royal carriage was passing, the King caught sight of the camera, and turned in my direction. When I had developed and printed it, I sold about two hundred postcard-sized copies of the photograph to friends and neighbours.

Before long, I was doing other work. Pub outings, known as 'beanos', were a feature of pub life in those days. All the men or all the women (never both) who were regulars at a pub gathered outside it early on a Sunday morning, filled a coach with crates of beer, and drove off down to Southend for the day. They would stop on the grass verge on the way for a booze-up, and probably spend most of their time in Southend in pubs. But before they set out, they liked to have a group photograph taken as a memento of the occasion (later on, they'd be too drunk to stand up), and that was where I came in. I went along with one of my old plate cameras, gathered them all in front of the coach, and took a picture. I'd develop it, and later in the week go back to the pub and sell a postcard-sized print to all the people who'd been on the beano.

As a family, we were still poor enough for all of us, mum and dad and seven kids, to be living in two rooms in Priory Buildings, so I suppose that every little bit I could earn must have helped. We certainly didn't have enough money to pay out for things like boots and items of clothing all at once, so we had to buy them from the tally man. The tally man was a sort of door-to-door hire-purchase agent; you could buy things from him and pay him back over a period of weeks, but you had to pay terrifically high rates of interest on the credit he gave you.

My suit came from the tally man, but even though it was paid for, I only ever wore it on Sundays when I went out with my mates. On the Monday morning my mum regularly took it along to the pawn shop, where it was folded up and wrapped in brown paper, and she was given five bob for it. Then, on the following Saturday, I would go and get it out of pawn again, for the next day: but everyone could tell where it had been, because it was so badly creased where it had been wrapped up in the parcel.

Most Sundays, wearing my suit, I used to go with my girl-friend and my mates to the cinema. Usually, we went to the Central, nicknamed 'the bake' because it was so hot and steamy. It had only one floor, and a woman pianist in the pit accompanying the films. What went on in that cinema in the dark was nobody's business, although it usually stopped short of anything too naughty: partly because we were too young, and partly because there was an attendant who came round flashing his torch on us and trying to catch us out.

The other cinema we used to go to, Gatti's in Westminster Bridge Road, was a bit more special. It had three floors: a pit, a circle, and a gallery; and there was usually an act between the two films. Our regular treat there was to buy monkey-nuts and eat them, throwing the shells over the edge of the gallery into the pit below. In the end, the hail of monkey-nut shells became such a problem that the management fitted a wire-mesh screen over the pit to protect the patrons.

King George V and Queen
Mary, taken on a ten-shilling
pawnshop camera.

In the week, I started to go to evening classes in wood-work, petrol engines, and gymnastics. I still do woodwork; the man who gave the petrol engine classes was more interest-ed in talking about sex; and in gymnastics I learned how to do hand springs and somersaults, but still didn't satisfy my growing need to take part in some sort of competitive sport.

The family struggled on, and, at last, when I was sixteen, we were able to afford to move from our two rooms with a scullery to a proper house not far away in Lancaster Street. Suddenly we had three floors: downstairs we had a front room, used only on holidays and festive occasions, and also for courting (we could sit in there provided we kept the light on); a big kitchen with the fire always burning and a pot of tea always on the hob: and a scullery. In the back yard was a lavatory which we didn't have to share with any other family.

On the first floor was my parents' bedroom and the very first room I ever had to myself. This was useful for my devel-oping and printing business, and also because my girlfriend Dora preferred watching me at work in my darkened room to sitting in the brightly-lit parlour. I was very grateful.

On the top floor were the rooms where my brothers and sisters lived.

I think I had a lot to do with getting that house; by that stage I ran the family quite a bit. On the first Saturday after we moved in the rent collector came round to see if we were getting on all right. I was standing at the door with my dad talking to him when he suddenly said 'Who's in charge here? You or him?'

My father quickly said 'No, he's not in charge. I'm in charge,' and shoved me back indoors.

Apart from photography, my other significant discovery at this time was cycling. I had soon found that the quickest way to go round the chemists' shops was on a bicycle, and I bought my first machine in the Cut on a Bank Holiday. It cost ten shillings, and it was in bad condition. Since there was nowhere open to buy oil, I had to grease the chain with Vas-eline to make it go round.

I stuck with that bike for about six months, cycling hap-pily round the West End; and every time I passed a certain policeman with a pompous air and a big moustache on point duty by St Martin-in-the-Fields, I used to yell out 'Watcha, Jackson', and poked my tongue out at him.

Then one day as I was coming out of Chancery Lane into Fleet Street, a taxi ignored a policeman's directions and drove straight into my bike, buckling the front wheel. I wasn't hurt, and although I had to carry my bike back to the office, I was happy enough when the taxi driver agreed with the policeman to pay me back for any damage he had done.

I went out and bought a really good lightweight alumin-ium wheel from F. W. Evans in the Kennington Road, and sent the bill off to the taxi company. When there was no reply, I wrote again. When there was still no reply, a friend told me to try the National Cyclists' Union. I wrote to them, and they took up my case, and, lo and behold, the taxi com-pany sent the money.

At the same time, as I have mentioned, I had begun to feel that I really wanted to get involved in a sport. I had never had time or energy to learn one at school, but now I began to feel terribly active. Gymnastics alone didn't satisfy me, and I realised that the only thing I knew how to do was cycling.

I looked in *Cycling* magazine, found the toughest all-male cycling club, and joined it. It was called the Norwood Paragon.

Above: This was used on the front cover of *The Bicycle*, whose caption read: '''. . . on the far horizon . . .'' Two charming cyclists outlined against the sky.'

Below: My brother Sid in a Norwood Paragon 50-mile time trial. He proved to be faster than me.

The Norwood Paragon was about half-an-hour's cycle ride away from Blackfriars. I got myself a good bike, and began to go out with them on their regular Sunday club runs. When we stopped to eat our sandwiches by the roadside, I used to entertain the other chaps by doing somersaults and handsprings. And I began taking photographs for the club with my old plate camera – group photographs, like the 'beano' pictures.

To my delight, when I sent some of these photographs to a new cycling magazine called *The Bicycle*, they used them.

It wasn't long before I could turn an afternoon's ride into a profitable outing by taking scenic shots of the countryside, which were frequently used on the back cover of *The Bicycle*. And eventually, when I went on cycling holidays in North Wales, staying at National Cyclists' Union approved Bed and Breakfasts for half a crown a night, I was able to finance these by taking a few photos of the mountains. I used to get thirty bob for a full back page, with a credit line: 'Photography by A. Hardy'.

I soon got to meet the staff photographer on *The Bicycle*, George Moore. George was a quiet, methodical chap of about my age. In the early days of the magazine, as a promotional gimmick, they started to give away 15″ × 12″ enlargements of photographs of well-known racing cyclists. George was responsible for making these enlargements, and being such a careful, patient sort of man, he was doing them very carefully, one at a time, and it was taking him all week to produce a batch of fifty, which would be given away just like that.

When he heard that I worked in the developing and printing business, he asked me if I would help.

Now my experience of making enlargements was limited to doing hundreds of prints from copy negatives of actors appearing in West End theatres. At Central Photographic Service, speed was essential, and we used to develop twenty pictures at a time, in shallow glazed pie-dishes from Woolworths, by jiggling them around with our fingers. Then we put them into the hypo tank and held them down with a wooden stick which had a lump of cloth tied to the end.

Moore was horrified by my techniques – he never did like that kind of high-speed work. But at least we got the enlargements done, and we still got on well enough for him to show me a lot of beautiful 15″ × 12″ prints of his photographic work.

What really struck me about them was the sheer technical quality. In those days Road Races started almost before it got light on a Sunday morning, so it didn't interfere with the traffic; and in addition, cyclists' clothing was supposed to be inconspicuous, so they usually wore black tights and a black alpaca jacket, all of which made taking pictures at the start of Road Races very difficult. But in George's pictures there was a tremendous amount of detail: you could even see the difference between the rim of a wheel and the tyre, which was just a blur in mine. So I asked him, 'How do you do it George? What do you take them on?' And he showed me his camera. It was a 35mm camera, a Leica.

From then on I saved every farthing I could until I was able to afford to buy a second-hand Leica from Constantine and Jackson's, in Chancery Lane.

Unknown to me, the influence of 35mm or 'miniature' camera photography was beginning to make itself felt at this time. German photographers like Kurt Hutton and Felix Mann had come to England and were working for *Weekly Illustrated*, edited by Stefan Lorant (who was later responsible for the successful launch of *Picture Post*). With its fast lens and speed of operation, it was able to capture a feeling of intimacy and movement which hadn't been open to photographers before. Lorant in fact was to base *Picture Post*'s format on the proportions of a 35mm negative.

I found out very quickly how to use the Leica for cycle racing. Swinging the camera with the movement and using it in general as an extension of my eyes came naturally to me. I also discovered by experimenting that it was possible to take pictures in practically any light — even candle light; and because I couldn't afford to buy made-up developers, I made my own 'super-soup' out of paraphenylene-diamine, metol, glycin and soda sulphite. This enabled me to force development, so that even when pictures were very under-exposed, I could still get something out of them.

Pretty soon I was almost doing poor old George Moore out of a job. It now being summer, Herne Hill race track was in full swing on Saturday afternoons. Jock Wadley and I would meet there on our bikes and cover the various races, especially if there were some of the noted continental stars riding. After the main events had finished we would cycle back to *The Bicycle*'s offices in Doughty Street, where I would develop the film and print the most important shots. By this time it would be about ten p.m., so after a meal and a short rest, Jock and I would get a new stock of film and cycle through the night to cover a road racing event known as a time trial. In this particular case it was a very well-known race run every year, the Bath Road Hundred, which started at about five o'clock in the morning. The competitors set out from a fixed point, normally near Newbury, and raced around the lanes and roads, finishing back at the starting point after a hundred miles.

Jock and I would cycle to convenient spots, usually turning points, and photograph the race, which finished at about eleven in the morning. We then cycled about sixty miles back to Doughty Street where again I processed the film and made prints. By this time Bill Mills, the editor, was making up the paper ready for next day's publication. I was paid thirty shillings for each of these jobs.

The experience I was gaining was not only photographic. *The Bicycle* sent me on my first foreign assignment: to cover the world cycling championships in Copenhagen.

The sea crossing was rough, and I was sick all the way there. The job involved spurts of hard work, though I could take time off between the different events. The main excitement of the visit apart from the cycling happened at a party which took place in a seventh-floor flat.

Above: Myself and brother Sid in our cycling plus-fours.

Below: The printed caption read: 'Garnering wealth in the Welsh wheatfields — a picture of simple harvest beauty taken near Bridgnorth.'

There was a beautiful girl there, a real cracker. I wanted to drink champagne from her shoe, the way I had seen it done in films. She didn't want her shoes ruined by being filled with alcohol (they never seemed to worry about that in films), and we had an argument which resulted in me pulling off her shoe and throwing it out of the window. The situation could have turned nasty, but the girl took it fairly well. So, I am pleased to say, did her husband. I afterwards found out that he was the strong man at the Tivoli Circus.

My luck was still in on the journey home. In contrast to the journey out, we had a smooth and sunny crossing, and a party of cyclists, journalists, promoters and businessmen sat on deck and played pontoon.

I was worth about ten shillings, betting in threepences and sixpences, and doing quite nicely until I got the bank.

On the first round I broke even. But on the second, two or three players went bust, one had pontoon, and three had five cards under twenty-one. There must have been twenty pounds against me on the deck.

I turned my own cards up: a five and a seven. I twisted a five. I twisted again: a three. I had twenty with four cards; there was nothing I could do except twist again and risk going bust. I twisted. It was an ace. The man with pontoon took the bank, and I took the twenty pounds.

All this time, I was still working for Central Photo Service. I worked for them for a total of nine years, and by the time I left my pay had risen to £2 7s 6d a week. But I was beginning to get some recognition. For one job covering a six-day cycling event at Wembley Stadium, I decided to try out a new flash system designed to synchronise with the shutter of a plate camera.

Previously, the lens cap had to be taken off, the flash powder ignited, and the cap put back on again. This meant that only the most static subjects could be taken, and even Prime Ministers on the steps of 10 Downing Street learned to freeze for the press photographers' cry of 'Caps off!'

Now, with the invention of flash bulbs and an electric system of ignition, it was possible to synchronise the flash and the opening of the shutter more precisely.

The bulbs were about the size of modern 100-watt light bulbs, and filled with crumpled shiny magnesium paper; they cost about one shilling each. I bought a cardboard box of fifty of these, and took them along to Wembley. Not one of the fifty shots I took came out. I went back to the shop, and they were very good and replaced the bulbs. On the second occasion, I had the same complete lack of success. Again the shop replaced the bulbs, and made some adjustments to my camera. Finally, on the third attempt, out of fifty shots I obtained two pictures.

The pictures were used in *The Bicycle*. They were fabulous pictures – even the cyclists thought so. And to prove the point, the editors printed a tribute by some members of the Belgian team saying that they were the best cycling pictures ever taken of them.

Although I was doing quite a bit of work for *The Bicycle*,

My boss A.F. Duke and his wife visited friends on the Isle of Sheppey, where I was camping at the time, and called in for a cup of tea.

and earning some extra money for it, Mr Duke, my boss at Central Photographic Service, was not aware of it. It was a time when I learned a lot about photography: the importance of quick reactions in getting a good shot, and a willingness to experiment technically; and an appreciation of what can be done in the darkroom to bring out the best in a picture taken in less than perfect conditions; also I discovered such clever devices as the 'join-up', which was to be an important aspect of my later work for *Picture Post*.

Finally, when I was twenty-three, I got back together with my girlfriend Dora, and we decided to get married. Mr Duke was not at all happy about this: he was embarrassed at the idea of a man trying to keep a wife on what he was paying me. So, to save himself any further embarrassment, he gave me the sack.

In the week before I was due to leave I went round asking everyone I knew who had Fleet Street connections if they had heard of any jobs going. At that time Central Photo Service used to do enlargements for a Mr Sheed, who ran an agency which supplied photographs of well-known personalities to all the newspapers. Mr Sheed decided to play a joke on me and told me that a certain William Davis, who ran the General Photographic Agency, was looking for a miniature-camera photographer. He didn't tell me that Davis was well known for his use of large-format cameras, and had certainly never touched anything smaller than a half-plate camera in his life.

So, without the slightest doubt or hesitation, I went along to the offices of GPA and applied for the job. Soon, I knew, I would be moving to Kennington with Dora. The Blackfriars where I had grown up, and its warm, light summer evenings, with all the women standing in their doorways talking, waiting for their old men to come home from the boozer, and all us kids sitting on the pavement, would become part of my past.

Cycling

Because of my early interest in cycling, I photographed a variety of events throughout my career. Above is a six-day race at Wembley. On the next two pages are a record of Ken during his successful Brighton-and-back record attempt. First is Ken at crack of dawn turning on the Brighton front. Bill Mills, editor of *The Bicycle*, is on the right. Beneath is a picture of Ken Joy snatching a drink, actually taken the night before the event. It's obvious why I posed this. In order to get the focus right at night time for the third shot, I pre-focused on a piece of paper and took the picture as he passed it.

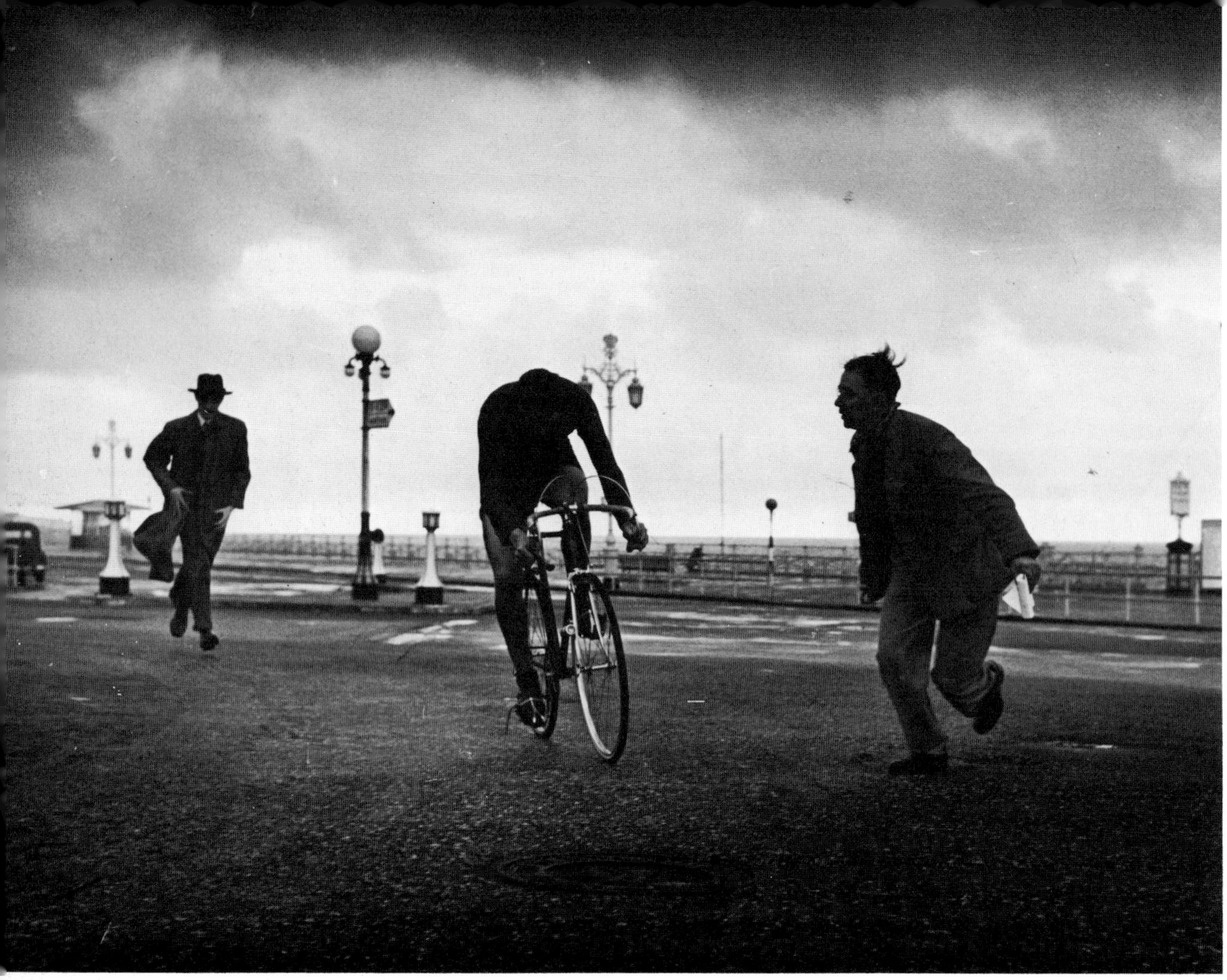

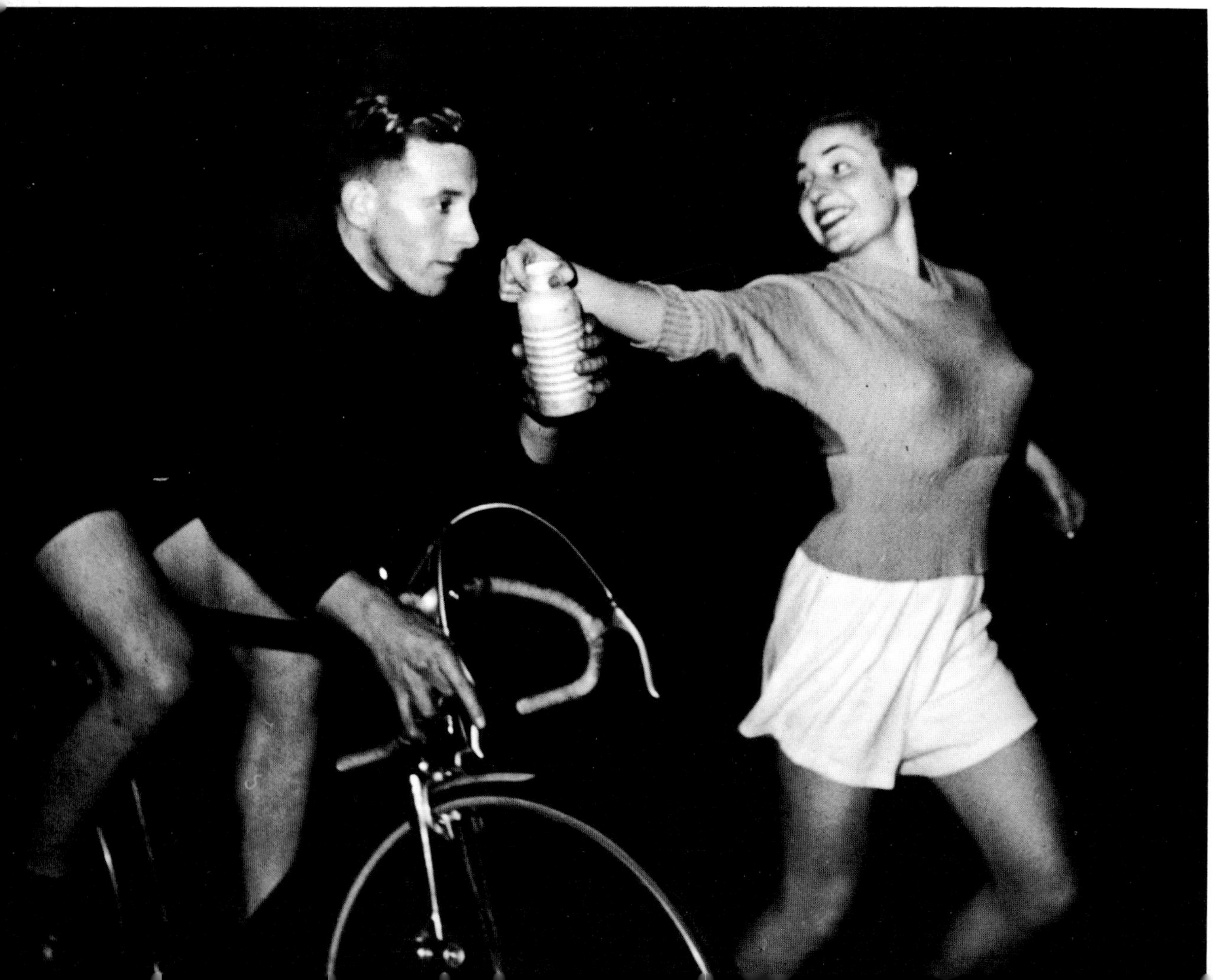

3: GPA and Criterion Press

William Davis was a tall, good-looking man. He wasn't exactly an eccentric, but he was certainly a striking figure and known to all as he strode along Fleet Street wearing his usual broad-brimmed hat and his high, starched-wing collar.

On the Monday after Mr Sheed told me about the vacancy, I went along to the building where GPA had its offices, climbed the stairs, and knocked at a half door, like a stable door with a counter on it.

A manager popped out and asked me what I wanted. When I had explained, he went and fetched Davis.

Feeling that I had nothing to lose, I said:

'I hear you want a miniature-camera photographer, sir.'

Davis looked puzzled.

'A miniature camera? What's that?'

'35mm, sir', I explained. 'It makes negatives of about one inch by an inch and a quarter.'

He finally understood: 'That's not a *camera*, that's a *toy*! Come with me: I'll show you what real photography is.' His office was dominated by a huge, hand-tinted photograph of King George V lying in state, which he had taken. He got out a lot of his big, very static pictures, all done with flash and a camera on a tripod: still-lifes, buildings, and famous people. There was no doubt that the quality was very good.

'Now show me what you can do', he said.

I took out some 15" × 12" prints of landscapes and cyclists and showed him. He squinted closely at them:

'What did you say you took these with?'

'A Leica, sir, 35mm.'

'Can you prove it?'

'I can only show you the negatives, sir.'

That seemed to satisfy him. He told me to come back that afternoon, when he would give me a job to try me out.

When I went back, he told me that he had arranged a photocall with a Hungarian comic actor called Szakall, who had just arrived in London, and was staying at the Mayfair Hotel.

At six that evening I was already outside the Mayfair Hotel for my seven o'clock appointment, carrying my camera and equipment in a little cardboard attaché case. I

Above right: William Davis, taken with a long-range lens (hand-held) as an experiment. He was the man who, unfortunately, started me smoking.

Below right: My first darkroom, in a broom cupboard, with a Leica Valoy enlarger.

Below: Herr Szocke Szakall.

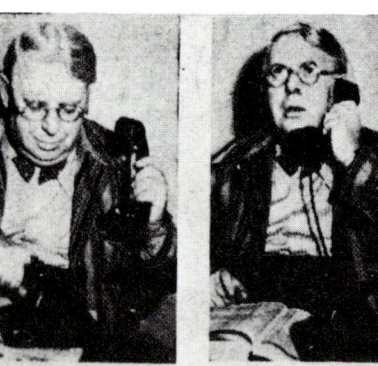

'E speeka de Engleesh not zo goot . . . but he gets the right number first time on the Tryon Terror! He is HERR SZOCKE SZAKALL (pronounce it how you like), funniest comedian on the Continental stage, and the only man to make Buster Keaton laugh. Has come to London to make a film.

prowled up and down for an hour, while the commissionaire in gold braid and epaulettes glared at me suspiciously. At last it was seven, and I summoned up my courage and went in.

To my surprise I was allowed to go up to Szakall's room. Following Davis's suggestion, I got Szakall to ring down for cream cakes while I set up my photoflood lamps. I worked away for an hour or so while the tiny room became hotter and hotter, and Szakall sweated more and more, and finally began to look quite ill.

When I had finished, I rushed home to Blackfriars and developed the films. The next day I took them to Davis, and he liked them. That very same day he managed to sell a sequence of four of the pictures to the *Daily Mirror*, so he signed me up. My contract was a good example of Davis's financial cunning: I was guaranteed one job a week for 30/-; if I did a second job, he'd pay me £1; and if I did a third job I'd get 10/-; for each further job I would also get ten shillings. But he added a clause to the effect that, however many jobs I did, 'under no circumstances' would I be paid more than five pounds a week.

Dora, after having promised me that she wouldn't give up working if we got married, now gave up her job in a clothing factory, so I had to support both of us on what I earned at GPA. Yet with my Leica, I was not in a position to compete as a Press photographer. A plate from a plate camera could be developed *and* printed, still wet, all within the space of a few minutes. The prints themselves could be rapidly dried by dipping them in methylated spirits and setting light to them, and it was not unusual to see messenger boys rushing between darkrooms and the offices of newspapers with prints still alight. Developing 35mm film took longer, so I tended to follow Davis in doing non-news pictures for newspapers and glossy magazines.

Press photographs make themselves, but our kind of work involved *making* pictures. Davis and his salesman Bertram Collins used to go through the papers every day looking for items which we might be able to turn into a good picture. We also did a regular feature for the *Sunday Graphic* which linked up with a popular wireless programme called 'In Town Tonight', providing photographs of whoever had been on the programme.

I went to Streatham and photographed a singing mouse; I took pictures of a shepherdess called Mary Lamb; and I took my bike by train to a remote part of Essex and cycled twenty miles from the station to photograph a wart charmer in his local pub (this was one trick I could believe in). When I got back to the station, I found the last train had gone, and I had to cycle all the way back to London.

A man in Suffolk who put stones in flower pots and watered them daily, claiming they grew, and 'the man who hypnotizes alligators' were two more favourites which were taken by the Press.

In addition, we had a certain number of 'seasonal' stories: every summer we did something on 'Foreign Visitors to

London', which involved tracking down tourists in unusual national costumes; and every Christmas there was a picture of an out-of-work actor dressed as Father Christmas lying on a bench, with a caption like 'Found Late Last Night in London'.

I discovered I could easily match Davis and Collins for silliness. One story of mine was entitled 'Britain's Only Bird Surgeon', which was published in *Weekly Illustrated*, showing a budgerigar tied with elastic bands to a piece of wood, supposedly about to undergo surgery, and there was the even more ridiculous 'A Fish Goes to Hospital', which made a four-page spread in an early issue of *Picture Post*.

I took one picture of a fish lying on its side in cotton wool, which was supposed to show it falling asleep under the anaesthetic. Collins' caption said 'after twenty minutes the goldfish becomes unconscious'. Another picture showed a fish bought from the fishmonger's actually being cut open.

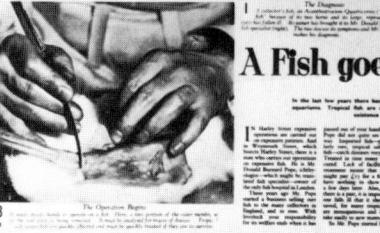
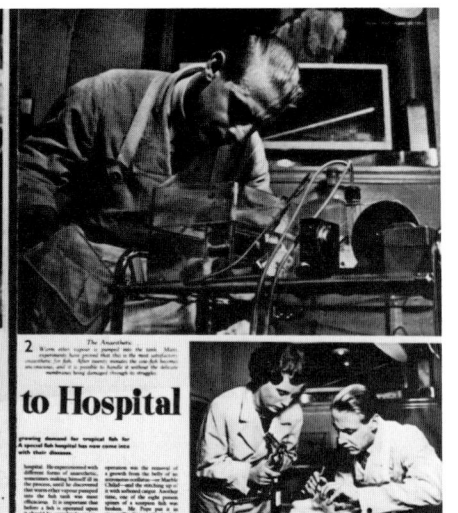

Above: I fear that at least one fish may have given up its life in the service of photojournalism. I hope I'm wrong.
Below: Dorothy Rolls, shadow dancer, at the Coliseum.

And the last showed a completely different fish swimming around in its tank, which was supposed to show the same fish restored to health.

But while I was always trying to think up ideas for stories, I was also looking for ways to increase the range of my photography which 'The Singing Mouse' and 'The Man Who Grows Stones' could not satisfy.

My experiments with synchronised flash on plate cameras for *The Bicycle* made me think about the possibility of having the same kind of arrangement on a Leica: imagine the increase in flexibility this would bring. The standard flash unit which Leica made for use with the camera worked on the principle that the shutter opened, the bulb fired, and the shutter closed again. This meant that the fastest speed available was the speed of the flash bulb, which was approximately 1/60th of a second. I thought that if I could synchronise the shutter blind so that it went across in the middle of the flash, I would be able to take much quicker exposures.

I fiddled around with a soldering iron, and after a few experiments, managed to doctor the Leica flash unit so that I could now take flash pictures at speeds of up to 1/1000th of a second. This opened up new possibilities for action shots in conditions of artificial light.

To make good use of my spare evenings, I used to go to the Coliseum and buy a 6d. ticket for the gods whenever there was a promising-sounding variety act advertised. If it was suitable, I used to go round to the stage door afterwards and arrange a photo-call with the artist.

Balliol and Merton had a dance act which consisted of Balliol throwing Merton up in the air and catching her, and Merton winding her legs round Balliol's neck while he whirled her round and round. By lying between Balliol's legs and taking shots with my high speed flash while all this was going on, I managed to get some highly unusual pictures.

My first pictures ever used by *Picture Post* were of a girl who wore billowing skirts and turned cartwheels on stage,

calling herself 'The Human Pinwheel'. I also took pictures of a novelty shadow dancer: a girl with a magnificent figure who danced about with hardly anything on, on the other side of the curtain from the audience, lit from behind so you could only see her silhouette. I was lucky: I had to take the pictures from her side of the curtain.

In 1937, Dora and I moved from our two-roomed flat in Kennington, to the ground floor of a house in Brixton, where our first son Michael was born. Baby pictures always were, and still are, popular. I took some high-speed flash photographs of Dora throwing him up in the air and catching him. To make sure they would sell, a good caption was important. The truth was less important, and Collins excelled himself on this occasion when he wrote:

BRITAIN'S FINEST BABY?

Doctors despaired of the life of this baby when born a year ago, but today he is claimed to be the best developed child in Britain, due to special physical exercises developed by his mother, Mrs Hardy of Brixton.

The story duly appeared in the *Daily Sketch*.

Another inspired moment took place when Davis sent me to the Arsenal Football ground on a Saturday afternoon to take a picture at the match for the feature page. To catch the next day's paper, I could only spend thirty minutes at the ground before I had to get back to the GPA darkroom. I was standing thinking 'What on earth can I take?' when my eye settled on a scruffy little kid. I fished in my pocket for a sixpence, and showed it to him: 'See this? If you run onto the pitch and kick the ball, you can have it.' The little kid's eyes nearly fell out at the sight of the sixpence. He couldn't oblige quickly enough: he ran out onto the pitch, and was immediately grabbed by two burly policemen.

I took my picture, the boy got his sixpence, and Collins wrote a story about a little boy called Percy who was only 3' 6" and had been helped by the police when he went onto the pitch to get a better view.

The story duly appeared in the *Sunday Graphic*.

After babies and children, the next most popular subject for pictures is animals. At this time, whenever I had no other story to do, I used to go and hang around the zoo in Regent's Park. A lot of photographers used to make special friendships with particular zoo-keepers, who would then tell them if anything that seemed likely to make a good picture was happening, in return for a small back-hander.

I was especially known to the girls in Pets' Corner, and I got on so well with the zoo's Public Relations man, Mr Doubleday, that he even gave me his cast-off suits for my dad to wear.

Through my connections, I was able to get exclusive pictures of the baby gorilla which they had just acquired playing on the grass with a chimpanzee in a toy train belonging to my son Michael. These appeared in the fourth issue of *Picture Post* with my Human Pinwheel pictures.

Above left: This was when I first synchronised a flashbulb with the back blind of a Leica at one-thousandth of a second.

Below: Anne and the Chimp: this series ran for about a year in the *Sunday Graphic*.

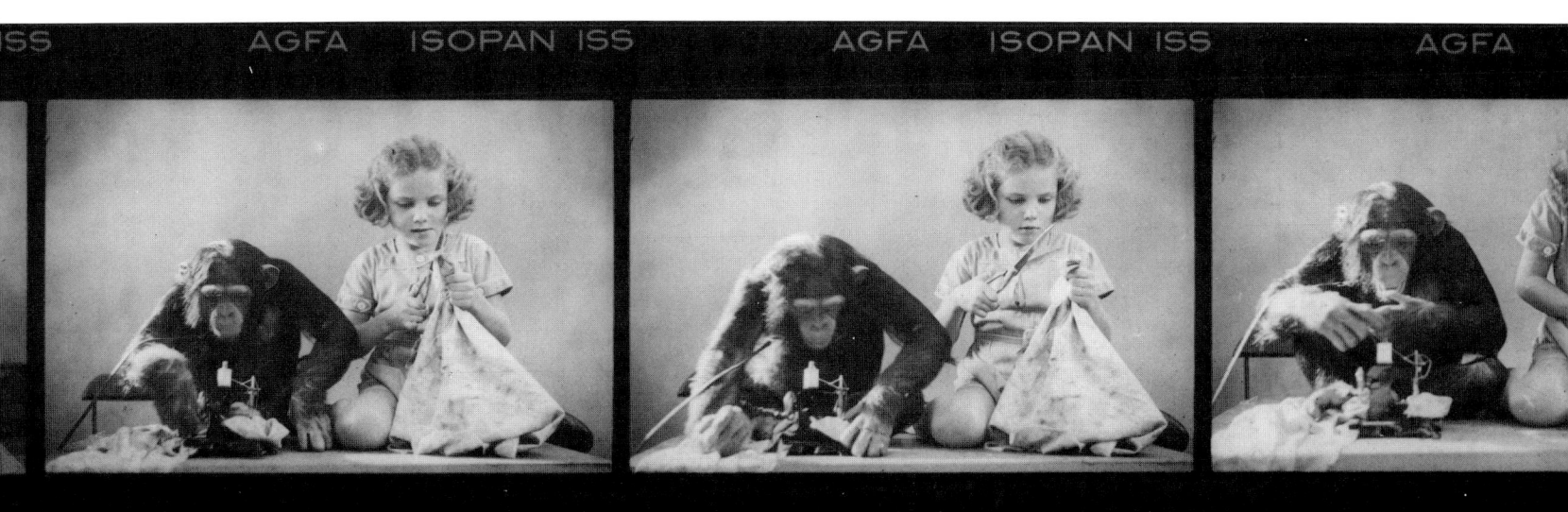

I also just happened to be at the zoo one day in July 1939 when Princesses Elizabeth and Margaret came to visit. I found out from Mr Doubleday that they were going to visit Pets' Corner, and quickly arranged with the Lady-in-Waiting to be the only photographer allowed in with them.

I got some pictures of them playing with a panda, but my best shot came later on, when they had left Pets' Corner and the rest of the Press had arrived. All the other photographers saw it, but, with my Leica, I was the only one fast enough to get a picture of a penguin treading on Princess Margaret's foot. But such lucky breaks were the exception rather than the rule. Getting pictures at the zoo was usually more like hard work. To get a sequence of pictures of the gibbons in action, I had to wait all day outside their cage. They seemed to be rather tired that day, and only swung from branch to branch sporadically; and half the time when they did swing, they were at the wrong angle so that other branches were in the way of my shot.

I also did some regular features: one was a series called 'Animal of the Week' for the *Sunday Graphic*. Another was a long-running series of picture sequences relating the adventures of a little girl (who was the daughter of a woman journalist on the *Sunday Graphic*) and a chimpanzee: this was called 'Anne and the Chimp.'

Although the original idea was Davis's, I had to think up a new story every week: no easy task.

One week I managed to persuade a shop in the Charing Cross Road to lend me a lot of musical instruments: trumpets and drums and so on. I took them up to the zoo in my motorcycle sidecar, and did a story with them. By the time Anne and Chimp had finished with them, they were all battered and dented, and the drum was torn. When I took them back to the shop I dumped them down and buggered off quickly.

For another story I got Claude Butler, an old acquaintance from my days at *The Bicycle*, to make me a special miniature tandem for the girl and the chimp to ride on.

Later on, when that series finished, I started another one, this time featuring my own son Michael, and the panda, called 'Peter and the Panda'. Periodically, the panda used to lose its temper and go berserk, so there was always a keeper standing by with chains to fasten him to the wall until he

Michael dressed up for a story on a Red Indian and his tracker.

calmed down again. But I don't think many people really appreciated how dangerous pandas can be, with their long and extremely sharp claws, apart, that is, from insurance companies. When Davis tried to insure Michael's safety, none of them would have anything to do with it.

In spite of Davis's contract, I must have been feeling more secure financially. I began buying a Ford car on the never-never – a 'de luxe', which meant that there was a metal cover over the spare wheel on the back. And we moved to a brand new house in Eltham at the end of a road beside some woods. It was built by Biltons and cost £700, which I was paying back to the Halifax Building Society at 1 guinea a week.

There were always some tensions between Davis and myself. One Saturday in August 1937 I had spent the entire day wandering around the streets of the West End looking for exotically dressed foreigners for the 'Foreign Visitors to London' story. I think the only likely candidates I had found had been some girls in Austrian national dress.

By the middle of the afternoon, I had had enough. I decided to go back to my mum's at Blackfriars via the Strand in case there were any foreigners hanging about, and have a cup of tea.

Outside Woolworths I noticed a crowd of people huddling round something. When I asked one of them what they were looking at, he told me that someone had just stabbed the newspaper seller. I pressed to the front of the crowd and took a picture of the man lying on the pavement. I was just congratulating myself on having got an exclusive, when two policemen marched up leading a man between them. This was really something: not only had I got a picture of the victim, but now I could also get pictures of his attacker.

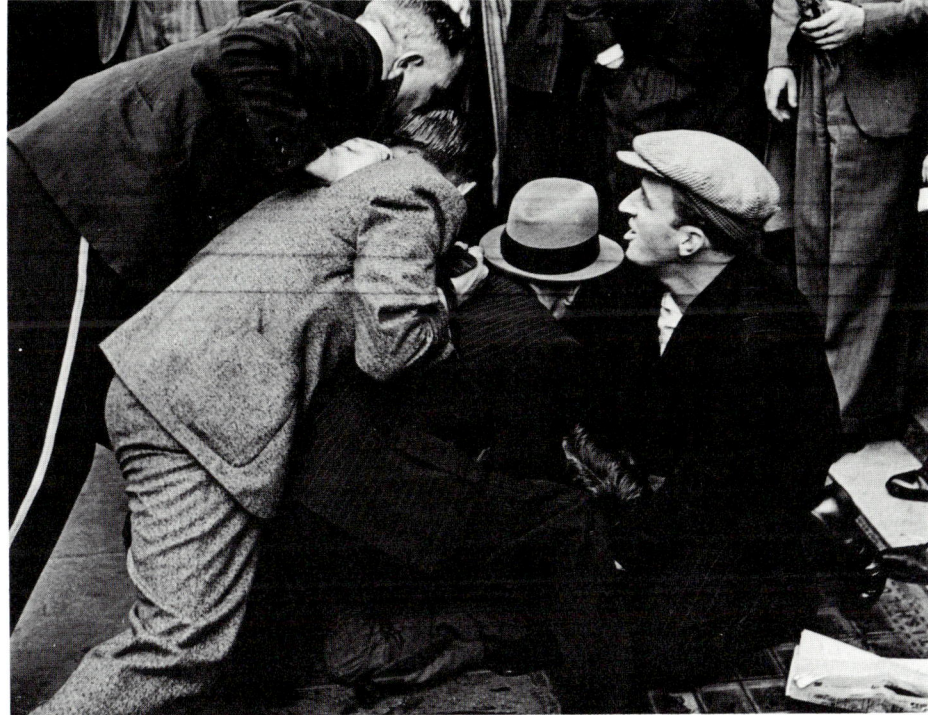

I walked backwards in front of the two policemen and the man they had arrested all the way to Bow Street Police Station, taking photographs.

I then took the film quickly back to the GPA darkroom and developed it.

I now had to decide what to do. Being a Saturday, Collins was not about, and I would have to sell it myself.

I must have visited practically every Sunday paper, and received a polite refusal from all of them (the man had not been charged yet), before I went to the *Sunday Express*. They quickly agreed to take them, gave me £5, and despatched a reporter to Bow Street Police Station.

The next day, all the *Sunday Express* placards read:
STABBING IN THE STRAND: EXCLUSIVE PICTURES
and I had a full back-page spread.

On Monday morning Davis was going through the weekend papers when he saw the story. He slapped the paper down on the table:

'That's the sort of pictures you ought to be doing, Hardy: news pictures.'

I said:

'Yes. I did those.'

'What? How much did you get for them?'

And he rushed round to the *Express* and got some more money out of them, although I never saw any of it.

I was receiving what is sometimes called 'a Fleet Street education'.

Sometimes Davis would take me out on jobs with him to hold the flash and help out. He was always the majestic and dignified photographer who had taken pictures of Queen Mary's apartments at Buckingham Palace, while I was the humble assistant. Davis always worked in the same way. When we did a photocall at a club called the Florida, in the West End, there was a jazz band and dancing couples. Whenever he wanted to take a photograph, the couples would have to freeze, and I would have to fire the flash.

Afterwards, while we were packing up and Davis was chatting to the proprietor, he said why didn't I run along and take a few pictures of the band with my little camera? So I went and took a few pictures using natural light, and got the names of the musicians – one of whom was Edmundo Ros.

Then we went back, and Davis developed his big plates, and I developed my roll of film. But, funnily enough, the only pictures we sold out of the entire afternoon's work were my shots of the band, which made a two-page spread in *Picture Post*.

In the meantime, almost without my noticing it, war was approaching.

Only two weeks before war was actually declared with Germany, I had a picture story about a carefree day trip to Calais, 'Channel Crossing', which made seven pages in *Picture Post*.

I had the idea for the story, wrote to the boat company, and got two free tickets: one for my brother-in-law Charlie and one for me. We went across for the day, had a lot to drink, met up with some girls, and I took a lot of photographs.

At the end of every week I used to go to Davis to get paid. That week he said to me:

'You haven't had a very good week this week, have you? As it's such a bad week, I'll give you 30/- for the Channel Crossing story.'

The pictures I took at the scene of this stabbing and arrest could probably not be printed in similar circumstances today.

During the war, every civilian had to carry a gas mask. Note that this was published over a year before the outbreak of war.

Later, I found out that he had already sold the story to *Picture Post*, who had made seven pages out of it, which meant that they would have given him £26. It was bad enough that whenever any pictures of mine were used, they were credited either to GPA or even to William Davis, but to get thirty shillings out of £26 was the last straw. I went and had it out with him, and arranged that in future I would get more like my fair share of the money he made from my pictures.

I began to do more stories which hinted at what was coming. On the bus from his home in Streatham one morning, Davis saw people queuing outside Brixton Town Hall to collect their gas-masks. He sent me down there straight away, and my picture, taken with a plate camera from the top of a ladder (a standard item in the Fleet Street expense-fiddler's repertory was 'hire of ladder'), made a full page in both *Illustrated London News* and *Life* magazine.

An ominous picture of mine of someone in a gas-mask appeared on the cover of *ARP News*.

Davis now began to be filled with terrible fears about the future. He took the view that as soon as war was declared, London would be bombed into the ground, all business would grind to a halt, and chaos would result. Because of this, he felt that the most sensible thing he could do was to leave London and retreat to his weekend cottage at Rottingdean. Collins and I would run the business in his absence, just in case things weren't as disastrous as he thought, and any money we made after expenses had been deducted, would, of course, be shared three ways.

I spent the day war was declared – 3 September 1939 – hanging around Downing Street trying to get any pictures I could of the Prime Minister.

In the late afternoon I went back to Lancaster Street to see my mum. She was in a full state of war-preparedness: the front room was full of buckets of water, tinned foods, and first-aid equipment. Even the table had been made into a short of shelter, with a mattress underneath it to sleep on.

Pretty soon the railway stations were filled with children with labels on their coats being evacuated. Michael and Dora, who was pregnant with our second son Terry, were evacuated to Melksham in Wiltshire.

I tried to join the RAF, but was rejected on grounds of bad eyesight. This was probably the most ridiculous reason possible, since my sight was probably at its best at the time. Perhaps the chap testing me had poor vision. Anyway, they failed me and I went back to work.

I tried to drive down to Melksham to see Dora whenever I could, but with petrol rationing in force it was not easy. In January 1940, Terry was born and I drove down in the Ford with Charlie to Melksham Hospital.

The roads were covered with black ice. At the top of a hill outside Calne, I stopped the car and got out to see what the surface was like. Although I had left the handbrake on, the car suddenly started to slide forward, slithering across the road, turning round, and ending up on its side in a ditch.

I tied some cloth round my feet and padded along the icy roads until I came to a garage. They took one look at the weather, and said that they wouldn't come out.

I wasn't going to give up so easily. After all, the car was half paid for.

I struggled back to the car, and Charlie and I were discussing what to do next, when along came a couple of big strong farm labourers. They lifted the car out of the ditch without any difficulty, and pointed it the right way.

We thanked them, and set out again. Only now added to the problem of the black ice was the fact that the off-side front wheel had broken away from the steering and kept wobbling all over the place.

I remember the look of fear on people's faces when they saw the car weaving and lurching towards them in the little narrow lanes.

When we finally got to the hospital, the sister there was very chilly towards me when she found out I had driven down, as if the mere fact of having driven a car in wartime made me some kind of spiv. Happily, when I at last saw Dora and Terry, they were both in good health.

In the spring, the expected bombing of London had not happened; Dora, Michael and Terry came back to Eltham. Davis also seemed to feel that it was safe to come back and take control of GPA again.

He had decided that he didn't like the way Collins and I had been running things: we had been earning far too much money. I had been getting as much as £20 a week, whereas when he was around I had been averaging more like £6 or £7. At the end of April, he gave us both the sack.

Collins and I put our heads together and decided that we wouldn't let this worry us. We would take all the business we had gathered and set up on our own as 'Criterion Press'. Davis kicked us out on a Thursday, and by the following Monday we had a little office at 172 Fleet Street, complete with a darkroom, all for 10s a week. Sid helped me make some benches, and my dad made some bits and pieces for the horizontal enlarger. I bought a desk for £3 10s and borrowed a typewriter, and by Wednesday the first pictures supplied by Criterion Press were used in the *Evening News*.

Things were not always easy. One week we only had thirty shillings between us. I then decided to sell the Ford in case I found myself unable to keep up the repayments.

Collins used his contacts, and we carried on doing the usual laid-on stories. There was a growing feeling against the Japanese and the import of Japanese goods, and Collins arranged for a woman to go into the branch of Woolworths at the Angel and scream anti-Japanese slogans just while I happened to be there with my camera. I took a few pictures and we left quickly. We had a drink with her afterwards in a pub.

But now I was no longer working for GPA, magazines like *Picture Post* started to discover that the person who had been taking all the GPA pictures they had been using was me, although my pictures had been published over Davis's name in many publications. When *Picture Post* decided to do an

The caption in *The Sphere* read: 'By means of a special camera it was possible to secure this very clear picture of Piccadilly after dark during crisis days last week. The khaki escort was once again in evidence.' The picture was published on 9 September, six days after war was declared.

issue on Air Raids, a couple of months after Criterion had started up, they commissioned me to take photographs of shelters.

There had been an isolated raid on Newcastle, so I was sent off up there. I travelled overnight, and arrived at about six o'clock on a sunny Sunday morning. I immediately took some photographs of the empty streets which would do to show the streets deserted during an air raid.

Nobody seemed to know anything about any air-raid shelters, though. Eventually I asked the landlady of the bed-and-breakfast place where I was staying, and she remembered that there was a shelter in a culvert where nervous people sometimes went at nights.

The culvert was a huge brick-lined tunnel with dim little light bulbs twinkling high up every ten yards or so. I had no flash and no tripod, but went down there and took what pictures I could with my Leica, hand-holding it for exposure times of about a quarter of a second.

Afterwards I also took some pictures of workmen building a subway, by the light of their acetylene lamps. These would also do for shelter pictures if the others didn't come out.

The next day I caught the train back to London. I arrived late at night and hurried straight to the Criterion darkroom with my precious films clutched tight in my hands.

This was my first proper commission for *Picture Post*, and I was feeling nervous. I knew they were well under-exposed, so I put them in my 'super-soup' and gave them half an hour instead of the usual sixteen minutes.

When I looked at them in the green safelight, there was nothing at all to be seen. I put them back for another half an hour. When I looked at them this time, I could just about see the faintest pin-point of light; so I put them back again.

I was feeling tired and a little bit edgy by this time. Rather than wait around for another hour, I decided to go to my mum's. I walked back over Blackfriars Bridge and let myself in. Everyone was in bed, so I called up 'Mum, it's Bert', then went to the kitchen and made myself a cup of tea. Perhaps I dozed off, I don't remember. But by the time I got back to the Criterion office, the films had been in the developer for four hours. This time when I took them out, there was nothing more I could do. I fixed them and dried them.

When I printed them up, they were very grainy but I felt the lighting had a Rembrandt-like quality. *Picture Post* were very excited about them. With the addition of some pictures of shelters which had been built in the middle of the street in Camberwell, I had four pages in that issue. *Life* magazine also used the pictures.

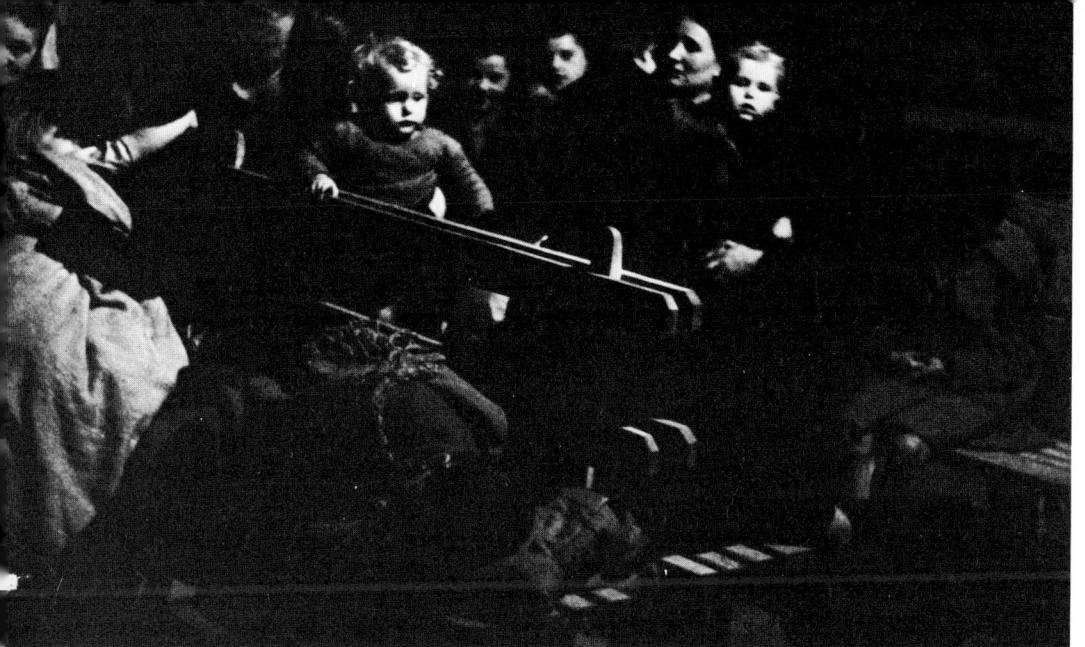
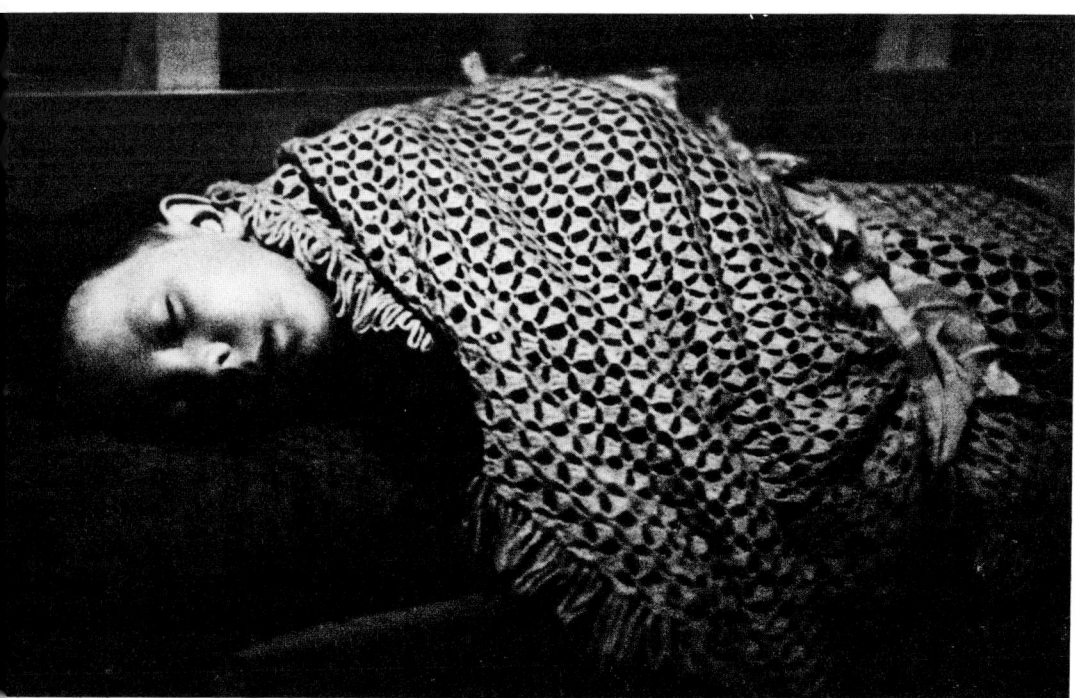

4: Early Days at *Picture Post*

The German bombing was most heavily concentrated in the areas around the City and the docks. Quite a lot of bombs fell in and around the Blackfriars Road, and my mum was shaken up. Although bombs fell close enough to shatter the taped-up glass in the windows, Lancaster Street, itself never received a direct hit.

The East End also received heavy punishment, and *Picture Post* responded by sending me out to take pictures with Bert Lloyd, who was then a journalist.

Bert Lloyd was one of the most brilliant men I have ever met. He came from a large and poor family, most of whom had died of TB. He was shipped off to Australia as a young boy in the hope that the climate would be good for his lungs, and started his working life there on a sheep farm. Then he worked on whaling ships, spending six months at a time at sea.

He was a card-carrying Communist, but for all the right reasons. He just didn't think that money should matter. He didn't keep account of anything borrowed or lent, and he was a kind and generous man. We became very good friends.

He was a natural linguist, and also had a terrific memory for everything he had read. Once, in a cinema in Cardiff, after we had seen a film about the discovery of penicillin, he gave me such a long and detailed talk about venereal disease, its symptoms and cure, that I felt sick. Later on, he became a great authority on folk music.

From the point of view of *Picture Post*, his greatest asset was his ability to win peoples' confidence instantly, and to talk to anyone. This made him the best man to send along to places like the East End of London.

'The East End at War' was the first story we worked on together. Our technique was just to wander around talking to people and taking pictures of anything which caught our eyes.

The spirit of the people was tremendous, and there was a strong determination to carry on as if nothing had happened. After having taken so many 'laid-on' pictures, I almost hesitated to photograph scenes like the girl in the clothing workshop still at work on her sewing machine, in case it didn't look 'real' enough.

Even the Post Office managed to carry out its duties in the middle of all the destruction. The man I came across filling in his tax form in his bombed-out house was amazed to have received it. I don't think it amused him greatly, though.

Meanwhile, Bert Lloyd and I visited an old music hall called the 'People's Palace' which had been turned into a reception centre for homeless people; and I took a photograph of an elderly man and woman, one sitting on a chair and one standing, outside what I took to be the ruins of their home.

After I had taken the picture, the old woman looked at the old man and asked me 'Who's he?' Still, at least they looked like a lovely old couple.

In the middle of all the bombing, the *Picture Post* darkrooms were damaged, and put out of action. Bill Pearson, the Picture Editor, asked me if they could use the Criterion darkrooms, and I was pleased to help out. In addition to commission work, I was helping by giving room to the woman in charge of developing and printing, Edith Kaye.

Edith was the wizard of the *Picture Post* darkrooms, and had worked for the magazine since the days when Stefan

These pictures show the spirit which pulled us through in the time of heavy raids.

Lorant was Editor. The story of how she got the job was odd. Born in Germany, she arrived in Britain at the same time as a lot of the first 35mm cameramen, such as Kurt Hubschman (later Hutton), Felix Baumann (later Man) and Tim Gidal.

Tim Gidal had done a story using 35mm film, and was looking for somebody to process it, when Edith's name was mentioned to him. He telephoned her, and made an appointment to meet her under the clock at Victoria Station.

Edith, slightly worried by the strange approach, went along, but took a friend with her. All was well, Gidal gave her the films, and she went away and processed them. But when Gidal went proudly along to Lorant and asked him what he thought of his pictures, Lorant looked at them closely and said: 'Never mind your story, who did your printing for you?'

He contacted Edith straight away and hired her to run the *Picture Post* darkrooms, where she remained until the magazine closed in 1958, by which time she had taught many talented printers their job.

Throughout this time of heavy raids Dora and the boys were still in London, so I used to go back to Eltham at nights. I spent a lot of time mending the roof: the tiles were always being shattered by shrapnel, but if I had time I'd go for walks in the woods with Michael and my wire-haired terrier Toby. Several more weeks of intensive bombing followed before the authorities decided that it would be a good idea if women and children were evacuated after all.

In October, Dora, Michael and Terry were evacuated to a place called Greenfield, about twenty miles outside Manchester.

My circumstances must have been known to Tom Hopkinson, the editor of *Picture Post*. Having found out that Dora had been evacuated up North, he tried to give me commissions nearby so that I could drop in and visit her. This sort of concern was typical of him.

Around this time he sent Bert and me up to Liverpool to do a story on the ferry. On the way back we were sitting next to the door of a compartment on a crowded corridor train. I asked Bert about the funny type they used in Germany, and he wrote my name and some phrase in German on the dirty steamed-up window.

When I got back to the *Picture Post* offices the next Monday, I was told that there were two men waiting to see me. I went into the editor's office, and I was immediately cross-questioned about why another man and myself had been writing in German on railway compartment windows. After they had finished with me, they still saw fit to question Bert Lloyd.

Somebody had reported us as being spies, and we had been traced by our special railway Press passes. Happily we were let off.

Our next story was 'The East End Parson', and the subject was the Reverend French, Rural Dean of Stepney, who was doing tremendous work for the people in his parish whose homes had been destroyed by the bombing. The kids all loved him, and really did run after him in the streets, although I had to ask them to do it again for the camera, just to make sure of getting the picture I wanted. However, that was the only picture which was in any way 'laid-on'.

Then Bert Lloyd's own folk interests took us up to a pub at

Liverpool: a sequence of pictures appears at the end of the chapter.

The Rural Dean of Stepney
with some of his flock.

Right, top: The chart room in
the Admiralty.

Centre: More paperwork on
the way in the Admiralty.

Bottom: Early morning at the
War Office.

Leiston in Suffolk, called 'The Eel's Foot'. It was famous locally for its singing and dancing on Saturday nights, and people used to come from miles around to join in.

Bert had heard about the place from a wealthy Communist friend of his, who lived in a smart modern house in the village with big picture windows. (The villagers hinted darkly that he used the windows in some way to signal to enemy aircraft.) We did the story and I took pictures in the pub, which was only lit by oil lamps – but by now I was a bit of a specialist at awkward lighting conditions. Then, risking being taken for spies again, we stayed at the house of Bert's friend. I am pleased to report that we survived without arrest.

It would be difficult to imagine a more complete contrast to Bert Lloyd than Macdonald Hastings. If Bert was a man of the people, Mac definitely liked to be upper crust. He was very tall, and well turned out, and he had all the assurance of his education and background.

Picture Post used to send Mac Hastings on all the posher stories: ones involving military or government officials, for example. I went with him to do a story about the War Office.

It was quite a difficult story to bring to life. After all, a map room is not a very interesting place to photograph if you are not allowed to show any of the maps. I was allowed five minutes to photograph Eden, then Minister of War, stiff and formal in his office. Then, as I walked around the underground corridors, I saw the charladies at work on their hands and knees, advancing slowly towards me.

This was just the sort of thing I needed to put some life into the story. I fixed up a single photoflood lamp high in the ceiling at the far end of the corridor, and when an officer came along in his uniform, I got my picture.

Any bits of map that were left showing in my pictures of the map room were touched out later by the censors, in case they were of use to the enemy. However, I didn't really find censorship too much of a problem at this time.

There were a few other examples of them interfering with my pictures. When I took photographs of a field gun for a story called 'A Gun is Fired', the shape of the gun was changed by careful retouching. And when I went down to Plymouth with Mac Hastings to do a story on our preparations for a counter-invasion of France, 'Invasion Rehearsal', the censors were not so much worried by the enemy knowing that the invasion would take place in rowing boats (!) as by a picture I took of the lads who had taken part in the exercise sitting outside a pub afterwards, having a drink with their Commanding Officer, a charming man called Captain Rickie. It wouldn't do for the enemy to discover that members of the armed forces have a taste for alcohol.

I had a real taste of action when I went to do some pictures of an Ack-Ack [anti-aircraft] battery at Putney. It was a Saturday afternoon, and everyone was feeling tired and bored. I worked hard, persuading the crew to take up action stations and look as if they were firing at an enemy aircraft. Then, just as I had got it all set up, there was a droning above us in

the sky, and we could make out some aircraft approaching.

Suddenly the battery realised the planes were German, and started firing at them. I rushed backwards and forwards taking pictures: it was the first time a 'laid-on' story had turned into a real one. This was in complete contrast to a story I did later: 'Training a Rear-Turret Gunner'.

The training consisted of a man sitting in the rear gun-turret of a simulator and learning how to fire his gun. I found it difficult to make the picture of man in a glass bowl look interesting, until I remembered the model of a German aircraft I noticed in the mess, presumably used for aircraft recognition. It was only about two feet long, but I got somebody to fix it on the end of a pole and hold it up outside the simulator. Then I took a picture from behind the gunner,

Air gunner's view of the enemy – on the end of a pole!

looking along the barrel of the gun at the model aircraft on the end of a stick.

When the picture was used in *Picture Post*, the pole was carefully touched out and the propellers made to look as if they were spinning, to give a thrillingly authentic look of an action picture.

While I was doing all this commission work for *Picture Post*, I was still working for Criterion, which meant I had to split everything automatically with Collins, who was supposed to be the salesman, although he didn't have very much to do. I began to feel that he was doing more with our money than he was doing for it. I started to wonder whether it was time to form a more direct link with *Picture Post*.

By now I knew most of the people who worked at the magazine's offices at 43 Shoe Lane, and I liked them. I always got on well with the journalists, and I felt happy about working with them as a team.

Anne Scott-James was one of four women journalists working on the magazine at that time. She was tall – almost as tall

as Mac Hastings, which I suppose was why she eventually married him – elegant, and terribly refined. As a woman, she was put in charge of a *Picture Post* scheme for readers to knit woolly socks and mufflers for the armed forces, which we then presented to them. (Male journalists still don't seem to write about knitting, do they!) She was very conscientious: when I used to beg her to let me have a particularly nice scarf, she always said a very firm 'no'.

Eventually she took all these things up to Harwich to present to the crew of a ship moored there, and I went with her to photograph the occasion. The sailors were very touched, and as a gesture in return, gave us each a pack of 200 cigarettes.

I didn't know she smoked, and carefully packed both lots of cigarettes in my bag.

Later, the two of us rode back together in the train. We were alone in the compartment, and I was rearranging my bag when I suddenly heard a woman's voice saying: 'You dirty rotten thieving bastard!' At first I thought it must be someone in the next compartment – I couldn't believe that such an elegant lady could let go with such a mouthful. But it was Anne Scott-James all right. I gave her back her cigarettes very quickly.

While Dora was away in Greenfield, I often used to go and stay with Bill Pearson and his wife in their house north of London. They were both very generous. From there I could sometimes go and watch *Picture Post* being put to bed at the printers in Watford.

When I did get back to Eltham, I nearly got into trouble. I had acquired a sporty little open-topped M.G. with a strap across the bonnet and an appetite for petrol. Dora and I had made friends with a neighbour who worked for Payne's, the chocolate manufacturers, near Tower Bridge. One Saturday, he asked me if I would collect him from work.

When I arrived at lunch time, he was clutching a large cardboard box, which he quickly put out of sight underneath the hood at the back. I told him that I wanted nothing to do with what he was doing, and that if we were going anywhere, he would have to drive.

We had a liquid lunch, and were speeding towards Greenwich when we ran straight into a speed trap, and were flagged down.

Panic now set in: not only were we speeding, but we were also carrying stolen goods, and searches of cars were not unusual then. I had to think quickly: I told my friend to tell the police that my mother was ill, then I jumped out of the car and wandered up the road with my face buried in my hands like a man in distress.

Incredibly, the trick worked. Seeing my desperate condition, the police hardly bothered to look at the papers before waving us on.

I think my friend was summonsed by the Police for speeding, and fined five shillings, but I expect the black-market value of the chocolate more than paid for that.

I couldn't use the car when I went up to Greenfield to see

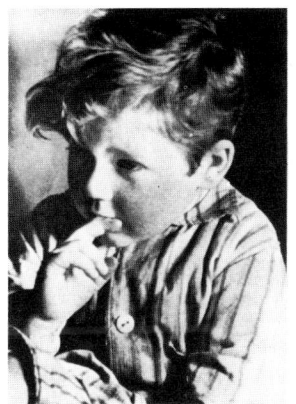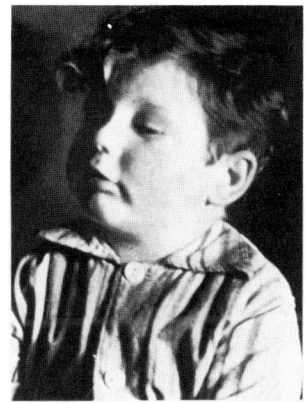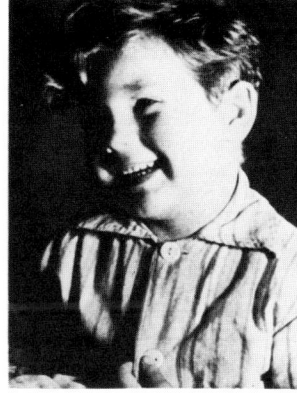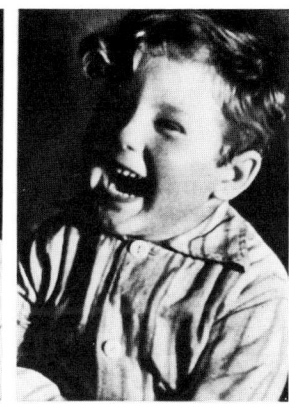

This little piggy went to market . . .

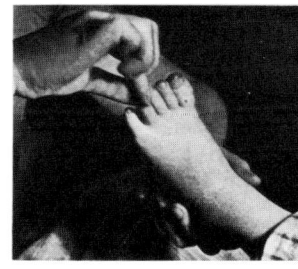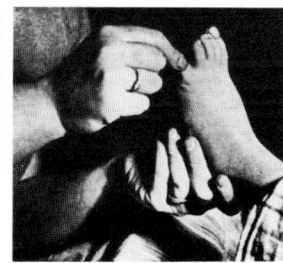

Dora, because of petrol rationing, so I had to take the train to Manchester and catch a bus from there.

Arriving in Manchester late one Sunday night, I found the place in flames after a bombing raid, and all buses cancelled. I was too impatient to wait the night in the railway station, so I set out to walk. Being Manchester, it was raining cats and dogs, and I soon got wet through and freezing cold. Eventually, in the early hours of the morning, I was forced to admit defeat and take refuge in a telephone box, first standing, then attempting to sit on the telephone shelf.

Arrived home the next day, I did a sequence of pictures of Michael's toes and his facial expressions while Dora played 'This Little Piggy Went to Market' with him, which was used over two full pages in *Picture Post*. This story more than paid for the trip.

The last commission I did while I was still working for Criterion Press was a story about the Blitz. I hung around the headquarters of the London Fire Brigade near Lambeth Bridge for a few nights, and took photographs of the operations room. But at that time, early in January 1941, there was a lull in the bombing.

I decided to stay at my mum's house in Lancaster Street so I would be close by, and I arranged for a driver from the fire brigade to come and pick me up when the action started.

On the night of 11 January 1940, heavy raids started once again. My mum went off to shelter in the Elephant & Castle underground station, and I waited for my driver. When he didn't turn up, I walked to the Lambeth fire station, and a driver took me out in his car.

We started along the riverside, south of Blackfriars Bridge. A row of warehouses were on fire, and I went down into the cellar of one of them with a fireman.

I was working away when a beam suddenly gave way behind us and the roof collapsed, blocking our way out. We both started looking desperately around for an escape route. At last we found a hole in the floor.

We scrambled down through it into a dark tunnel which ran along beneath the warehouses, and wriggled along it until we found a way out. We emerged from the burning buildings about four warehouses along with nothing worse than a few holes burnt in our clothing. Back where we had started out from, the firemen were already beginning to dig for us in the rubble.

Afterwards, we moved north of the river to the city. I must have gone up onto the roof of one of the buildings to get pictures of firemen fighting the fire from the tops of ladders, but I can't remember anything about it.

After some hours, I ran out of film, so I asked the driver to give me a lift back to Lancaster Street where I kept some spare rolls. There I found my sister Lily rushing about with buckets of water doing her best to put out fires started by incendiary bombs. The driver had to go back to headquarters to replace the car tyres, because his had all been destroyed by shrapnel, so I stayed and helped Lily for a while until he came back.

By dawn the raid had stopped and I went to see my mum at Elephant & Castle tube station so she knew I was all right. My suit was burnt and my camera was damaged, but *Picture Post* paid me the cost of replacing both of them. When the story was published a couple of weeks later, Tom Hopkinson gave me the first photographer's credit ever used in the paper: 'From our rule of anonymity we except these

Firefighting: the picture sequence is at the end of the chapter.

Churchill welcomed at the
Russian Embassy by Boris
Karloff's double.

Right: A moment later,
Maisky signalled me to
leave.

pictures. They were taken by A. Hardy, one of our own
photographers.'

My disagreements with Bertram Collins about money had
now reached the point where I thought it would be best if we
parted company. As part of the agreement I let him have the
office and all the equipment, including my Valoy enlarger.

On 3 March 1940, I joined *Picture Post* as a staff photographer on a freelance basis. The rates of pay for a story in the
paper at that time were £8 for a single page, £6 for the second
page, £4 for the third, £2 for the fourth, and £2 for every ad-
ditional page used after that. So that if, as had already happened, I had nine pages in a twenty-five page issue, I would
get £30 that week. Tom agreed to guarantee me £8 a week,
even if I had nothing used that particular week, to be deducted from weeks when I had more than one page used.
As it turned out, we never needed to worry about this
arrangement.

As a staff photographer, I used to join the journalists
every morning when ideas for new stories were kicked
around, and just about everything else. And when I was in
town, I went along with a group of journalists to lunch at the
Little Acropolis Restaurant in Charlotte Street. Having finished my education at fourteen, I found their conversation
full of interest. I expect they learnt a few things from me as
well.

Tom Hopkinson was my boss now, and also my critic. I
had a tremendous respect for his opinions; everyone did.
Tom's office was guarded by Paddy Brosnan, his secretary,
and nobody could see him without her permission. But occasionally we'd be sitting around and Paddy Brosnan would
come up and say that Tom wanted to see one of us. Everyone
would stop what they were doing and hold their breath
while whoever it was went into Tom's office, and wait until
they came out again to see if they were smiling or looking
fed-up.

Going to see Tom always made you a little apprehensive.
He was not aggressive, far from it. He sat you down in a chair
in front of his beautiful desk, and offered you a cup of tea
which Paddy then brought in. He'd put down a little mat for
your cup, so you didn't spoil the leather top of the desk.

Often he simply wanted to say that such-and-such a story
was very good. But if he did criticise, he would only need to
say 'Are you sure you got the best pictures you could out of
this?' That was really giving you hell. You felt so dreadful
that you couldn't sleep. You knew that something was
wrong somewhere.

Most of the time, though, he contented himself with sending a little note. If you were lucky, it might say: 'First class,
Bert'.

Although Tom could be fairly tough about money, he was
always generous to a fault about my expenses. I was soon
well known for my expenses. The *Picture Post* accountants
used to glare at me whenever I handed them one of my
expense sheets, but as long as Tom had okayed it, there was
nothing they could do. The man I had to be careful of was

Charles Fenby, the assistant editor. Once I had put down '3/6d for tea'. That was a lot for tea in those days, and Fenby queried it with me: 'How on earth did you manage to spend three and sixpence on tea?' 'Well', I said, 'I had a couple of boiled eggs'. That stumped him: eggs were black-market items in those days, so 3/6d wouldn't be unreasonable. I'm glad to say he didn't make any more trouble after that.

My next story with Bert Lloyd came about because of Bert's communist contacts at the Soviet Embassy. Ambassador Maisky was giving a big reception, and we were the only British Press boys to be allowed in.

Maisky took us aside and said he didn't mind me taking photographs of the arrivals if we were tactful in how we went about it. I took up a position in the entrance hall behind a pillar and waited for the guests to come.

Churchill and Eden came in, and their coats were taken by a huge Russian retainer with a face and build not unlike Boris Karloff. Then, as they walked forward past me, I stepped forward to get a picture. Churchill frowned in my direction and said to Eden: 'Who's that man? I've seen him somewhere before.'

That was supposed to be that, but I thought it would be good to have a picture of everyone sitting down to lunch, so I approached Maisky. To my surprise, he agreed, so long as I kept myself hidden and promised to leave when he gave a pre-arranged signal.

I was able to take pictures of all the great and noble guests, diplomats and financiers, arms dealers and heads of state, and finally got the crowning shot: a picture of Maisky and Churchill touching glasses. Then Maisky gave me the sign, and I disappeared.

Churchill was so respected then that seeing him in the flesh was like seeing a legend. Just the sound of his voice on the wireless at lunchtime made people stop what they were doing and sit up and take notice. One *Picture Post* idea was to send all the photographers out to get pictures of people listening to one of his speeches. I went to a pub called *The Black Dog* in Shoe Lane.

J. B. Priestley's series of wireless talks 'Postscripts' also used to be eagerly listened to. He also used to do a story each week for *Picture Post*, and I was the photographer who went with him most often.

We went to factories and theatres, and each story always had a picture of Priestley in it to show that he really had been to the place he was talking about.

He was enormously popular, and not much interested in photographs, except of himself. Everywhere we went, people instantly wanted to talk to him, so he would be taken off by them, and I would be left to try to get a picture as well as I could. I think he found it difficult to accept that *Picture Post* was a picture magazine, so there was not much co-operation between us.

I got a bit fed up with this in the end, and complained to Charles Fenby, the assistant editor (I didn't dare to discuss it with Priestley). I wasn't trying to make trouble, I just

J.B. Priestley's voice was known to millions through his radio broadcasts, but his face only became famous through his 'Picture Post-script' series.

wanted Fenby to mention to Priestley that the photographer had a job to do as well.

Fenby wrote a letter and gave it to me to give to Priestley.

Priestley and I were doing a story on ENSA at the Theatre Royal, Drury Lane. He was sitting chatting with Basil Dean, the head of ENSA, when I handed him the letter. He opened the envelope and read it.

The letter must have been rude, extremely rude. As he read it, Priestley said nothing, but slowly grew redder and redder with rage. After that, though, things worked out a bit better.

Once, when we were staying at a hotel in Chester together, we had just signed the register when a woman came up to him and started talking to him as if she knew him well. Priestley must have looked rather blank, because the woman suddenly stopped and said: 'I'm so sorry, I thought I was talking to *the* J. B. Priestley', and walked off. Quick as a flash, Priestley was running after her: 'But I am! I am!'

By late October 1941, I was working flat out, seven days a week, for the paper. The last week of that month and the first in November show roughly how my time was spent.

On Sunday, 26 October I went up to Edinburgh with Bert Lloyd to do a story on a Council Meeting, but we arrived too late.

The next day we went to Leith where a Russian ship was due to berth the following day. We met up with a woman interpreter who was supposed to understand the various dialects spoken by the seamen. On Tuesday we did the story of the Russian ship. The woman interpreter got hopelessly confused with all the different dialects, and in the end Berty Lloyd was interpreting for her. That day I received a message from *Picture Post* to travel to Machynlleth in Wales, so I left Bert and travelled down overnight.

I got two hours sleep in Shrewsbury bus station before

POST

HULTON'S NATIONAL WEEKLY

In this issue :

A TRAWLER IN WAR-TIME 3ᴰ

MARCH 21, 1942   Vol. 14. No. 12

On most jobs I took a portrait in the hope that it would be used on the cover. This one worked.

catching the 4 a.m. bus to Machynlleth, where I was met by Macdonald Hastings, fresh and immaculate after his night in a hotel. We then took part in an old-fashioned type of fox-hunt without horses, which involved dashing about for about twenty miles all over the mountains. We didn't even catch a fox.

On Friday, I went to Neath to cover a miners' meeting, and on Saturday I travelled back to London, arriving in the early hours of Sunday morning.

On Monday I took my films into the *Picture Post* dark-rooms, and found that they had made one of their rare mis-takes in developing my foxhunt pictures. Instead of putting the films back to back in the developing tank, they had put them face to face, and ruined them. I would have to do the pictures again.

On Tuesday I went down to Brighton with Anne Scott-

James to do the out-of-town opening of a show with George Lewis. On Wednesday I went to the zoo, and on Thursday I did a story about Land Girls at Hassocks in Sussex. On Friday I returned to Machynlleth to repeat the foxhunting story. This time we caught a fox, and, because I was a bit fresher, my pictures were better. One of them was used by Tom for the front cover, which was always a thrill, and meant I was paid an extra five pounds.

Probably because of his experience on whaling ships, Bert Lloyd was always sent on seafaring stories. Early in 1942, we were sent up to Fleetwood to do a story on trawlers fishing in the North Sea.

Before we went on board, we took the precaution of buying a lot of second-hand clothes, so our own wouldn't permanently stink of fish. The trawler itself was a tiny, dirty, stinking little tub – all the best boats had been taken over by the Navy to be used as mine-sweepers. When the crew turned up they were completely pickled. Some could barely manage to stagger up the gangplank, but soon we put out to sea.

The North Sea was particularly rough that week. I was all right, but funnily enough (since he had been a seaman), Bert was sick as a dog. We spent a couple of days getting pictures and talking to the blokes, and then, having exhausted all the possibilities in that direction, settled down to spend the rest of the week being bored (though not by the weather).

The boat did everything but turn over. We slept at night in cupboards around the walls of the tiny little cabin, listen-ing to the rats scuttling along the bulkheads above us. We ate at a table in the middle of the cabin, although no one ever put their plate down on it: you had to hold on to it and lean with the motion of the boat if you wanted to have any food left. But only old hands were able to keep any food on their plates when, instead of going up and down, the boat sud-denly leaped from the crest of one wave, left the water and hit the next wave with jarring force.

Sometimes I tried to hang around the little galley, where the day's fish dish was being prepared (it was a case of fish with everything) to keep warm; but the cook always kicked me out.

At one stage we had to shelter from a storm with a lot of other trawlers off Bear Island, but finally, after ten endless days, we arrived back at Fleetwood. The crew headed straight for their drinking club, to spend their wages and top up their livers before their next trip. Bert and I filled our kit-bags with fresh cod, and headed back to London.

By this time, Tom Hopkinson was fending off attempts to call me up for active service. He thought I could do more for the war effort by continuing to take photographs.

He managed to get my call-up deferred a couple of times. If he could delay it until I was thirty, I would be able to become a proper war correspondent; if I got called up before that, I would have to do whatever the forces decided they wanted me to do.

In any case, I was doing a fair number of stories about the

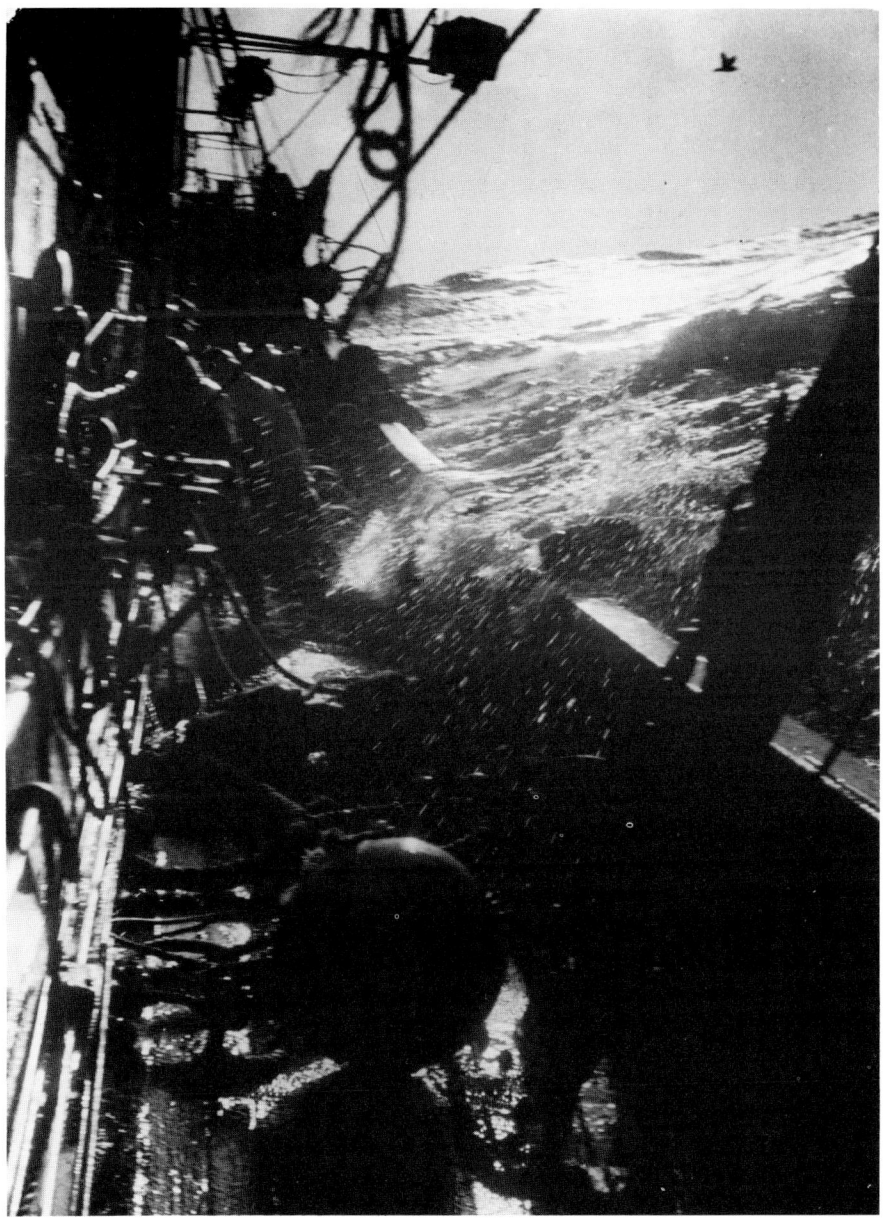

services. Shortly after the trawler voyage, I was sent up to Scotland for a sort of photocall which was to take place on board the aircraft carrier *Illustrious*, showing her going through her paces.

The jaunt on the *Illustrious* was intended to last one day, but when we got out to sea, a storm blew up, and we were unable to get back to port for five days. On about the third day – perhaps we were beginning to look a bit dog-eared – someone must have realised that none of the Press corps had a change of clothing with them, and we were given permission to go to the quartermaster's stores and buy as much underclothing as we needed at ridiculously low prices. There was such a feeling of luxury in buying and putting on all this top quality American underwear, that it almost seemed worth spending all that time at sea in a storm.

Shortly afterwards I was sent with Mac Hastings to do a story on a 'Battle school' at Ilfracombe in Devon. Once again all the press boys were there with their plate cameras, this time set up at various points along the assault course. With my Leica I was not hampered by the need to stay in the same place, so I decided to try a different approach and go round the course with the soldiers, stopping at each obstacle and taking pictures.

Mac cheered me on as if he was at a school sports day, while I scrambled round. When we came to the final obstacle, a bit of cliff about thirty feet high, he yelled out: 'Go on Bert, you can do it!' I did, and when I got to the top, I turned round and took a photograph of the next man up crawling over the edge, which made the cover of *Picture Post*, and an extra five pounds.

Later on, when it looked like everything had finished, all the Press boys headed as one man back to the mess to drink away the thirst that watching all that hard exercise had given them. But I had the feeling that something else was about to happen, so I hung around.

That something else turned out to be a rare exercise with live ammunition. The idea was to get the soldiers used to the feeling of having bullets flying close to them. A machine gun was set up on a fixed position, and the men formed a line along the beach at right angles to the gun. At a signal from their officer, they all fell face down onto the ground, and the machine gun opened fire on a line a couple of feet in front of them.

I knelt up and took pictures of them lying there, but my best shot was the one I took of the imprints left by their bodies in the sand after they all got up and moved on.

Above left: Bert by the other Bert (Lloyd).

Above: Why the other Bert was sick!

Paddington station: an elderly lady being escorted to her carriage. Anne Scott-James is on the left.

Wartime Terminus: further pictures at the end of the chapter.

When I got back to the mess, the pity felt for me for having missed valuable drinking time was soon converted to jealousy when the word got round about what I had been up to. For the time being I had an exclusive, but so great was the outcry, the exercise had to be repeated for them the next day.

Doing another story on a two-day survival exercise at Ilfracombe, I was invited by some soldiers to have some of the stew they had managed to cook up even though they were living rough. They gave me a big plate of the stuff. It tasted delicious, like rabbit. 'Did you enjoy that?' they asked when I had cleaned my plate.

'Lovely.'

'Do you know what it was?'

'Yes, rabbit.'

'Wrong. It was cat.'

On that trip, I discovered that I was a good shot. I had never done any shooting before, except with a five-shilling Daisy air-rifle as a kid. Now someone gave me a .38 rifle adapted to fire .22 bullets, and I had a go at hitting shoe polish tins thrown in the air.

When I hit the first one, they said it was beginners' luck.

When I hit the second tin, they were more interested, although they still thought it was a fluke. To test me, they fixed a penny to a telegraph pole, and we retreated a good distance away. This time, when I hit the penny, I began to be treated with a certain respect.

Later on, when I did shooting practice with the Army Film Unit at Lingfield, it turned out that most of the photographers were good shots. As an army photographer, I was only armed with a revolver, but I am glad to say that I never shot anyone with it, and, better still, no one ever shot me.

One of the last stories I did as a civilian was about Paddington Station: 'Wartime Terminus'. The large picture of five platforms which was used over two pages was the type of join-up which I had learned under Davis, and was probably made from three separate shots.

In some of the pictures of touching farewells, you can see the tall figure of Anne Scott-James in the background. In the best tradition of photo-journalism, we used a model for one of the principal figures, to add a bit of dignity.

After the story was published, a man kept trying to contact me at the office. When he finally caught up with me, he told me that by chance I had taken a picture of his unfaithful wife saying goodbye to her lover. He was absolutely convinced of this, and it was only when I told him that the woman was a model known to me that he gave up the idea that I could help him to trace his wife.

At last I couldn't be kept out of the army any longer. I think the Army Film and Photographic Unit was in the process of formation, and it was decided to call up a number of people like me in readiness.

There were sentimental scenes at *Picture Post*. Mac Hastings bought me a green wooden pipe from a shop in the Burlington Arcade, and Tom Hopkinson threw a farewell party for me at a Hungarian restaurant in Piccadilly. When I was dancing with one of the girls there, a toffee-nosed lady came up to me and told me off for being so rude as to dance with a big cigar in my mouth. I was just having fun.

Tom also arranged, entirely voluntarily, to have *Picture Post* pay five pounds each week into my bank account for the entire time I was in the army. This eliminated any worries I had about being able to keep up the mortgage repayments on the house at Eltham on my lowly private soldier's pay.

On 18 June 1942, with my green pipe in my luggage, and two hundred cigarettes given to me by a girl who saw me off from the station, I travelled up to Newark Army Camp, where I was to do eighteen weeks' basic training with the Royal Engineers.

Firefighting

One of the most frightening nights of my life. The streaks in the sky are actually molten metal.

THE HEIGHT OF THE BLAZE : *Eighty Feet up in the Air a Fireman Strikes at the Heart of the Fire*
Stark and grim is the climax of the fire fight. Blazing walls are crumbling. The fire is bursting through. Overhead, guided by the flames, the German bombers are circling. One after another they release their load of death. Unmoved, unflinching, the firemen run out their ladder. One man mounts, higher and higher, till he is alone above the flames. There, eighty feet up, he strikes at the very source of the fire.

14

THE MAN ON THE LADDER : *In Clouds of Smoke and Steam He Faces the Fire Alone*

All night long they have fought the fire. They have fought it in the streets streaming with water. They have fought it within buildings blazing like a furnace. On to the flames they have poured a hundred thousand gallons of water, concentrated at colossal pressure. And still the fight goes on. From our rule of anonymity we except these pictures. They were taken by A. Hardy, one of our own cameramen.

Wartime
Terminus

The complete story
made six pages in
Picture Post.

Liverpool

Over the years I did several stories on the city. It was, among other things, where I first learned to appreciate Chinese food. The Chinese seamen used to live in really dreadful conditions and I did a really strong story about them, though at the last moment *Picture Post* decided not to publish it.

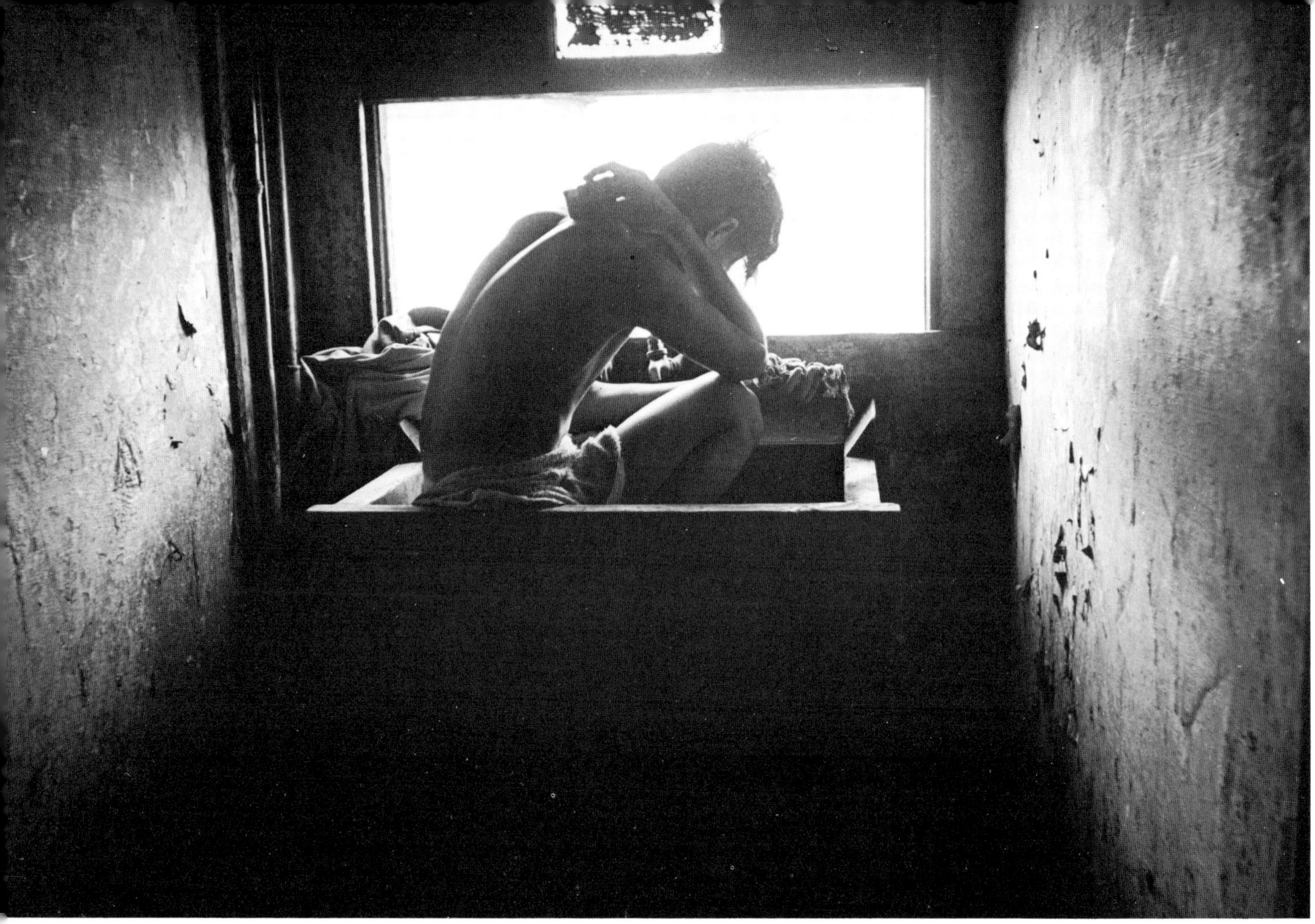

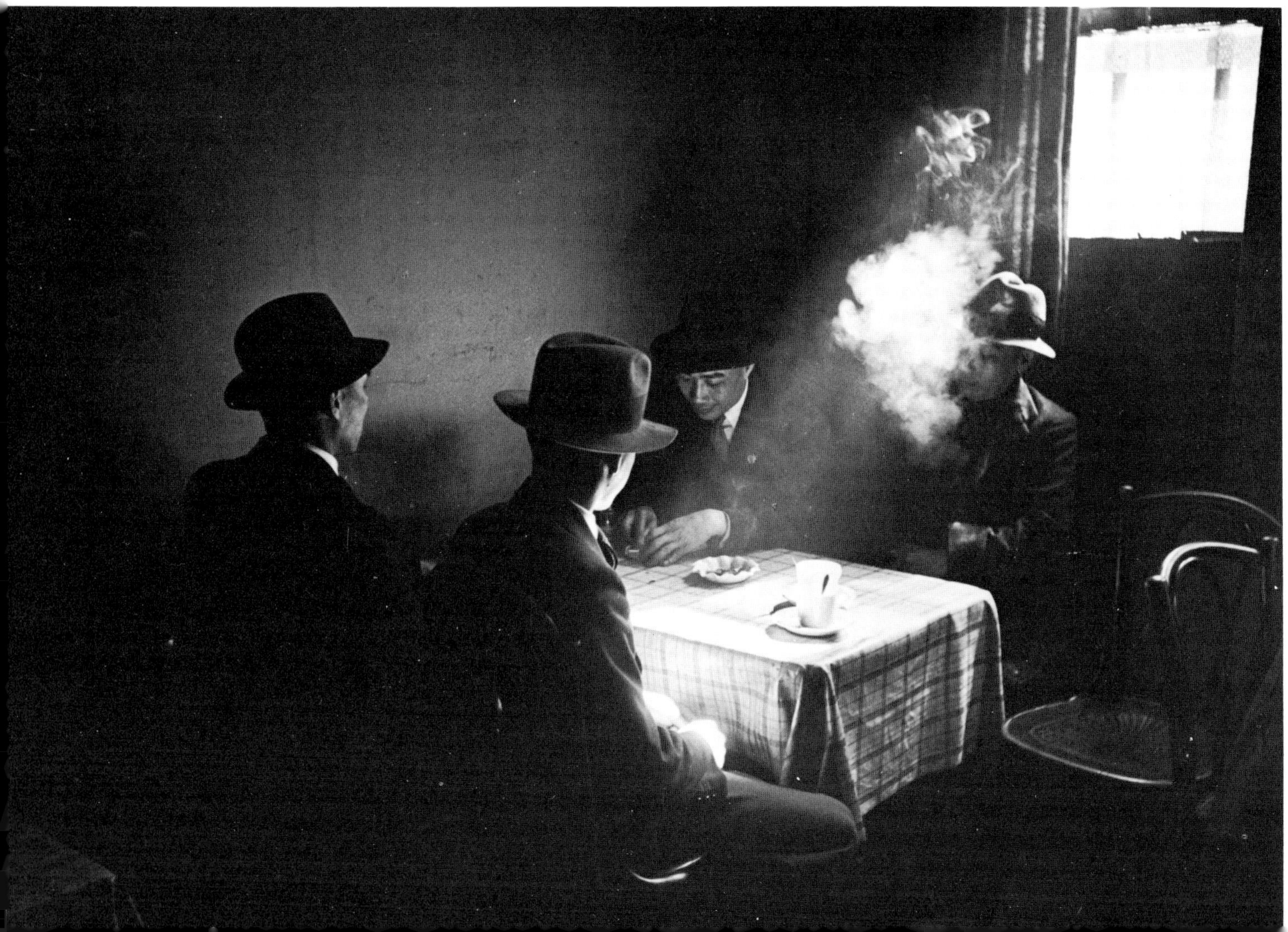

5: Army Life

I hated my introduction to the army. Going from the comparative freedom of being a roving photographer for *Picture Post* to the persecuted existence of a rookie, the lowest form of life in the army, was a big shock.

We did the usual square-bashing, and they tried to teach us to salute. I never did master that art, but I did learn that, for the time being at least, sergeants and I were natural enemies. It soon became clear that the only way for me to stay out of trouble was never to cross their paths. At Newark, if I saw one on the horizon, I used to scurry behind the nearest Nissen hut.

The training seemed to go on for ever, but then, after only three weeks, without any warning, I was told that I was being posted to the Army Film and Photographic Unit [AFPU] in London. I had to hand back my rifle and collect my civilian clothes from stores. (I always wondered what happened to all the civilian clothes handed in that were never collected.) Next I had to collect my day's food ration from the cookhouse: one small tin of bully beef and three raw potatoes. I put the three potatoes in my empty locker, and, pausing only to ask a friend to give my apologies to the girl in the NAAFI canteen and tell her that I wouldn't be able to go for a walk in the woods that evening as arranged, I dashed off and caught the train.

Shortly after I left, there was a surprise kit inspection. I was later told that the officer conducting it was so incensed at finding three raw potatoes in my locker that he wanted to fetch me back and have me put on a charge.

Blissfully unaware of the trouble I had escaped, I arrived in London and proceeded to the transit hotel in Marylebone, where I was pleasantly surprised to find that we could come and go as we liked. One of the first things I did was visit *Picture Post*: I think they were a bit shocked to see me back so quickly. I also used to go home to Eltham as often as I could.

One evening I was walking calmly down the front steps when a voice called: 'Ah, sapper, where do you think you're going?'

My blood froze: it was a sergeant. 'Out, sir.'

'Oh no you're not. Come with me.'

I followed his strutting form to the basement, where he pointed to a great mound of potatoes on a table beside a sort of hopper.

'See those potatoes? Peel them.'

I peeled as fast as I could for an hour, thinking that if I could get them all done quickly, I might still have time to get home and see Dora. At the end of the hour I heard boots on the stairs, and the sergeant reappeared:

'How are you doing?'

'Nearly finished, sir.'

'Oh, have you?' he said. And he pulled a lever at the side of the hopper, and another mound of potatoes as big as the one I had just peeled came tumbling down.

'Carry on, sapper.'

I didn't get home that evening. But after that I always took care to leave by the back entrance.

After a few days I went for an interview at AFPU headquarters in Curzon Street, Mayfair. One of the interviewers was Harry Deverson, who would take over Bill Pearson's job as picture editor of *Picture Post* after the war. With typical army efficiency, I had been put down to be trained as a movie cameraman, but when they looked at the form I had filled in and saw who I was, they hastily changed their minds and decided that I had better be a still photographer after all.

I now had to attend a six-week training course, where it was felt I should be told all about how to take a photograph. The school was run by Captain Houghton, formerly of *The Times*, assisted by Lieutenant Malandine, a staff photographer on *Illustrated*. Malandine came from the same sort of background as me, but by volunteering at the start of the war he had obtained the honorary rank of Lieutenant. We began to get on each others' nerves at once, and his dislike of me affected practically the whole of my army career.

There were about thirty of us on the course. Judging by some of the people there, anyone who had sold films across a chemist's shop counter must have qualified for training; but I soon palled up with a couple of chaps who were in the same boat as me: Bill Wooldridge, who had worked for Reuters, and Ron Holloway, who had worked for a newspaper in the Midlands.

We were all equipped with the standard-issue army camera, the Super Ikonta. It was (ironically) a German folding camera with a non-interchangeable f2.8 lens, and a press-type open viewfinder on the top. It took eleven pictures on a 120 film $2\frac{1}{4}$ inches square, with a top speed of 1/250th second. Winding on the film was a slow business, taking about two or three full seconds. The camera packed away in a bulky leather carrying case with room for a half a dozen 120 films (if we wanted more we had to carry them in our pockets) and a ridiculous flimsy tripod that wouldn't even stay still at 1/100th of a second. It was quite a contrast with my own cameras and equipment. At first I used my Rolleiflex, but when it was damaged, the army wouldn't repair it, and I had to use the horrid Ikonta.

After we learned all about our cameras, we were given projects. I did one story on a park in wartime, and another on an ATS girl. For one of these projects I was using my own tripod when Captain Houghton came up to me and asked me what I thought I was doing. I explained that the army one was so wobbly that I could get a better picture if I used my own. He was not impressed: 'We can't have that, Hardy, that's cheating!'

At the end of the course I passed out top (without cheating). Bill Wooldridge was second, and Ron Holloway was third. The rest of the students went on to Pinewood for further training, but Bill and Ron and I were posted straight away to Army Public Relations in Cadogan Gardens.

On our first morning there, we were told to report to the Colonel in charge, and marched into his office: me first, Ron second, and Bill third, and gave a wrong salute. The orders we received were to prove fateful.

My story on an ATS girl was made while I was being taught how to take photographs by the army (by then I had been in the business for fifteen years).

The first thing he told us was that we were all sergeants now, so we should put up our stripes straight away. I could hardly believe my luck – after only a couple of months in the army, I was free from bullying sergeants.

Then he went on to say that he knew what we Press boys were like, and how we would be bound to fight over who did what job, so we would do the jobs which came along in rotation, starting with Hardy, then Holloway, then Wooldridge.

A day or two passed, and the first job, which was mine, came up. It was very routine: I had to photograph a cadet at the Duke of York's Barracks across the road in Chelsea, for *Cadet* magazine. Even though it was so straightforward, Ron said could he come along and watch. He did, and the whole thing was over in ten minutes.

The next job to come up, on 16 August, was Ron's. He was told to pack all his kit and prepare for a long trip. He had been in the army a bit longer than me, and had lost his army knife, so I lent him mine.

Bill's job came up next, and then I was sent on another: I went down to the coast with an officer I shall call Captain Smith to photograph wounded commandoes returning from the Dieppe raids. If he hadn't stopped at a club for three hours on the way down, while I sat outside in the jeep, we might have been in time to get some pictures. Luckily Captain Houghton knew me well enough not to blame me.

When I got back from this pointless jaunt, I was told that Ron had taken part in the raid, and had been killed. He was the first casualty from the AFPU. No other dangerous jobs came up, though, and life in Cadogan Gardens settled into a lazy routine.

We lived on the top floor of a huge house. There was an ATS [Auxiliary Territorial Service, really the female version of the army] barracks next door where they giggled a lot (especially at night), and kept us awake, but we didn't have much to do with them. During the day, Bill and I used to go and sit in Joe Lyons tea shop in Sloane Square and play cards. Everyone knew where we were, and we could easily be got hold of if a job came up. In the end we knew the waitresses so well that if we fancied a bit of haddock for our tea we could take it in and they would cook it for us.

After five o'clock our time was our own. I sometimes went to a cafe which was owned by an Italian. He was a compulsive gambler, and often left his wife alone in the evenings, so I got to know her quite well; too well for him, in fact.

But most nights, Bill and I used to go out on the town. One evening we started at seven o'clock in a pub near our billet, drinking pints of beer with whisky chasers. I don't know how many we had, but after an hour we went off to a dance hall in the Tottenham Court Road where we used to go to pick up the popsies. I can remember sitting for a while watching the girls dancing, then I was horribly sick. I don't think the manager was very pleased.

Bill managed to get me to a taxi, and by eight-thirty I was back in Cadogan Gardens flat on my back fast asleep.

Things didn't always end so messily. One night when Bill and I came staggering out of Sloane Square tube station, Bill dared me to climb the war memorial in the middle of the square. There was nothing much to get a grip on, but by drunkenly embracing as much of the plinth as possible and scrabbling with my toes, I had managed to get a fair way up when a couple of coppers came along.

I abandoned my attempt on the sumit and accepted their invitation to accompany them to Sloane Street Police Station.

We fully expected them to charge us with being drunk and disorderly, but the funny thing was that by the time we got to the Police Station we were getting on so well with them that they didn't bother. In fact we got on so well that after that evening they often used to join us on our nights out when they were off-duty.

Friendships were easily made and easily broken in the war. Bill and I had a surprisingly innocent relationship with a couple of ATS girls whom we used to meet regularly in a pub in the Kings Road. They were very keen on us, but I suppose we must have been rather busy at the time. They used to do little tricks like taking one of our handkerchieves and hiding it in the front of their blouses, or up the leg of their knickers, with the general idea of us trying to get it back again. The one I was friendliest with was Scottish – both her parents were surgeons working in London. One night when we were all out together, she complained that she didn't feel well. Then she admitted that the reason was that she had been inoculated that day because she was going off on a foreign posting the next day.

I offered to see her home. We got a taxi to her billet in a mews near Hyde Park, and, for the first time, some touching scenes took place. When we arrived, she told me to wait a minute. She disappeared, and then a minute later rushed out with a tartan plaid cape which she wanted me to keep to remember her by.

I faithfully kept the cape, which got slowly more tattered and bedraggled, in the bottom of my kitbag until the end of the war, but I never found out what happened to her.

None of the photographic jobs I was given to do at this time were very interesting. I spent more than a month at Gairloch Head on the West Coast of Scotland, taking pictures of the construction of a Mulberry Harbour, a prefabricated metal platform floating on barge-like bases.

The camp seemed to be in the middle of nowhere. I had just arrived and installed myself in the Sergeants' Mess, when the Sergeant-Major came up to me. He wanted to show me a card trick, and what was more, he was willing to bet me a pound that I couldn't tell him how the trick was done in the space of an hour.

He was in charge, so I watched dutifully, and accepted his bet. He had gone out to leave me to it when another sergeant came in and saw me looking puzzled at the deck of cards. He quickly realised what was going on: 'That Sergeant-Major's a bastard', he said. 'He played the same trick on me.' And he quickly showed me how the trick was done.

Now I felt a bit worried about how to convince the Sergeant-Major that I had solved the problem without any help, so I got a sheet of paper and covered it with all sorts of complicated mathematical-looking formulas.

When the Sergeant-Major came back after an hour, I showed him how to do the trick and he was astonished. No one had ever managed to do it before. But before he handed over his pound, he demanded to know how I had done it. I produced the piece of paper and explained:

'Look, it's easy: if $x + y = z$, and $a - b = c$, then . . .'

He thought I was a mathematical genius, but in the weeks that followed he won back all his money and more besides.

The only other sources of entertainment apart from cards was an ATS barracks about ten miles away. The chaps from our camp and the ATS girls used to meet at a pub halfway between the two, run by a nice old couple. It was so busy that I volunteered to help out behind the bar. I suppose it was just as well that I had so little else to do: by the time I had walked five miles to the pub, helped behind the bar, walked a girl five miles back to the ATS camp (stopping on the way), then walked the whole ten miles back to our camp, I felt quite buggered.

For light relief, it was possible to go to dances at the nearest town. I had a bit of a thing about a girl I used to see there at dances. I used to have a few drinks and she used to teach me to dance the Scottish reel, which as far as I can remember seemed to involve me regularly being thrown to the floor.

In due course, I returned to Cadogan Gardens. Life was so leisurely that I worked far harder for *Picture Post* on my occasional leaves than I did while on duty. We filled in time in various ways. One of Bill's interests was old cars, and sometimes, just for something to do, I used to go with him to garages to look at cars for sale. On one of these trips, I acquired a real grand prix Bugatti for £200. I found out later that it had formerly been owned by an Italian count. I kept it at home at Eltham, and only sat in it occasionally, and sadly never got to drive it on the road.

Another day, Bill Brandt, whom I knew from working on *Picture Post*, told me that he was looking for a strongly-built man to model for some photographs. I immediately thought of Bill Wooldridge, who was well over six feet tall, and he agreed to help Bill Brandt out.

We both went along to the session, and I remember how astonished Bill Brandt was when we suggested he paid a fee for Bill's time. In the end, though, I believe he was reluctantly parted from his money.

There was so little to do that autumn (in 1943) that when Mac Hastings told me that he was going to Scotland to do a story on a stag hunt for *Picture Post*, and that he needed a photographer to go with him, I skipped off for the weekend to do it.

Legally or not, I travelled up with Mac to Cannich in Inverness, wearing civvies. We were staying at a posh baronial hall with a lot of right honourables and lords, and that sort of thing. I didn't find it at all awkward: I have always got on well with the real upper classes and the lower classes: people who have no 'side' to them.

Stag hunting was a difficult business: it seemed to be a question of peering over the tops of rocks at stags with lovely antlers, miles away. All the time we had to notice whether the wind was coming towards us or them. There was no chance of getting anywhere near them unless we first performed an enormous detour. We spent all day doing this, and covered a tremendous mileage; but we never shot anything.

The next day we tried again. This time we shot three stags. The people who had shot them were happy, and so, for a different reason, were Mac and I. The whole thing had made a good story, and now we had free time to relax.

Relaxation meant fishing. Mac was an enthusiastic angler: he used to buy his fishing tackle from a shop called Hardy's at the bottom of St James's Street where it enters Pall Mall, and on this occasion he had the very latest type of reel with a special slip-clutch to prevent the line from breaking when there was a sudden tug on it.

There was nothing much for me to do: the only fishing experience I had was years earlier when I caught an eel at Westbury-on-Severn on a Country Holiday Fund holiday, so I wandered up and down the river bank watching everybody else.

Eventually, somebody noticed me doing nothing, and sent the gillie to fetch me a spare rod. Now I needed a fly, so a man called Bertie Pallant (who was the King's dentist) lent me one, and I tried my hand. After catching the line in the branches of a tree once or twice, I got the knack of casting so that the fly landed on the surface of the water like a real fly.

The river looked beautiful, with rocks and leaping fish. As I cast my line I began to see the attraction of the sport for all those other fishermen, thoughtful and intense, and Mac with his up-to-date tackle. I was just wondering if anyone ever caught anything with all this concentration, and whether it really mattered, when suddenly my fly dipped below the water and there was a tug on my line. I had a bite.

The King's dentist was at my side in an instant. He told me to dip my rod, and in doing so I dropped to one knee. I played the fish for a half an hour in this position. When I tried to stand up again, I found my leg had gone dead.

At last, after an hour, the salmon gave up the fight. I got him to the edge of the river, and Mr Pallant gaffed him for me. It was hardly a monster at seven pounds, but he breathed a sigh of relief: he hadn't thought I would catch anything, so he had given me a fly with a dodgy hook. As for me, I was pleased as Punch, even though the traditional penalty for catching a salmon on your first attempt was to treat everyone else to a drink. It proved to be the only fish anyone caught that day.

The gillies wrapped my salmon up expertly in hessian for me, and I was presented with a pair of stag's antlers as a souvenir of the occasion. On Sunday Mac and I set out to return to London.

Below: A battle course with live ammunition. I am pictured on the far right.

Bottom: While waiting for some kind of action, I experimented with different kinds of improvised lighting. This was lit by a car's headlamps.

My leave was up on Sunday night, but wartime conditions meant that all the trains were terribly delayed, and I didn't arrive back at Cadogan Gardens until ten o'clock on Monday morning. Still in civvies, and carrying my salmon wrapped in hessian under one arm, and my stags antlers in the other, I crept into the house and up the stairs, past the Colonel's office on the first floor, and the other offices on the second, to my quarters at the top of the building. I was telling the others my fisherman's tale, when a sergeant came marching into the room: 'The Colonel's waiting to see you. He's been looking for you since eight o'clock.'

I quickly got into my uniform and clattered down the stairs. The Colonel addressed me gruffly: 'Where have you been, Sergeant?'

'Sir!', I said, 'I've just got your message!'

He told me that I had been appointed photographer to Southern Area Command, and that I was to proceed to their Headquarters at Salisbury right away. I though of my salmon and my stag's antlers upstairs, so I said: 'Beg pardon, Sir, but I've no clean underclothes. Permission to go home and fetch some?'

To my astonishment, he agreed. I took my trophies home to Eltham, and left the salmon to Dora's tender mercies. I had no time to taste any of it, because I still had to get to Salisbury that evening.

Salisbury was boring. I had now made arrangements with Mac Hastings for him to rent my Baby Austin from me for one pound per week; it was so rusty that the seats had to be bolted to a bit of wood underneath the floor, because there wasn't much of the floor left. I took my bike to get around on.

The PR offices were at the edge of the town, and my lodgings were a ten-minute walk away. I was the only NCO in the office, and for the most part I was treated as such. We used to sit around all day doing very little. At lunch time I used to walk home to my lodgings for lunch, and in the evenings, because I had no friends in Salisbury, I often sat and read the latest novels to my landlady Mrs Newman and her crippled son Tim.

The only relief from the monotony was going back to London at weekends, which I usually managed to fix by saying that I had some films to go to the AFPU darkrooms in Curzon Street, and that I couldn't risk sending them by train.

By January 1944 I had had more than enough of Army Public Relations. I don't think that many of the army PR men would have lasted five minutes as PR men in the outside world. It was largely a waste of time, and the appeal of the easy life had long since worn off. I knew that D-Day was in the offing, and I knew that PR would certainly not be going over very quickly, so I requested a transfer back to the AFPU in the hope of seeing some interesting action.

As soon as my transfer came through, I was sent with the rest of the AFPU on a toughening-up course at the Irish guards' barracks at Lingfield. Practically the first person I bumped into was Bill Wooldridge: we agreed that the leisurely life we had been leading since joining the army had made us really unfit, so at the beginning of the course, we shook hands and took a solemn oath not to dodge or complain about anything, however tough it got.

It was tough: there were assault courses, cross-country runs and survival tests. Because of our oath, Bill and I were probably the only ones who made a point of not troubling the medical officers with complaints about blisters. The officers didn't take part in the courses at all. At Lingfield our instructors from the Irish Guards were impressed by the fact that cameramen seem to make very good marksmen. Not that this was always the case: when I fired a smoke canister from a mortar for the first time, the instructor said, 'You've just hit East Grinstead. I hope you didn't kill anybody.'

The two-day survival exercise at the end of the course just about finished everyone off. We got back to the barracks after a forced night march with all our equipment at about 5 a.m. As a special concession, we were allowed to miss reveille, and get up at eight o'clock, when we were told that, for a special treat, we were all going on a five-mile cross-country run.

about three weeks old, from Tilbury. When we were about to leave I quickly ran down the gangway and snatched a pebble from the quayside to keep as a reminder of England, and as the ship sailed down the estuary of the Thames I watched Shooters Hill near my house in Eltham going past, with a sick feeling in my stomach. In my diary, it says: 'Cheerio London, for now.'

I had been parted from Bill Wooldridge again in the weeks leading up to D-Day, when he went off to the Middle East. I palled up with a chap called Robinson: Robbo for short. The

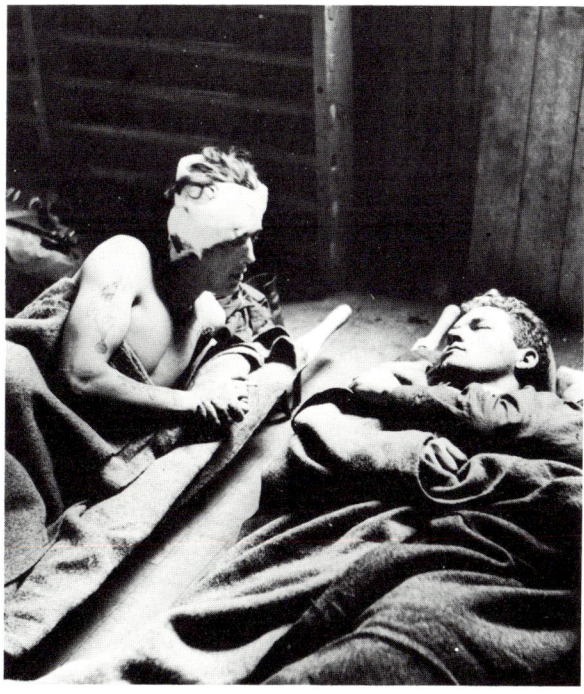

The shot on the left, of one of the first of the wounded arriving back from Normandy, was used as a *Picture Post* cover. The wounded men on the right were waiting to be flown back to England from makeshift airstrips.

The queue for the Medical Officer to get sick notes was made up of almost all the Unit who were under training except Bill and me. We stuck to our agreement, and struggled round the five-mile course. When I went home on a few days' leave afterwards, I was so fit that I felt uncomfortable walking. I ran the two miles from the station to my house.

D-Day came on 6 June 1944, and I went down to Gosport to photograph the arrival back in England of the first of the wounded. I had seen plenty of people injured and killed in the Blitz, but now I began to get a sense of what it meant to be involved in the fighting.

Now came a lot of waiting around at various army camps, until we ended up at a concentration area at Leytonstone, east of London. Although we were about to go across to France at any minute, we were still allowed a fair amount of freedom. I was even able to get back to see my mum at Blackfriars, where I saw a doodlebug for the first time. Everybody used to watch them very carefully, hoping the engines wouldn't cut out over their house.

We finally went across on 1 July, when the invasion was

AFPU was working in teams: one still photographer, one movie photographer, and a driver, with a jeep. I was the still photographer, Robbo was the movie man, and our team was to be attached to Headquarters.

Our first night in France, the fourth of July, was spent in the loft of a farmhouse at Cully in Normandy. The Allied troops were still bottled up, and German shells were whistling low over the roof. For the first time in the army, I was terrified: this really was war.

A week passed, and we began to get used to it. Then one Sunday, Robbo and I were sent out to do separate jobs for the day. I wanted to do a story on what happened to a soldier after he was wounded in the front line: how he was taken back to a dressing station, then to a field hospital. Finally, if he was seriously hurt, he was taken to the beach and flown back to England. Robbo was sent to do something a bit safer behind the lines.

The Germans were putting up a terrific fight for Caen. I went out in a Regimental Aid Post jeep with a Medical Officer, two stretcher-bearers and a driver. We were driving along a scarred and cratered road in the Lebeze Woods,

My first frightening encounter with the enemy came in Lebeze woods when we were heavily mortared. I came closer to death, however, when I nearly detonated a land mine in my efforts to seek cover.

In this makeshift maternity hospital there were only oil lamps for lighting. I was terribly impressed by the calm and gentle way the nurses managed to cope with conditions which were really very poor.

George Formby, whose wife went everywhere with him.

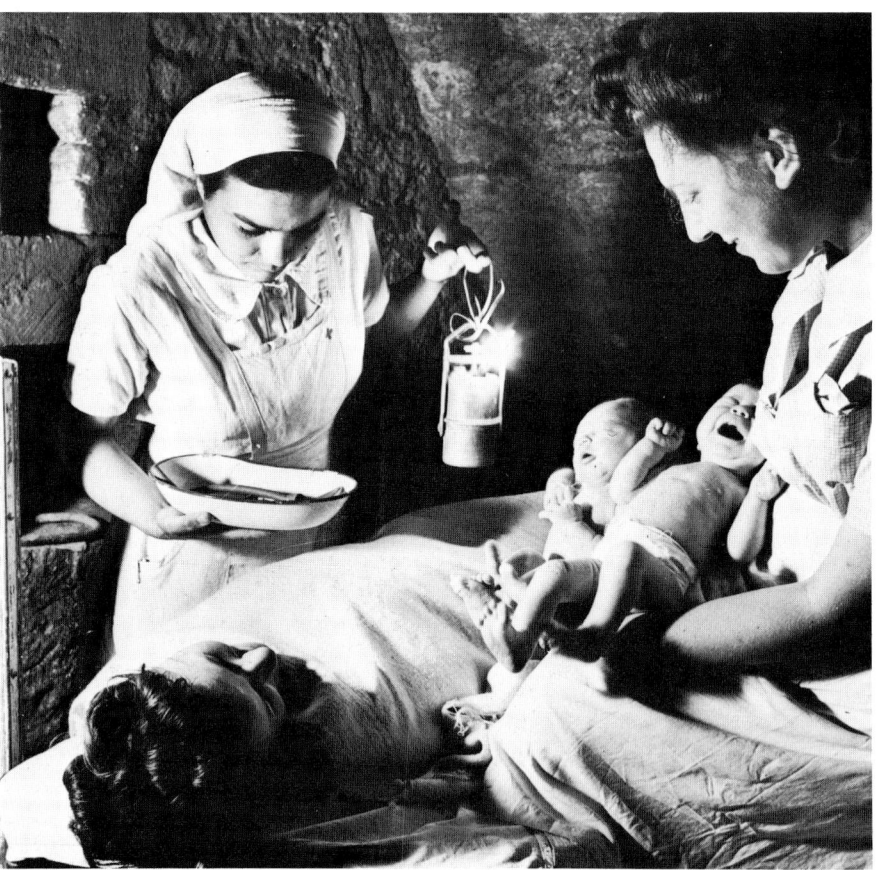

overlooking Caen, when we were stopped by a tree which had been felled across the road. With some difficulty, we managed to bump the jeep through the projecting branches of the tree and get going again, when the Germans opened up with a tremendous mortar barrage of 'moaning minnies'.

Suddenly, we began to feel very scared. Shells were falling all around us, so we leapt from the jeep, and found what cover we could. I spread myself flat on the ground just in front of the jeep, and scrabbled desperately at the earth with my fingers, trying to dig myself in.

As I dug, my fingers uncovered something smooth and metallic. Something told me to stop digging.

At last, the bombardment died down, and we were able to come out of our hiding places. Luckily, nobody had been hurt. Now I had a chance to see what I had been scrabbling at. It was a Teller mine. If the jeep had gone another foot, we would have been blown up.

We didn't stay around: we carefully reversed in our own tracks back to the tree, and bumped through it again. Then we left the jeep, and set out on foot down the hill towards the front line, where we found plenty of wounded men, and I did my story.

I accompanied a wounded soldier to the field hospital, where there was a lot of blood, and then to the beach which the Dakotas that were flying back the wounded used as an airstrip.

When I got back to Headquarters, I went to find Robbo and tell him about my close scrape. Somebody told me: Robbo was killed on his job. He was the second AFPU casualty, and the second friend of mine to be killed on duty. It didn't seem to affect me much at the time, but the next day when I was eating, I began to shake so uncontrollably that the fork dropped from my hand.

All this time I was keeping very busy. I had decided that as well as my army work, I would try to do a story for *Picture Post* and one for *Illustrated* every week.

Later in July I photographed a maternity hospital which had been set up in a cellar on the outskirts of Caen, and after Caen fell, I did a story on homeless people living in the Cathedral. British bombers had destroyed most of the city but the great Cathedral had been left intact.

Being just a sergeant had its drawbacks: if I had been a commissioned officer, or a war correspondent, I would have had a lot more freedom. But then again, as a war correspondent entitled to use my own cameras to do my own stories, I probably would have taken more risks, and I might not be here now to tell the tale.

When George Formby came across to entertain the troops, I was assigned to go with him in his jeep and take pictures of him getting on with everybody; but wherever we went some officer would come up and say, 'Ah! Mr Formby, come and have a drink', and haul him off to the officers' Mess for a good time, while I had to sit outside waiting in the jeep missing a golden opportunity to take good pictures.

Later on, when George Silk of *Life* and Bob Capa came over as war correspondents, I met up with them. They both knew me and told me they liked my work. They stayed in some luxury at the billet obtained by the canny officer in charge of Army Public Relations, who was very talented at that sort of thing; but when they invited me to come and have a drink with them, I wasn't allowed to – the Mess was for commissioned officers and war correspondents only.

We other ranks had our moments. Some of the boys discovered a cellar filled with Calvados. They didn't know anything about any fancy French liqueurs, so they knocked it back as if it was wine. One man managed to drink a whole bottle before collapsing. He was out for three days, during which time we had to keep him in his tent, out of sight of the officers. At night we had to sit on him, because he began to think he was somebody else, and would rush out of the tent shouting and screaming at the top of his voice. I think he recovered all right, but he stuck to beer after that.

After putting up a fierce fight for Caen, the first airfield to be taken, the Germans' resistance suddenly collapsed, and they went on the run. The Allied troops had them bottled up at Falaise, but since Paris was also about to fall, a section of us from the AFPU were detailed to go and record the event.

We travelled in two jeeps, four to a jeep, and took eleven days to reach Paris, stopping at little farmhouses along the way (photographing de Gaulle at Chartres), and receiving a tremendous welcome wherever we went.

We finally entered Paris on 25 August. The Free French soldiers marched in first, followed by the Americans. It was a terrific sunny day and there was a carnival atmosphere. Cheering crowds lined the streets and boulevards, and we didn't mind driving slowly along receiving our share of

Me with some new German friends.

Below: A British corporal, aided by a member of the French Resistance, taking prisoners.

A sequence of pictures of the Liberation of Paris can be found at the end of the chapter.

adulation. Eager hands thrust bottles of wine into ours, and eager girls leapt up into the jeep to hug and kiss us. Our faces were red with the sun, the lipstick, and the wine.

At last our heads began to spin a little, and we felt like getting out of the noise. The excitement of Paris, the lovely girls with beautiful legs cycling with their skirts billowing up round their waists, and the noise and the crowds were all too much for us. We turned down a side street to rest for a while with the engine turned off.

But even as I was standing there, a smartly dressed woman accompanied by the most beautiful young girl came walking by and stopped to give me an enormous bouquet of flowers: 'These are for your mother', she said. Then the girl showed her gratitude by yet another barrage of hugs and kisses.

When I had time, I wrote and told my mum what had happened. It must have really touched her, because she carried the letter in her handbag until the end of her life.

That night officers put up at the Hotel Scribe, while the NCOs and drivers were left to fend for themselves. It was impossible to find anywhere, and in the end, rather than leaving me to sleep in the jeep, Lieutenant Malandine gave me permission to sleep on his floor. By the next night we had found a nice little hotel in the back streets, where we stayed in comfort. I even had a room to myself, which I was able to put to good use, as there were other girls anxious to show their gratitude.

The next day General de Gaulle arrived in Paris, and walked all the way from the Arc de Triomphe along the Champs Elysées to Notre Dame. I had seen a huge Union Jack hanging from the window of a house, and I asked the woman who owned it to give it to us, or at least lend it to us. She finally gave in when I told her that it would be hung from our jeep and driven along the Champs Elysées with us as a

part of de Gaulle's triumphal procession. My pictures of the Film Unit boys in the other jeep waving the flag make the liberation of Paris look like a British affair.

Then, when we came in sight of Notre Dame, there was a sudden flurry in the crowds of people. It took me a little time to understand what was happening: there were German snipers firing at de Gaulle from the roof of the Cathedral.

The whole mood changed. People were diving for cover, or desperately trying to run away. For a while there was confusion; I was able to take a series of pictures of what happened until, after about ten minutes, the snipers were rounded up.

This was the only serious reminder of war during my stay in Paris. For the rest of the time I enjoyed myself in company with my new friend, Ernie Water, who had taken the place of Robbo. We realised for the first time the terrific black-market value of cigarettes to the tobacco-starved French. This gave us a handy source of income.

After four days, we moved on again. I travelled north towards the coast with Ernie Water and Captain Derek Knight photographing flying-bomb sites. We then took part in the liberation of Brussels, receiving another tremendous welcome. After staying the night, we drove along a road littered with the bodies of German horses, to Antwerp, where we found the usual reception, and I did a story on the entry of the British troops.

The German withdrawal left their collaborators high and dry. While I was in Antwerp, *Picture Post* sent out Jennie Nicholson and we did a story about them. The Belgian Resistance had rounded up all known collaborators and put them in the lions' cage at the zoo. They took out the lions first, of course.

Ernie Water and I went along to have a look. There were all these terribly well-dressed men behind bars, and I said to Ernie: 'Look at the lovely watches they're all wearing.'

A member of the resistance standing next to us happened to overhear what I said. 'You can have their watches if you like', he said. So he gave orders for all their watches to be taken away and handed over to Ernie and me.

For a while, we had cornered the market in watches.

Our Headquarters were in Brussels for the next few months, overseeing the despatch of films back to London, for censorship by the Ministry of Information. I moved around the area, often working with Captain Boulting, who later became famous with his brother as a film producer.

We recorded the fall of Calais, one of the last places held by the Germans on the Channel coast. We also photographed a Gestapo torture chamber at Charleroi.

We were still conquering heroes as far as the people of Brussels were concerned. Ernie Water and I were out one evening when a man came rushing up to us and begged us to come with him to a students' café in the backstreets where they didn't see many allied soldiers. He wanted to buy us a drink and thank us properly for liberating his native land.

I don't remember much about the evening, so it must have

These women had their heads shaved to show that they had been collaborating with the Germans.

Top left: A German atrocity discovered in Belgium. As we advanced, we uncovered further horrors.

Above left: These collaborators seem to have lost their watches!

Top right: A French couple return to their village with mixed emotions.

Above right: A Russian beats up his Nazi oppressor.

ATS girls were welcomed in private homes.

ing the prettiest girl we could (Who thought of it? Was it me? Or was it Mac?) and showing what it was like on the day Brussels was liberated through a sequence of pictures of her facial expressions.

We found the girl we were looking for in a large department store in the centre of the town, and persuaded her to come up onto the roof of the building where we could take the pictures. When I tightened her sweater by pinning it at the back to emphasize her figure, she asked with touching innocence: 'Why are you doing that?' I just said, 'Don't worry about it.'

I don't know what happened to the pictures, but pretty soon Yvonne and I were firm friends, and I saw her as often as possible. Although her English wasn't bad, I was able to help her to improve: over coffee in cafés she used to ask me about words which particularly puzzled her, and I tried to help her by spelling them out, and helping her with pronunciation. I think I taught her quite a lot.

For long afterwards, I used to see Yvonne every time I went back to Brussels. That is, until she too discovered the attractions of the officers' Mess and forgot poor Sergeant Hardy. I never forgot her.

With the Allied advance into Germany, the AFPU Headquarters moved to Eindhoven in Holland. Here, for reasons best known to our superior officers, Ernie Water was promoted but I was not. When Ernie had put up his pips, he was told to stand on the steps of the billet which had been taken over as the officers' Mess so we could see that he'd been promoted.

When I duly walked past, I stared at Ernie, and Ernie stared at me, but we didn't say a word. For the time being, I had lost another of my friends.

With the final push into Germany, my life began to get a bit more dangerous again. One day I was working with Mac Hastings and the driver Harry Flower near the border. All hell was going on. We came up to some infantry troops and asked one of them: 'Where's the front line, mate?' He pointed ahead of us down a long country road, and we drove off in that direction.

We continued to drive for a mile or two until we could see a church spire in front of us in the distance and we came to the outskirts of a village. As we passed the first couple of houses we noticed that women came to the doors and stared at us. Something told me that we should turn round, so I said to Harry, 'Stop the jeep, turn round as quickly as you can, and don't touch the bloody verges – they're probably mined.'

We drove back the way we had come as fast as we could. If we had driven another half a mile or so, we would have run slap-bang into the enemy, or at least fallen foul of snipers in the church tower: a trick the Germans often used.

When we got back to the troops who had directed us, we told them what we thought of them: 'You said our front line was down there.' 'It was', they replied. 'You *were* the front line. What's it like down there? Anyone get hurt?'

been a good one. The man who invited us in the first place was a professor at the University. At the end of the evening, he insisted that I went home with him to spend the night.

I went back with him to his house. He had a lovely Jewish wife. They were parted from each other, though they still shared a house because it would have been too dangerous for her if they had split up while the Germans were still in control. She and I seemed to get on very well together.

That night, I slept downstairs in the large kitchen area. As the city had only recently been liberated, there was still some difficulties over mains services, and the gas supply was only turned on at night, which was when any cooking had to be done. When she came down to use the kitchen it wasn't only the clattering of her pots and pans that kept me awake. I saw a lot of her in the next month.

In November, Mac Hastings came over to Brussels as a war correspondent to work on some stories for *Picture Post* with me. It was good to work with him again. Permission had been obtained for me to use my own cameras and not the soppy army-issue Super Ikonta, so we wired London to send on my Contax and Rollei cameras. However, everything wasn't quite like old times, because Mac, being Mac, had officer status. Instead of being able to discuss stories in a natural and relaxed way each evening, we had to split up, and he went to the officers' Mess and I went to the sergeants'.

In spite of this, we quickly came up with the idea of find-

On the next day, 18 November 1944, we entered Germany for the first time, crossing the border near Beauchamps. Mac and Harry and I had to leave the jeep and follow the advance across the fields on foot, being careful only to walk in the tracks left by our tanks, so we didn't step on an unexploded mine.

There was smoke everywhere, and the smell of cordite, and every now and then a German soldier would loom up with his hands on his head, surrendering. The troops didn't bother much with them: they just took their weapons away, and told them to keep walking to our rear.

Beauchamps itself was a pile of rubble. The fighting was still going on: German soldiers hidden in the basements of houses were putting up a rearguard action, while our boys were trying to flush them out by chucking grenades and firing machine guns into the ruins.

Suddenly, in the middle of all this, a German soldier came out of the ruins of a house with his hands on his head. Our troops quickly surrounded him, and he looked worried. He was probably afraid that he might be shot. But the soldiers were thinking of other things at that particular moment: the German was armed with a Mauser automatic pistol, for which there was a ready market.

No sooner had he been disarmed, than Mac was in there, doing a deal with the soldier for the Mauser (What a catch – better than a seven-pound salmon. He'd certainly be able to impress the boys in Fleet Street with it).

The German seemed mightily relieved that he hadn't come to any harm. An officer said: 'Take him back, and don't shoot him'.

Just as they were marching off, Mac shouted: '*Stop!*'

You could see the German's face drop: had his captors changed their minds?

Mac ran up to him: 'I need the holster. You must have the holster for a Mauser.'

Mac was now headed back to London, and I went with him as far as Brussels, where we did a story on an English soldier enjoying his leave. I suppose the pace of things must have been slowing, and soldiers on leave used to head for Brussels where they had the time of their lives. I took the opportunity to see Yvonne.

I showed the soldier having his first bath for ages in hot water, having a meal, and taking a girl out for the evening. The last picture was more difficult, because Brussels was still blacked out at nights, so, not for the first time, I had to take my light from an improvised source. Using a Contax with an f 1.4 lens, I photographed the couple silhouetted against the slit headlights of a car.

The picture went back to London for developing and printing, and censoring by the Ministry of Information, and then came back to the AFPU office. It just happened that I was in the next room when Major Stewart and Lieutenant Malandine were going through them. The pictures taken in the blackout seemed to amaze them, and I could hear them saying: 'How does he do it? How on earth does he do it?'

The Rabbi held the interest of the children who were evacuating from Holland to England. He kept their fears at bay with his wonderful stories. They were also distracted by the continual flow of passing ships.

After Christmas I did a story on the evacuation of Dutch children to England, which landed me in Tilbury, where I managed to obtain a nine-day leave pass. During my leave I went home to Eltham, where I celebrated Dora's birthday, and built a yacht for Michael. I also had lunch with Tom Hopkinson, who told me that from now on he was going to put £100 in my bank account every time *Picture Post* used a story of mine, whether it was especially commissioned or not. I then went to see Len Spooner, the editor of *Illustrated*, who had also been commissioning work from me. He

Smokescreen on the Rhine: the atmosphere of smoke with silhouetted tanks and figures made for marvellous pictures.

The Rhine Crossing: a further sequence of pictures can be found at the end of the chapter.

thanked me for the pictures, and offered me a free copy of any issue of *Illustrated* which contained a picture of mine.

My leave came to an end all too soon. I went back to Strachen, in Germany, where Mac Hastings joined me.

As usual, it was difficult to discuss ideas for stories because of our separate messing arrangements, but we had heard that the British were going to put up a huge smoke screen when they were crossing the Rhine, to make it more difficult for the Germans to see what was going on.

After our first day's work at Xanten, I bumped into Lieutenant Malandine when I arrived back at the office. As curious as ever about my movements, he asked me what I had been up to. 'Oh', I said. 'Just some pictures of the smoke screen.'

'I don't suppose there was much in it, was there?'

'No, nothing at all. Just smoke.'

When I had finished the story, the pictures duly went back to London, where they were looked at by the Ministry of Information. A message quickly came back to the AFPU headquarters saying: 'Hardy's pictures of smoke screen good. Are holding'. They didn't want *Picture Post* to have them exclusively before the AFPU had had a chance to take some pictures on its own account, which could then be used by the rest of the Press.

The AFPU then sent out another sergeant photographer –

who later became famous as a television cameraman – to take a set of pictures. These were then sent back, but the men at the Ministry still preferred mine. Finally they decided that a couple of my pictures would have to be released to the daily Press at the same time as *Picture Post* used them, so *Picture Post* didn't seem to be getting an exclusive of such a good subject as the preparations for a major offensive. The crossing of the Rhine actually took place on 24 March 1945.

Mac and I spent the whole night before the crossing on the heights at Staaland, taking pictures of the river.

There was barely a soul about apart from ourselves. The river was crowded with barges and landing craft. There were fires on the far bank, and the odd red tracer bullet from far off was flying slowly (as it seemed) through the air. The moon seemed to shed an eerie light over the whole scene.

I was working with my Contax on a tripod, using long exposures to get the feeling of it all. Suddenly Mac, who had been standing beside me, dived to the ground, and shouted at me: 'Bert! For God's sake get down!'

Lazy red tracer bullets were winging towards me.

'I can't', I said. I'm giving a time exposure!'

But I didn't hang around for long after my shutter clicked.

When Zero-hour for the crossing came, it was difficult to imagine where so many soldiers had come from. I was crossing with the troops, going forward with them taking photo-

graphs, then returning and taking pictures of the largest Bailey Bridge being built.

On one of these return trips General Dempsey spotted me. He was just about to make history by becoming the first Allied General to cross the Rhine, and he wanted a record of the occasion. He ordered me to go with him.

We went across in two small motor launches. I took a few photographs, and then went ahead, so I could get ashore and take pictures of him stepping out of his boat. Once these had been taken, we didn't stop long on the far bank. On the way back, I got into the same boat as the General, and sat in the prow so I could get pictures of him against the far shore.

When we were about halfway across, the Germans got our range with their mortar fire. Shells were landing all around us, sending up sheets of water. The engine of our little boat strained as we headed for the shore. A piece of shrapnel went spinning past me so slowly that I felt like reaching out and catching it like a cricket ball.

At last we reached the comparative safety of the shore. We were still being fired on, and General Dempsey and his entourage quickly took cover by diving into a shell hole. I was about to join them, but this was one picture that looked too good to miss: GENERAL TAKING COVER FROM ENEMY FIRE. So I stood up on the rim and took a few shots. Dempsey spotted me at once:

'Sergeant! Get down here immediately!'

'Yes, sir. As soon as I've taken this picture.'

General Dempsey hadn't realised that I was working for *Picture Post* when he asked me to take pictures of him, but he still made very sure that he saw copies before they were released for publication. It was a good scoop for *Picture Post*, and I was well pleased: I got a nice letter from Tom saying: 'brilliant stuff', and the picture I had taken from the prow was used on the front cover.

Our advance continued. Airborne troops had been dropped behind enemy lines, some twenty miles beyond the Rhine. We wanted to make contact with them in our eagerness to be where the action was, and on 25 March (the day after the crossing) we decided to try to get through enemy territory to meet up with them at a little village about seven or eight miles in front of the ground troops. We set off in a jeep, hoping that it was worth the risk. We were in luck. We encountered no enemy soldiers on our trip, though it was certainly a tense drive.

When we arrived, the troops were busy herding the villagers into a church hall so they would be out of harm's way if there was any fighting. Harry Flower and I had a look round while this was going on.

We wandered into a little factory. On a bench in an office we found an open safe with a lot of German money. We fetched a Press bag from the jeep and scooped all the money into it. No one would be any the wiser.

We hung onto that bag of money for the rest of our time in Germany. It was impossible to change it into any other currency, but it kept us and all our mates in beer and other luxuries, and when we left we just handed it on to our successors.

After we had got all the pictures we wanted, we drove back to the positions occupied by the ground troops, and told them what conditions were like up ahead. That evening, Mac went back to Brussels taking my cameras with him. Once again I was Sergeant Hardy of the AFPU, even though now I was a wealthier man.

I was issued with a special pass signed by General Eisenhower, which gave me leave to go wherever I wanted and photograph whatever I liked. I was the only NCO to get such a pass. Nevertheless, it was beginning to get difficult to find subjects to photograph. In the wake of the British advance, the British Military Government had been set up to administer the newly occupied areas. It was run by an unlikely selection of Colonel Blimps who suffered from the delusion that they had won the war single-handed.

Harry Flower and I drove in ever-widening circles from AFPU Headquarters in our search for stories. At the beginning of April, we found ourselves in the small town of Osnabrück. The whole town had been tidied up after the destruction, and it looked as if everything was getting back to normal. As we drove through the outskirts, we passed a unit of the Pioneer Corps sweeping and cleaning.

We were driving past the bombed-out remains of a de-

General Dempsey on the way back across the Rhine. The top picture was used as a front cover of *Picture Post*. In the lower picture, he takes cover from the mortar fire.

Osnabrück: when help arrived, I was free to take pictures of these Russians being rescued from the smoke-filled cellar. Most of them survived.

partment store, a mass of rubble and twisted girders, when we noticed that something was up: smoke was drifting from the basement of the building; and when we slowed down to have a look, I thought I could hear voices crying for help.

We stopped instantly and leapt out of the jeep. I clambered through a hole in the pavement, down a metal ladder, and followed the direction of the cries along a dark, smoke-filled passageway. The dense fumes made it impossible to see and almost impossible to breathe, and I was on the point of giving up when I stumbled into a human figure. It was a woman. I wasted no time in grabbing hold of her and dragging her back along the passageway, then heaving her up the ladder into the fresh air.

Harry looked shocked. As soon as I had stopped coughing, I told him to hop in the jeep and drive back to the detachment of the Pioneer Corps we had seen to get help.

While he was gone, I went back down the hole again, and managed to heave up another half-suffocated woman. They lay gasping on the pavement, recovering from the effects of their ordeal. When Harry finally turned up with the Pioneer Corps, they were able to form a human chain and get the rest of the people out more quickly. Now they had arrived I was able to get on with taking pictures.

Later we talked to a couple of the survivors who had recovered enough and spoke a bit of English. They were Russian men and women who had recently been liberated from a slave labour camp a few miles outside Osnabrück by the occupying forces. They had walked into town in a group, and had come upon the ruins of the department store. One of them had climbed down into the basement and discovered a lot of new blankets and clothing. The rest had followed, and they started to help themselves.

After their years of hunger and ill-treatment, a simple thing like a blanket seemed like heaven to them; but while they were busy finding themselves clothing, along came two German policemen. (The British Military Government needed all the help it could get in running the country, so, after vetting, the German civil police had been allowed to continue to perform their duties.)

The two policemen ordered the former prisoners out of the basement, but they weren't taking any more orders from Germans, and told them where to go. Unable to think of any other way of asserting their authority, the policemen set fire to strips of paper and threw them down into the cellar to smoke out the looters. This caused the blankets to smoulder, but the looters were too busy to notice what was happening until it was too late, and they were trapped by the fumes.

The policemen had then cleared off. It was lucky that we had happened to be driving past when we did: although about twenty people had to be taken to hospital, we had saved the lives of most of them. Harry and I drove some back to their camp in our jeep. Later on I wrote down the details of the story, saying how German policemen allowed to carry on by the British Military Government had done this terrible thing to former camp inmates, and sent it back to England

Belsen: my most horrifying experience. The pictures explain themselves horribly clearly. The freed prisoners shown here are in fact from Fallingbostel. I have never seen such starved-looking people except at Belsen. Above them is a picture of the last hut at Belsen being burned down.

The coffin carried by the woman is for her own child.

with the pictures. But although the censor saw nothing wrong with the story, that was not the last I heard of it. When the British Military Government set up a Court of Enquiry a few weeks later, Sergeant Hardy of the AFPU was summoned to give evidence. I was questioned about the incident at great length before they were satisfied.

The slave labourers at Osnabrück and the Gestapo torture chambers at Charleroi were just a foretaste of what was to come. On 19 April 1945, on the day after the camp was entered by the Allies, I went to Belsen. I have seen some terrible things in my life, but this was the worst by far. Parties of photographers and correspondents, and various military personnel who had heard about the place and had to see for themselves, were wandering about staring in disbelief.

There were emaciated dead bodies everywhere: some piled in mounds where little children born in the camp played without realising the significance of what they were playing on. Others had been thrown higgledy-piggledy into pits the size of tennis courts by their comrades, whose turn would have come in a day or two.

Although I do not usually like taking pictures of corpses, I controlled my feelings of rage for long enough to take some: without such evidence, no one would believe that anything like this had ever happened.

The fate of the survivors was hardly better. Many were too weak to move: they grovelled on the floor with outstretched hands, begging for food. But you knew you couldn't give them anything, because the shock of the sudden intake of food into their systems might kill them. Most of them would probably die anyway. All I could do was feel terribly sad, and try to take a few photographs.

Dressed in rags, and infested with vermin, they stank from living in filthy huts without any form of sanitation. Only one woman with her child seemed different from the rest. They must have just arrived, because they looked clean, and their clothes were neat. They sat beneath the branches of a tree, keeping well away from all the other inmates, as if to avoid being contaminated by the whole nightmare.

By the time I reached the hut where the former guards of the camp were being kept prisoner, I was feeling bloody angry. I think even the guards must have been beginning to realise what they had done. They were standing huddled together looking furtive and guilty, surrounded by British personnel.

As I was standing there, some orderlies came in with food on trays for the Germans. The sight was too much for me. I couldn't bear to think that we were feeding these people after what I had seen. I picked up a plate of food and threw it right into the face of one of the guards.

He hardly reacted. I thought I would be in big trouble, but nobody else, not even the officers who were present, took any notice. They probably felt exactly the same way as me.

I still maintain that the average German did not know what was going on in places like Belsen. I made a point of

I spent a couple of days photographing Giles the cartoonist and we became friends (we have kept in touch ever since). Together we caught a chicken and plucked it, but the officers' Mess benefited, and I never tasted the chicken.

carrying a contact print of one of the most horrifying of my photographs around with me to show to Germans who didn't believe that such things had really happened. The authorities even posted up pictures of the atrocities in public places in German cities; but quite often the Germans still didn't believe it: they just thought the pictures were Allied propaganda.

VE Day came in May, by which time the AFPU was stationed in Lüneberg. I took pictures of the people of Lüneberg reading the proclamation of peace, and then settled down to enjoying myself.

We were billeted at the house of a high-powered SS officer whose wife still lived there. It was a very comfortable place to live, overlooking a park in a tree-lined avenue. If you sat on the balcony long enough, looking through the SS officer's high-magnification telescope, it was usually possible to observe the courtship rituals of German couples in the park.

The SS officer's wife kept herself to herself. One room in the house was kept locked up by her, and we noticed that she always kept a close watch on the door of the room.

One day while she was out our curiosity got the better of us, and I managed to get into the room. A number of suitcases were stacked up as if in readiness for a quick get-away. I sneaked one of these cases back to my room and opened it up: it was full of booze and looted articles.

We took the booze and put most of the rest back. There wasn't much the woman could say or do, because the stuff was all stolen in the first place. But I expect she was relieved when the AFPU moved on.

The war being over, celebrations were taking place everywhere. Since General Dempsey had already entertained the Russian General Grishin to lunch at Ludwigslust, Grishin felt duty-bound to invite Dempsey to a return match at Parchim, far to the east in the Russian sector. I was to go along and photograph the whole thing.

Harry Flower and I drove there, while General Dempsey

flew. The Russians laid on a real welcome for us: the road leading up to the building where the reception was being held was lined with a row of smart, blue-uniformed guards. I stayed around long enough to take some pictures of the English and the Russian generals toasting each other and swearing eternal friendship between themselves and their countries, then went off to have my lunch with the lower ranking officers (Harry Flower had to go off with the NCOs).

There was a small number of British officers, and very many Russians. We sat down at one o'clock and the toasts began immediately: we started with Stalin and Churchill, and worked down until we were toasting each other, our wives, and our dogs and cats. With each toast, we tossed back our glass of vodka with one gulp (the only way to drink the stuff) and it was instantly refilled by buxom serving wenches. In this way, a considerable amount of vodka was got through.

At five, nobody could think of anything else to toast, and so we rose unsteadily to our feet and staggered out of the building. The lines of blue-uniformed guards were still there standing proud and erect, and I struggled to maintain the dignity of the British Army by walking in a straight line and being careful not to trip over my own feet as I marched between them. When I finally located our jeep, I found Harry Flower stretched out in the back, half conscious. He had drunk almost as many toasts as I had, and made it plain not only that he could not drive, but that he would not drive.

How we ever got as far as Schwerin in the American sector that night, I don't know. I do have a vague memory of seeing a couple of pretty girls carrying bundles of firewood along the road, and offering them a lift to their homes. And I do remember feeling quite mystified for a while when I discovered two bundles of firewood in the back of the jeep at Schwerin. What happened in between has disappeared forever into the mists of time and vodka.

My days in Europe were running out. One day, for the

Marshal Zhukov decorates Generals Eisenhower and Montgomery at Frankfurt. Can they find room for any more medals?

hell of it, Harry and I drove deep into Denmark. After the devastation of Germany, it was like paradise. Everything seemed to be in plentiful supply.

We stopped in one village and bought toys for our children. In another village, we found a lovely café with tables outside and checked tablecloths. When we read the menu, we could barely believe our eyes: we sat down and ordered bacon and six eggs each, and fresh coffee.

All was silence while we ate, forgetting (for a while, at least) the taste of bully beef and tea like boot-polish. Then a thought crossed my mind. I leaned across to Harry and whispered:

'How're we going to pay for this lot? We haven't got any Kroner.'

A while later, the proprietor came nervously up to our table. He would be most grateful if we could possibly pay for our meal with cigarettes, because cigarettes were very scarce in Denmark at that time.

I don't suppose he knew why we looked so relieved.

On another occasion Harry Flower and I were returning to our billet along a wooded path at a place called Vloto when we heard the sound of girlish laughter in the woods. We were intrigued, and decided to investigate. In a clearing we came across three German girls lying around in the grass in languid postures which revealed, ever so discreetly, that they weren't wearing any knickers.

Despite the law forbidding fraternising with Germans, we considered this an ideal opportunity to make contact with the German civilian population. We soon discovered that their objective was to get petrol for their car, so they could get away from Vloto.

Thanks to our spare can on the jeep I believe they were able to get a long, long way from Vloto the next morning.

But if I had thought that I would finish my army service in Europe, I was mistaken. In June I was told that, along with a number of other AFPU blokes including Captain Derek Knight and Lieutenant Ernie Water, I was being posted to the Far East. Having survived the invasion and surrender of Germany, and knowing that the counter-offensive against the Japanese forces in Singapore was about to take place, I was not exactly pleased.

In July 1945 we set out with our equipment in jeeps to return to Pinewood in England and to fly on from there to Ceylon. On the road back to Brussels, I was sent ahead in my jeep to find a suitable place for the rest to have lunch.

After driving for a while, I found an ideal café; it was even on the right-hand side of the road, so I could leave the jeep outside to show the others where we were. We told the proprietor, and he began getting beer bottles out, and heating up the stove.

As we sat there, on a lovely summer day, three or four girls came through a curtain at the back of the room and went and stood in the doorway of the café. The sunlight shone through their dresses in such a way that it was impossible not to notice that they had nothing on underneath. The place was not just a café.

Although the others duly rolled up, and lunch was duly served, I can't say I enjoyed myself very much: my meal was ruined by the sight of those beautiful creatures, thinly dressed, placed forever beyond my reach by the restraining presence of my commanding officers.

The Liberation of Paris

De Gaulle set off from the Arc de Triomphe to a tremendous reception, as did our proud British contingent of two jeeps. I was taking an interest in some of the pretty faces in the crowds when the snipers opened fire from the roof of Notre Dame.

The Rhine Crossing

At first the only light was from the tracers, some of which came too close for my liking. Then a mass of powerful searchlights were turned on, creating a strange effect known as 'Monty's Dawn'.

6: The Far East

I had a month in London. I got inoculated against Yellow Fever, took Dora, Michael and Terry to the cinema a couple of times, and lost some money at Catford Dog Stadium. Everybody else's war was over, but mine wasn't.

On 17 August 1945, I took off from Mayfield Airport in an Army Dakota. The flight to Karachi in what was then northern India took four days. As there was nothing to sit on except a crude metallic shelf along the bare metal interior of the fuselage, the only thing to do was to lie on the floor and long for it all to be over.

At Karachi, we transferred to a train to make the trip to the Army's Far East Headquarters at Kandy in Ceylon; the journey would take us nearly three weeks in all. The officers travelled first class, while the 'other ranks' mucked in with the rest of the population in overcrowded carriages with wooden benches. After a night in those conditions, I had finally had enough: I managed to get a first-class compartment for the rest of us. Our only compensation was the fact Singapore had fallen to the British on the day we set out from Mayfield. The Atom bombs had been dropped on Japan, so we hoped we would now not have to risk our necks in combat conditions.

Kandy was still Mountbatten's Headquarters when we arrived. The man in charge of the AFPU Far East Command was Derek Knight, who was now a Colonel. It was easy to see that the place was hopelessly badly organised: Derek Knight's job meant that he had to keep moving around the Far East, so he asked me if I would lick the place into shape, and get it running, if possible, on Fleet Street lines. As well as developing and processing all the films taken by army photographers in the Far East, supplying them with captions, and syndicating them all over the world, we also had to cope with the job of printing endless copies of Mountbatten's portrait photograph, which he signed and presented to every officer who served under him.

Colonel Knight offered me a promotion to the rank of captain. However, by now I was a bit wary: I knew that if you

accepted a commission you had to stay in the army at least a year, and I reckoned that I only had about that amount of time left to serve. I agreed to sign the form providing it came through quickly: I didn't want to be in the army a moment longer than necessary.

Soon I had the job of supervising the packing of all our equipment and its transport to the new Headquarters in Singapore. There we occupied the floor beneath Mountbatten in the twelve-storey Cathay Building.

It was not all that easy to get the place running as efficiently as Colonel Knight would have liked me to. For a start, there were technical difficulties: the high temperature and humidity played havoc with the films and the chemicals used to develop them: we had to use refrigerators to cool down the developing fluid. Also, we had no plate cameras, so it was difficult to achieve the kind of speed in getting photographs to newspapers that was possible in Fleet Street. On one occasion, when Mountbatten gave the salute to a fly-past of the Royal Air Force, I had motor-bike messengers standing by to rush the film from my Super Ikonta back to the Cathay Building, where they were developed and printed wet, destroying the negatives in the process, so they could be rushed to the offices of the *Straits Times* in time to go to press.

There were also some staff difficulties. Few of the photographers had seen any action. In November a team of us went up to Surabaya in Java, where some final Japanese resistance was being mopped up. A couple of photographers were not at all keen to take pictures of the street fighting at close quarters. Without being in amongst it, though, you couldn't possibly get any worthwhile photographs. It took some talking to persuade Major Evans, a tough but fair man, that it wasn't their fault they hadn't been in action before, and that he shouldn't court-martial them.

Meanwhile, my long-awaited promotion failed to come through: the papers had got lost in the move from Kandy to Singapore. In the end I got fed up with waiting, and started to wear my Captain's pips whenever I thought they would come in handy.

That same month, I decided to do a story on the Great World and New World Amusement Parks, and the red-light districts of Singapore. These were strictly out of bounds to the men because of the alarming spread of venereal disease in the armed forces stationed there at the time. But I hopped in a jeep with a couple of other officers, and we drove into the forbidden areas, thinking that the rules wouldn't apply to us because (a) we were officers, and (b) we were doing a story.

As soon as we drove into the first forbidden street, we were pounced on by a jeep-load of 'redcaps', military policemen, who had been lurking in the shadows. You could see that they were very pleased to have caught some officers breaking bounds. They took us back to their Headquarters. By the time they got round to asking for our papers, my heart was missing a beat or two. My companions showed their papers, and then I had to take out mine. All I had was an AP 64, which was the ordinary soldier's identity card. Again

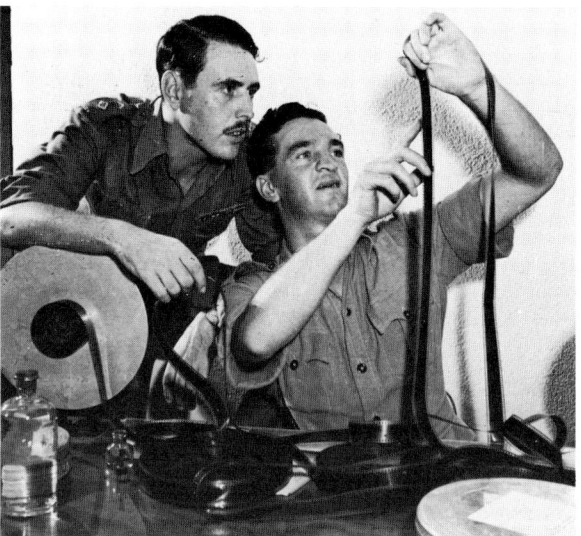

Colonel Derek Knight
and Major Evans,
two super blokes.

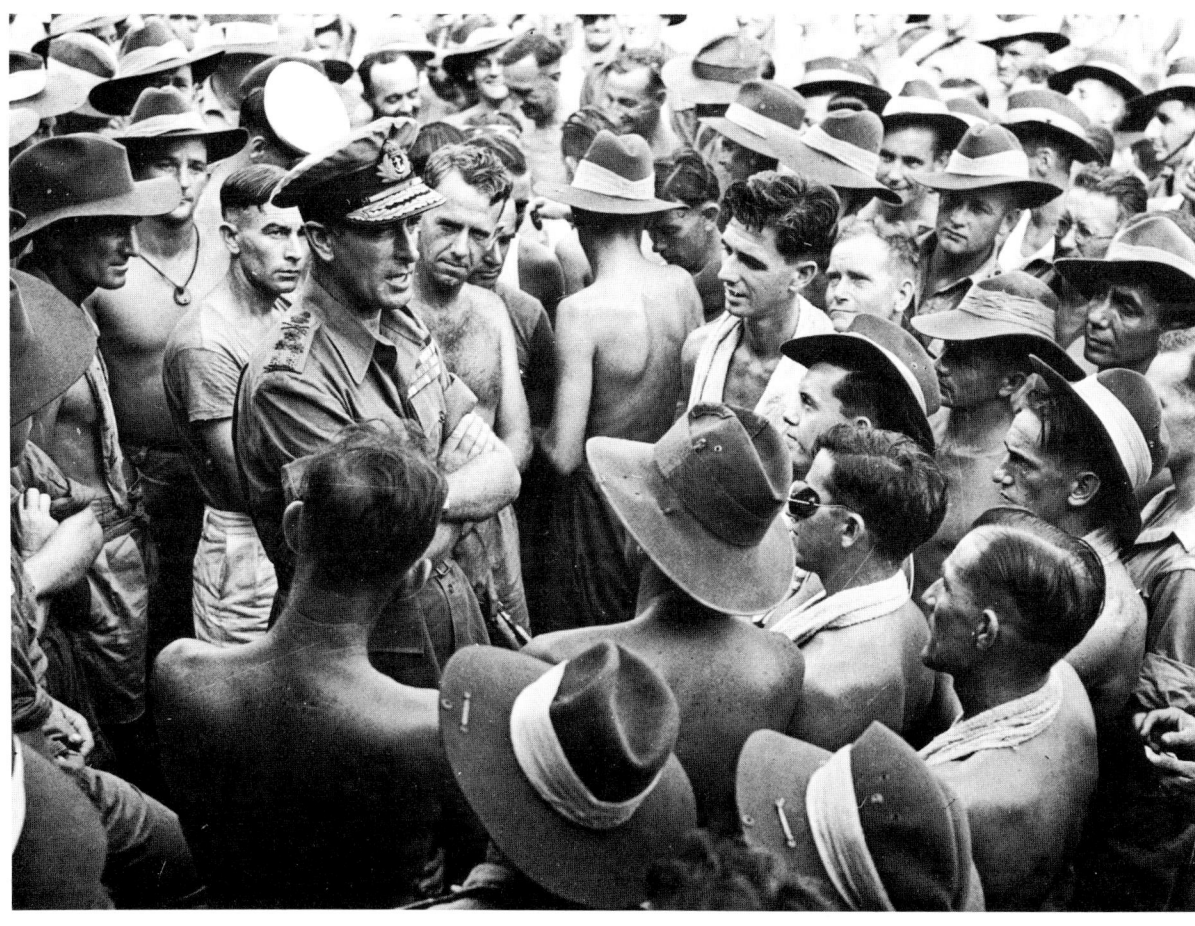

Mountbatten loved to meet and talk to the troops. Here he is with some Australians in Singapore.

you could almost see them jump for joy. One more item for the charge sheet: impersonating an officer.

Finally, after a lot of desperate explanation and argument, one of us got through to a Brigadier who was a friend, and he told the redcaps to forget what had happened. The three of us arrived back very late, very tired and very thankful that we were free.

I had risky moments of a different kind, too. Soon after, we heard that the RAF were going to fly supplies up to Kuantan in Malaya, which had been cut off by retreating Japanese who were still fighting. I decided to do a story on it.

A Sunderland flying boat had been especially adapted to drop depth charges, with strengthened wings and a light aluminium fuselage, and it was being loaded (in Singapore) with rice. When I saw the huge pile of sacks they were loading, I thought they'd never get them all in, but they managed all right. It seemed a bit much to me, but I assumed they knew what they were doing.

At last, bulging and straining, we tried to take off. As we taxied through the sea I thought we'd never get up into the air, but after about twice the usual run, we managed it.

The flight took a couple of hours. We could see the village of Kuantan surrounded by heavy jungle on a bend in the river below us. The pilot flew in low to survey the area: we would have to land in a short space, because the Sunderland couldn't turn round the tight bend in the river.

We came roaring in again, levelled off, and hit the water with a smart belly-flop. The thin hull of the flying boat, strained to breaking point by the load of rice, couldn't take any more, and promptly split open like a wet paper bag. The sacks of rice, so neatly stacked, tumbled through to the bottom of the river.

Water poured into the aircraft, so we all rushed up a gangway to the flight deck, which was on a higher level. The pilot

Rescued but riceless: our food had gone to the bottom.

rammed the throttle through the emergency gate to give the four engines an extra turn of power, which luckily carried us nearly to the river bank. As the plane sank slowly in the water, we all scrambled out onto the wings, and waited there until we were rescued by villagers in dugout canoes. Sadly, the river claimed all the rice.

Hairy flying was the rule rather than the exception in the Far East. When we took off from Kandy for Singapore in an aircraft containing all the equipment of the AFPU, the tip of our wing struck a parked aircraft a glancing blow, and I saw that the wing was damaged. When I told the pilot about it, he said calmly that he didn't think it would really matter.

Once, landing in a Dakota at Penang, we came in to land at a sharply slanting angle. We hit the runway on only one wheel, with a tremendous jolt. As I looked out of the window I noticed that the wing tip was only inches from the tarmac. There were no buildings at the end of the runway, which ran into the sea, so we were able to overshoot and pull ourselves up again for another go.

When we landed, I asked the pilot 'What the hell happened there?' 'I'm sorry about that', he said. 'My co-pilot tried that landing. He's not used to Dakotas: he's only just come off fighters.'

Fighting in the Far East had now more or less finished. In January 1946 I went to Bangkok to photograph Mountbatten signing a peace agreement with the King of Siam, who had been forced into the war on their side by the Japanese.

After the ceremony, three British war correspondents were briefly to be presented to Mountbatten, and they all wanted a photograph of the event to send back to their newspapers at home. Unfortunately, I had to explain to them that I would only have time to photograph one of them shaking hands: the Super Ikonta I was using took too long to wind on. In the end they had to toss a coin to decide who should be the lucky one.

While I was in Bangkok I was taken to the races by a royal prince. This was not such a rare honour as it might seem: the King of Siam had many wives, and many more children, and you seemed to bump into Princes and Princesses of the blood almost everywhere; one pretty Princess I met ran a shop. But having such connections did have its advantages: before each race, the Prince told me which horse to put money on, and I followed his advice. It is the only time in my life when I have backed six winners in six consecutive races.

I was keen to make the most of my remaining time in the army. Once, having done a job for the AFPU in Java, I decided to go on to Bali, which was out of bounds to most army personnel in the Far East. I took a week's leave, and packed my own cameras.

Bali was the nearest place to paradise I have ever been to. It was closed because it was just too pleasant: anybody who went there was sure to want to stay. Luckily, as I had a pass giving me the right to go anywhere, I set off in March of 1946.

A well known character there was a Belgian artist, Monsieur Le Mayeurs. He had originally gone to Bali for a holiday, but had stayed on to live, and married a Balinese girl. I was introduced to them, and was struck by their charming and friendly manner, their generosity and also by Madame Le Mayeurs's good looks.

Balinese women are extremely beautiful, and, in addition, have the distracting habit of wearing sarongs which leave their breasts bare. Everywhere around me, I seemed to see lovely photographs. Monsieur Le Mayeurs invited me to a marvellous dinner of sucking-pig with a general and brigadier, though none of us wore our rank.

We sat on the verandah in the warm tropical night, with sea lapping on the shore and the meat crackling as it turned on the spit. It was a truly unforgettable evening spent in good company. I was so struck by her beauty that I arranged, with her husband's permission, to do a picture story showing Madame and her servant bathing together.

The next day I returned with my equipment and photographed two lovely women together in a lily pond. They were happy and quite un-selfconscious, but they seemed somehow uneasy. I later discovered that the pool we had used was locally held to be sacred.

Back in Singapore, nearly four months after I signed the papers for my commission, I was enjoying a drink in the officers' Mess one evening when Colonel Knight told me it had finally come through.

When he broke the news, I thought hard: I certainly didn't want to have to spend another year in the army. Having considered the matter, I made one or two suggestions about what he could do with my commission, and where he could put it.

Bali: a sequence of pictures appears at the end of the chapter.

Someone's out of step! The King of Siam with Mountbatten.

Opposite: Japanese war criminals being hung outside Changi Jail.

He produced a set of pips from his pocket and suggested that I slip them onto the epaulettes of my shirt, just to see what they looked like (as if I didn't know already).

'They look good, don't they?'

'Yes, but I still don't want them.'

'What would you say if I told you that your commission was back-dated to the day you signed the papers, last September?'

'I think I'll keep the pips after all.'

I quickly moved into the officers' billet at Orange Grove Road, where I had my bed on the balcony, surrounded by my photographs of Balinese bathing beauties. Clad in sarongs, Ernie Water and I could at last sit around and talk freely again, without rank coming between us.

Although the war was finished, we hadn't finished with the Japanese. Trials of Japanese soldiers were taking place, particularly of those who had been in charge of Allied prisoners-of-war, and some were sentenced to death for war crimes. I had to go along to Changi Jail, where so many men had been kept next to starvation in appalling conditions, to photograph the hanging of these 'war criminals' on a specially constructed triple gallows.

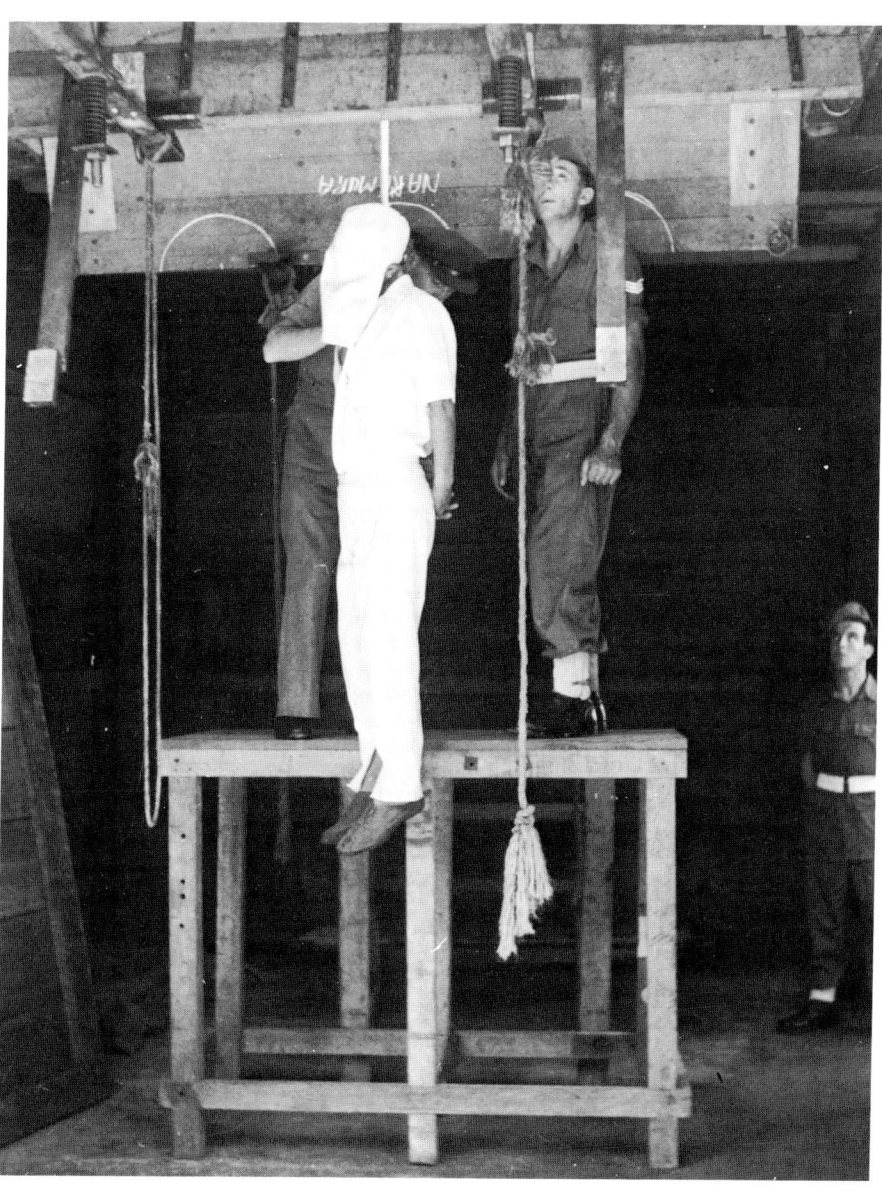

The executions were unemotional occasions, which made the physical awkwardness of the business more apparent. Because the ankles of the condemned men were tied together to stop them kicking or running away, it was difficult for them to stand properly and keep their balance; and because their wrists were tied together behind their backs, they couldn't use their hands to stop themselves from falling. So, right up until the last minute on the trap door, they had to be held upright.

A month or so later I had to attend another execution, this time of a general. In view of his rank, he was allowed to be shot, thus avoiding the disgrace of being hung. The shooting took place on the beach.

The condemned man was tied to a hefty stake, blindfold-

The execution of a Japanese General.

ed, and a piece of white paper was pinned over his heart to guide the aim of the firing squad. Before the officer in charge gave the command to fire, the general was permitted to shout 'Long live the Emperor' three times, which may have helped the Emperor, but didn't help him. At least he died happy and loyal, and didn't require the attentions of the military police officer with a revolver who stood by to finish him off if necessary. The redcap was none other than my old friend who had caught me and interrogated me when I attempted to enter the forbidden red-light district of Singapore.

By the middle of 1946 the military presence in the Far East was being reduced, and power was being handed back to the civilian authorities. There was less and less for me to do in my official capacity. Every night there seemed to be parties: parties to say farewell to this or that person, or to welcome this or that official. I began to feel very unfit. One morning I

Japanese Generals lay down their swords in surrender. These precious symbols had tremendous meaning for them, and this moment represented their ultimate disgrace.

got up early, jumped into my shorts, and set off for a run. I was only out for fifteen minutes, but it was a silly thing to do in such humid conditions: when I got back I felt terribly ill and had to lie down. I couldn't get up for the rest of the morning: all I could do was lie there with sweat pouring out of me like water out of a tap.

In May I photographed the installation of Malcolm MacDonald as the new Governor-General in Singapore; in June I took pictures of Mountbatten's farewell party at Flagstaff House; in August the AFPU (South-East Asian Command) closed down its operations in Singapore, and I prepared to return to England.

The *Monarch of Bermuda* lay lower in the water after all the heavy teak furniture I had bought, packed in all the heavy teak packing cases I'd had specially constructed, had been loaded on board (the wood would be handy, and worth a fortune, in England). I had already exported many pieces of furniture, some jewelry, yards of material and much else. One item I didn't trust to the porters was a lamp standard with an elaborately carved dragon's head. As I marched proudly up the gangway with my dragon over my shoulder, a cheer went up from the troops hanging over the side of the ship.

I arrived back in England at Liverpool on 8 September 1946, where I paid £2 3s 4d customs duty on my teak furniture. I then travelled through the night to Number 77 Military Demobilisation Unit, Guildford, where a further £2 'mess fee' was extracted from me and from every tired officer who couldn't wait to get home.

By nine o'clock that morning, fleeced, I was a citizen again, plain Bert Hardy. Later that day, I was standing on the platform of Eltham Station, with all my packing cases, and my dragon lamp standard, ready to tackle the first problem of my new civilian life: how to carry all that stuff two miles from the station to my house.

Bali

I took this first picture in one of my more artistic moods. Madame Le Mayeurs agreed to bathe for my benefit in the sacred pool with her servant. I thought it best to get her husband's agreement, too. The many beautiful women in Bali seemed happy to pose, and made wonderful subjects. Pictures of mothers with babies are the easiest of all.

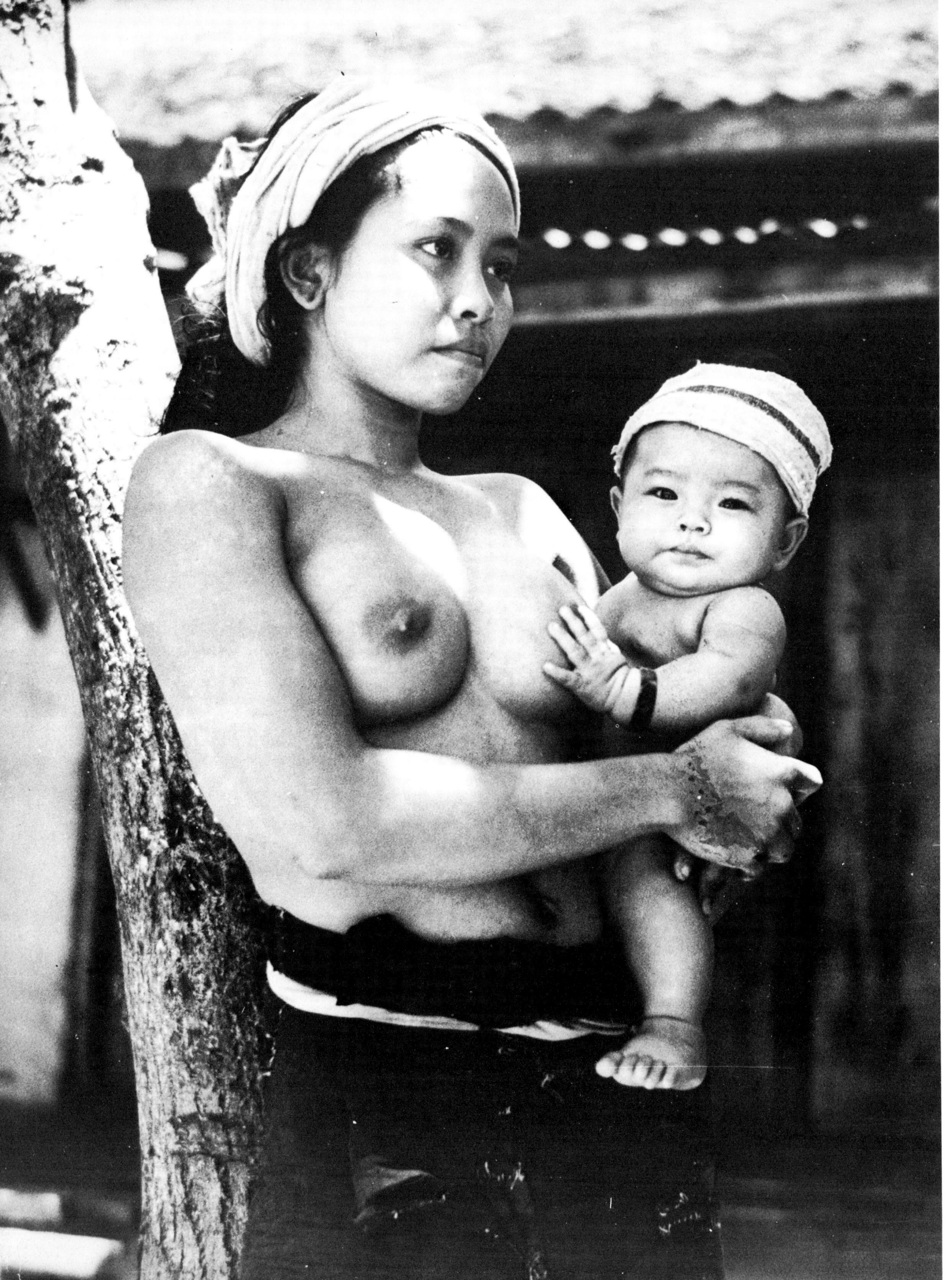

7: Back to *Picture Post*

Within a few days of arriving back in England, I got in touch with Tom Hopkinson and we arranged to have lunch together at the Bel Meunière in Charlotte Street, just like old times. He immediately offered me a job as a full-time employee of *Picture Post* at a salary of £1,000 a year. Although it was a lot of money in those days, I wasn't quite sure that it was enough to cover all my expenses, so I said I'd like to go and talk to my accountant about it. When we met again a week later, I'd found out that a thousand would be enough; but Tom had talked to the Directors, and was empowered to offer me £1,500 a year. It was an offer I couldn't refuse.

It was good to be back at work for *Picture Post* at a period when the paper was at its greatest. I kicked off with a story on Sid Field the comedian, which took me to his town of Birmingham, and I went to Denham to photograph the Boulting Brothers, whom I had last seen at the fall of Dunkirk. Then, after I had spent not much more than a month in this country, Tom must have decided that I had been at home too long, and sent me off to India for the opening of the first Constituent Assembly.

I went with Sidney Jacobson, now Lord Jacobson, but then just plain 'Jaco'. He knew India well, particularly Delhi, from his time there as a correspondent on *The Times of India*. We stayed at Maiden's Hotel, in the old part of Delhi. It was a beautiful, old-fashioned type of hotel. The only thing that put me off was when we were eating outside at tables with umbrellas, huge birds like vultures, which had probably just been pecking at the remains of dead people, would swoop down and snatch the food from our plates.

Before the opening of the Assembly, Mr Nehru granted us a ten-minute interview. Nehru was a fine man for whom I had a tremendous respect, but people's characters only emerge in their actions, or in certain facial expressions, and the photographer has to wait and hope for these to come. Sidney was talking to Nehru, and I was shooting away quietly when Nehru absent-mindedly picked up a rose from the bowl on his desk and sniffed it. I took the picture instantly: it was what I wanted. It said something about Nehru, and it made the cover of *Picture Post*. Tom thought very highly of these pictures.

What struck me most about India was the enormous contrast between the rich and the poor. At a party I saw a rich Indian take offence at the way a waiter had served him with a drink, and slap him hard across the face. I felt like giving him a taste of his own medicine.

But it would have been difficult to match the extreme wealth which we saw when we went up to Baroda for the Maharajah's birthday celebrations. As a part of the extravagance, two small cannon, one of solid gold and the other of solid silver, were set by the entrance to his magnificent palace. However, the climax of the celebrations seemed to be an elephant fight between two beasts who were in rut.

The fight took place in a huge stone-built arena. There were no easily portable long-focus lenses in those days, and I realised that to get any worthwhile pictures I would have to get as close as possible to the action. There were two stone islands in the middle of the arena, about three feet high and twenty feet across, with a small tree in the centre. I decided that I would have to stand on one of these. Jaco grudgingly agreed to come with me.

The savage elephants were led out into the arena and unshackled by their mahouts, who then ran as fast as they could for little openings around the edge, which were too small for the elephants. If the elephants had caught them, we were told, they would have picked them up with their trunks, thrown them on the ground, and trampled on them.

Jaco and I stood on our island and watched with interest as the elephants began sparring with each other. Everything looked set for a good clean fight until one of them suddenly caught sight of us, and decided he could do with a bit of trampling practice before the main bout. He lumbered over towards us, and began trying to reach us with his trunk. Suddenly, it wasn't so funny.

I took lots of pictures of Nehru, but this is the one that made the front cover.

PICTURE POST

HULTON'S NATIONAL WEEKLY   WE VISIT INDIA   HISTORIC PICTURES   FEBRUARY 8, 1947   Vol. 34. No. 6   4D

There was nowhere to retreat to: Jaco and I both backed up until we stood back-to-back on either side of the tree in the middle of the island. The elephant's trunk stretched, quivered, sniffed at us, stretched a bit more. He strained to reach us. I was dreading that he would be able to climb onto the island. The crowd roared their appreciation of the extra entertainment.

But then he abruptly seemed to decide that if we were going to play hard to get he couldn't be bothered with us, and moved off to pick on someone his own size. To our great relief, he forgot all about us, and continued with the main event.

The fact that I had formed an educational relationship with two English lady school teachers hardly made up for the fact that I had to spend my first Christmas as a civilian for five years in Delhi. On Christmas day 1946, by way of celebration, I ran twice up and down the steps of an old tower, the Qutb Minar just outside Delhi. You had to be pretty fit simply to get to the top just once, so I must have been in good shape.

Back in England I was sent on a slightly safer assignment with Patrick Campbell. We had to go and interview J. W. Robertson Scott, a vigorous, white haired eighty-year-old with a bushy beard, who was retiring as editor of *The Countryman*. His job was being taken over by the son of Sir Stafford Cripps.

On the way up, we stopped off at a tobacconist's shop in Oxford, and Patrick introduced me to a particularly smooth blend of pipe tobacco called 'Baby's Bottom'. Patrick was also a bit of a tippler, while I was not a particularly heavy drinker. Perhaps I am unfortunate, in that my nose, which has been compared to W. C. Fields' nose, made me look a worse offender than I was.

When we arrived, Robertson Scott offered us a glass of ginger beer, but then he must have noticed us shuffling our feet and looking awkward. He quickly realised the mistake he had made:

'Perhaps you'd like something stronger?' he asked, staring particularly intensely at me. Then he leaned over to Patrick confidentially, and whispered loudly: 'He looks like a man who likes his drink.'

In fact, I had only really started drinking when I arrived in Fleet Street. Before that, as a boy, I used to look through the doors of pubs when I walked past, and feel annoyed with all the men boozing their money away inside, leaving their wives and children to cope as well as they could. I still remember going to Olympia on an early job for William Davis at GPA; I was with a journalist, and he suggested going to the bar for a drink. I had one bottle of beer, and I could hardly stand up: I caught a bus home later in the day, and when I got off, I was still very wobbly.

But although I enjoyed a pint with friends, my favourite type of drinking was, and still is, wine drinking. If anyone is to blame for my developing a taste for wine, it was probably Bert Lloyd, who was quite a connoisseur.

In May, Bert and I were sent on one of our periodic trips to France, this time to cover the Gypsy festival of the Black Virgin in the Camargue.

We motored down, and put up at a posh hotel called the Julius Caesar, in Arles, where we did ourselves proud. Each day we drove the twenty or so miles to the little coastal resort of Saintes Maries-de-la-Mer, where the festival was taking place. St Marie was the black handmaiden of the Virgin Mary, and they had been seen together walking in from the sea at the place which had been named after her. St Marie stayed and died in France, and the coffin containing her remains was kept in the bell tower of the little church. She was especially loved by Gypsies, and each year they gathered from all over the world for the festival in her memory. At the height of the celebrations, her coffin was lowered down the bell tower (it was so dark inside that I couldn't get a picture), and afterwards the gypsies all waded out into the sea.

Of course, the Camargue is not only famous for the festival: it is a wild, marshy area, inhabited by flamingoes, wild horses, and bulls. Cowboys known as 'gardians', riding horses with big saddles like armchairs, look after the bulls. These are used for the local type of bull fight. Unlike in Spanish bull-fights, the bull isn't killed. The object is simply to snatch a flower from between his horns. As the bulls get older and more experienced, they get cleverer; and individual animals became famous for their qualities. In Arles there is even a statue of a famous bull.

In fact the respect for the animals' lives seemed rather greater than the respect for human life. Another local sport was known as a 'Bull tease'. Bulls with leather casing over their horns were let loose in an arena with the local young men who practised their skills in this way. I don't think the lesson of the elephant fight can have sunk in properly. I tried taking photographs from on top of the stockade, but I wasn't getting the feeling of the event, so I joined the men in the ring. Unlike Sidney Jacobson, Bert didn't feel it was his duty to join me: he was quite happy to sit it out in the front stalls.

Everything was going fine until a young bull failed to realise that I was only there to take photographs, and charged straight at me with his horns down ready to toss me. In spite of the cameras dangling around my neck. I scrambled up and

I just managed to climb the fence in time to reach safety and take the picture.

The bull tease, with the beast in hot pursuit.

over the wooden stockade in record time. Bert assured me afterwards that it was one of the most popular events of the afternoon.

We were having an extremely good time, working each day and returning in the evening to our hotel to sample the delicious food and wines. But then we had to dash back home because Bert's wife Charlotte was expecting their child.

We threw our stuff in the car, and I drove us back up through France as fast as I could. I still enjoy driving fast (though now with a turbo). But I remember that Bert was slightly ruffled when, coming down a long straight hill towards a level crossing, we suddenly spotted a man cranking down the barrier. We were going so fast that there wasn't the faintest chance of stopping. I jammed the horn down, and the man saw us and frantically started cranking it up again. We just about scraped through the space beneath it.

The round of good food and luxurious living continued. I was sent with Marjorie Beckett to the Imperial Hotel in Torquay to do a story called 'Grand Hotel'.

Before I set out, I was given strict instructions to buy a dinner jacket. I have never owned a dinner jacket. I don't like them. They sent me along to the Savoy Tailors' Guild in the Strand, but it seemed silly to spend all that money on a suit which you only put on for a few hours once in a blue moon. Then I saw a lovely checked woollen sports jacket, the sort I had always wanted, and never had. I bought that instead.

Marjorie Beckett was very refined, and quietly beautiful.

When we arrived at the hotel, we looked around a bit, thinking of possible angles for the story. I got talking with the head chef and asked him all about this business of dressing for dinner. 'You don't want to worry about that', he said. 'They're just a bunch of toffee-nosed gits.'

That evening Marjorie got into her fine evening dress, and I put on my woollen sports jacket, and we went down to dinner. She looked lovely. When we sat down at our table, everyone was staring at us, thinking 'who does he think he is, coming down to dinner in a sports jacket?', but then the head chef came through the doors of the kitchen and straight to our table, to discuss our meal.

You could see the change come over people's faces: I must be a very important chap to wear a sports jacket to dinner and have a personal visit from the head chef. This happened every night we were there. No one found out that as soon as dinner was over, the chef and I used to nip round the corner to the local pub for a pint together.

On my return, I again teamed up with Sidney Jacobson to go to Poland. We sailed on the *Batory*, a Polish luxury liner filled with prosperous Poles returning from America. We took full advantage of the luxury on board. I even discovered a taste for cocktails, especially White Ladies. But all that soon came to an end.

The customs officers left us in no doubt that we were entering a poor country: they even wanted to charge me duty on my cameras. Luckily they didn't find out about the extra two hundred cigarettes I was smuggling in. Sidney was quaking in his boots about it: he was always far too honest to have anything to do with that type of thing. But I had spent time before in countries where things had not got back to normal after war time, and I knew the value of cigarettes.

We had booked berths in a sleeping car on the Orient Express to take us on to Warsaw when we arrived, but the *Batory* had spent twelve hours on a rescue mission in the Atlantic, and was late to dock, so we missed the train. There were no taxis when we left the docks, so we had to carry all our bags and equipment to the main railway station in Gdynia. There we had to join a long queue for tickets for the Warsaw train. While we were queuing, Sidney's wallet was stolen, so we then had to report the theft to the police, before returning to catch the night train to Warsaw.

The train was crammed with people and their luggage, mostly packed in cardboard boxes, and we were forced to stand up all night. By the time we got to Warsaw we were already pretty fed up with Poland. Our hotel, the Hotel Bristol, was quite different from the sort of Hotel Bristol which I seemed to have found in every other European capital. For a start, they hadn't finished re-building it yet. You'd be lying in bed in the morning, and someone would come marching in and start to repair the windows. Another time, I was about to sit on the lavatory when a voice shouted up, warning me that it wasn't plumbed in yet! The food was scarce: for breakfast we got black bread and, if we were very lucky, an egg.

The story we were doing was about a Scottish girl who had married a Polish soldier in Britain, and had returned to Poland with him. It was difficult not to feel sorry for them. He was a poor man in a poor country. Prices were tremendously high. At the official rate of exchange, one pound would just about buy a glass of beer or a sandwich. I soon discovered that there were two exchange rates: on the black market I could get about ten times as many zlotys for a pound. As we mainly had traveller's cheques, we wired the *Picture Post* office, and they sent us some pound notes through the post, which, amazingly enough, reached us intact. From then on, with the addition of our income from the sale of cigarettes, we had no more money difficulties. Now our only problem was how to get about the country: it was impossible to hire a car, and all the trains were far too crowded. Then, suddenly, a Polish newspaper got in touch with us. They were shocked that we were unable to get around, so they placed a jeep (which was incredibly rare) and one of their journalists (much less rare) at our disposal.

We were now able to see the hard work the Poles were doing to reconstruct their country from the rubble of the war. We were also deeply impressed by the huge consumption of alcohol: it was about the only thing of which there didn't seem to be a shortage, and many men took full advantage of the fact. They used to carry around little half bottles of *Spiritus*, a type of concentrated vodka which you were supposed to dilute 3:1 with water, but which they swigged straight. In one station, we saw an engine driver being pulled free from his train, completely knocked out by the stuff.

Later that year England had one of its periodic fits of royalty fever: the wedding of Princess Elizabeth to Prince Philip at Westminster Abbey. There was a rota system, which meant that certain photographers were given set positions, and these had to make their pictures available to all newspapers.

On the day, it was just as well I was a miniature cameraman: I was crammed into a tiny gallery over the West Door between two agency men, each with three plate cameras on tripods. We arrived at seven in the morning, and had to wait until the early afternoon with no chance to leave our positions, and only a thermos flask to relieve ourselves into. (I was told that elderly dukes and so on at these events often have a rubber bag strapped to their legs inside their morning suits.)

But when the Princess and her bridesmaids arrived, I immediately had an advantage over my colleagues: with my small camera, I was able to lean over the edge of our perch,

One of my best pictures, taken in very trying circumstances.

and take a quick picture as they adjusted her train. Conditions were very difficult: it was dark, and there was a lot of movement. Using my Contax with an f 1.4 lens at speeds of about one-tenth of a second, I was able to bring out the softness and fluency of the Princess's wedding dress, and the movements of the bridesmaids around her, like a ballet. I had now come to use the expressive value of movement in pictures: later, when I worked in advertising, I took it much further.

After doing a story on the Irish elections with Bert Lloyd in April 1948 I was sent off to Athens with Maurice Richardson to cover the Greek Civil War.

We started off in Athens, photographing all the important people from Archbishop Damaskinos to Mr Papandrios, but pictures of important men don't make a story. We applied for permission to go to the front, but we were not allowed to. Instead, we were allowed to go up to Thessalonika.

In Thessalonika, a huge Court Martial of about fifty people was taking place. We also heard that executions were going on all the time. This sounded more like war, but we were not allowed to photograph the executions, only the Court Martial. We were beginning to get a bit desperate, but then Maurice managed to get permission for us to go to Drama, where we could work with the 25th Infantry Brigade.

Getting to Drama was not easy. The railway line ran through the mountains along the border with Yugoslavia and Bulgaria, and the Communists had set up a field gun overlooking the line at a place called Rhodopolis. Every time a train went past they loosed off a few shells and occasionally, if the wind was in the right direction, they got lucky and hit the line or even the train. On our first attempt to get through, they managed to hit the track, so we had to go back to the nearest town for the night while the line was repaired. The next day we set out along the same stretch again. As a precaution, we all lay face down in the corridor of the train. This time, the Communists were not so lucky, and we got through safely. We had seen our first bit of action, but it was action at a distance, and we still didn't have any war-like pictures.

We were not very welcome in Drama: the General Commanding proved as elusive as the war he was fighting, but at last we pinned him down, and he told us that if we went just a few miles further into the mountains, we might come across some fighting.

We got a lift in a jeep to the mountain he had told us about. If we had been unwelcome in Drama, we were even less welcome here. We were shown around quickly, and an attempt was made to send us back again. Only when we insisted that we were not going until we had got some action pictures were we allowed to stay.

The next morning there was a flurry of excitement: two prisoners had been taken. The enemy at last! I hurried to take some pictures of them, since we had been told that the forces we were with didn't take prisoners (whatever that meant). I expect that was why the prisoners were so terrified that they were going to be shot when I photographed them.

Later the same day, I managed to lay on some pictures of soldiers crawling forward through grass on their stomachs. I now felt that we had done the best we could in the circumstances. We made our way back to Drama, and from there took the train back to Salonika. Once again the Communist field gun was busy, and this time we had to go back and spend two nights in Serrai waiting for the line to be cleared. At this point we decided that the man in charge of the field gun was probably related to the owner of the hotel in Serrai.

After a trip to Lamia to photograph the King and Queen of Greece, our visit came to an end. The driving of the lorry driver on the tortuous mountain road back from Lamia was far more frightening than any threat from the Communists, and we were pleased to get back to Athens to catch our plane home.

At the airport we slowly became aware of the fact that we were being treated very respectfully. We noticed the porters standing back and looking at us, whispering to each other. We wondered what we had done to attract such attention.

On the plane home the VIP treatment continued. At last, we couldn't stand the tension any longer, so we asked the hostess whether the Press were always treated so well. 'Not all the Press, sir', she said, looking at Maurice. 'You know who I am, then?' he said, mystified. 'But of course, sir. Who does not know Mr Randolph Churchill?'

It was not always necessary to try as hard as I had in Greece to risk my neck. On my return to England, as a rest from all my war work, I went with the picture editor, Harry Deverson, to do a silly story on a young English couple having their honeymoon at a hotel at Interlaken, in Switzerland.

It was a pleasant and relaxing story to do, and they were a nice young couple. On the last night of the holiday, Harry and I and the couple had a drunken evening of celebration with the proprietor of the hotel. The pair had gone off to bed a long time before Harry and I finally took the lift to our room on the fifth floor in the early hours of the morning.

No sooner had we got in our room, which was just along the corridor from theirs, than I was seized with an urge to say good night to them. I was sure they were up to no good, so I thought I would give them a little surprise. In my drunken state, I clambered out of the window, shuffled along a ledge till I was outside their room, tapped on the window and said 'Boo!' Satisfied, I returned again the way I had come, and fell into bed.

The next morning I awoke with a vague memory of what I had done. I looked out of the window to see if it was possible. To my horror, I saw that the ledge was only nine inches wide, and five floors up; I felt absolutely sick.

In the summer of 1948, *Picture Post* helped me find a car. It was difficult to come by cars at this time, and the new Ford Prefect they offered me was a real luxury. I sold my old Austin 7, which had its rusty floor, and its exhaust held on with asbestos tape. All in all it had been a good car: I had got

a lot of miles out of it, and during my time in the army, I had rented it to Mac Hastings at a pound a week, which he paid in a handy lump sum. Now I placed an advertisement in the *Evening Standard*, and when I arrived home from work there was a queue of people outside my gate all wanting to buy it for £225. I sold it to the first man in the queue, who had his son with him and didn't even want a test drive. The following day I proudly collected my brand new car, costing £380 with all extras, from the Ford showrooms in Regent Street.

In October, I took my new Ford to the continent for the first time, with Bert Lloyd. We were going to Mont, a village near Orleans, to do a story on the wine harvest: obviously Tom thought we were the right people for the job. But first we stopped off in Paris.

Paris was very crowded: we seemed to have arrived in the middle of some sort of international convention, and every hotel was fully booked. After spending the afternoon looking around for somewhere to stay, Bert and I decided to give it a rest, and have a meal at one of our favourite restaurants: L'Escargot, on the Left Bank. We were great friends with the proprietor, and when we told him our problem, he immediately offered to help us.

For the next two hours, while we were eating and drinking, he telephoned everyone he knew, to find if there was a spare room. He even telephoned a couple of brothels to see if there was a spare bed, but we didn't have any luck.

There was nowhere to go, until he thought of asking the Italian dishwasher. The dishwasher was delighted to take us home with him. He had only one room, but it was easily big enough for the three of us. In fact, his bed was big enough for two people: why didn't one of us share it with him, then only one person would have to sleep on the floor?

Bert and I looked at each other, and decided that we would have to toss a coin for the honour. I'm glad to say Bert lost, and I slept on the floor.

The next day Bert managed to find us an empty room high up in a big house in the Rue Faubourg. Although there was no lift, and no mattresses, and we had to carry all our luggage and equipment up six floors at least there was no dishwasher.

We spent one more night in Paris, and then drove on to Mont. It was tiny, and there was no hotel. Once again we were faced with the problem of where to sleep. This time one of the farmers of the village invited us to stay at his house. In our honour, he and his wife vacated their room, and Bert and I shared their lumpy mattress for the rest of our stay.

We went out each day to take pictures of the grape picking in progress. Afterwards we would retreat with the grape pickers to the cellar where the farmer kept his own presses and wine, and taste the unmatured wine. We sat in a circle and passed a dirty aluminium cup (which was seldom washed) from hand to hand. The unmatured wine was a milky colour, and while the cup was being passed round, the farmer used to tell stories. I didn't care for the taste of it much at first, but I soon began to like it. His stories seemed to

Mont: a picture sequence appears at the end of the chapter.

Opposite, above: This is really more of a landscape than a war picture.

Below: Where is the war?

be good too, though I couldn't understand much of his French. They were certainly dramatic.

When I tried to take a picture of the scene, I decided to try to fix a photoflood bulb in the socket. But photoflood lamps use much more current than ordinary bulbs. Each time I fitted it in, the fuse blew, and we were all plunged into darkness. Each time the fuse blew, the farmer patiently went and repaired it. But after this had happened three or four times, he lost patience: he fetched a thick four-inch nail and jammed it across the terminals of the fuse box. I was able to get my pictures.

In the evenings we were given supper. We used to sit on benches at a great kitchen table which was still covered with the breakfast things. Supper was always soup, which you drank out of a dish. When you had finished your soup, you then had to turn your dish over, and eat the rest of your meal – meat and potatoes – off the bottom of the dish. Naturally everything was washed down with wine.

Bert and I had the time of our lives staying with the family, sampling the wine and listening to the stories. We became comrades of our Marxist host and his family in the two weeks we were there. To show how grateful we were for their hospitality, we offered to take the farmer's son Pierre back to Paris with us on our way home.

Pierre was delighted by our offer. He rushed off to put on his best overalls, while the farmer and some of the other people from the village said they couldn't let us leave with a dirty car, and gathered round and washed it for me.

That evening we arrived in Paris and took Pierre to a grand restaurant. He was amazed by it all: he had never been out of Mont before. But he was even more amazed when Bert and I presented him with all the French francs we hadn't managed to spend (a considerable sum) because we had been staying at his father's farmhouse. I hope he enjoyed himself.

For my first assignment in the new year of 1949, I was sent back to the Far East, this time with Woodrow Wyatt. On overseas trips of any length I usually got to know the journalist I was with pretty well. Sometimes this led to lasting friendships, as it did with Bert Lloyd, and later with Brian Dowling. Woodrow Wyatt, though, never became a close friend.

He could and would argue about anything. We were lying on our beds in our hotel room in Singapore one evening, and he was rattling on, attempting to persuade me that black was white, when I suddenly burst out:

'You may be able to make what you're saying *sound* like the truth, but I know it's a bloody lie!'

He was, of course, a successful politician.

We spent some time in Rangoon photographing well known Burmese personalities, and I made friends with U Ohn, a government figure who was also a devout Buddhist, and a generous man. He had a leather case made for me to carry my cameras in, and later, when he was made Burmese Ambassador to England, we went out for a Chinese meal once or twice.

There was a civil war going on in Burma at the time. Government troops were fighting the rebel Karens only ten miles from Rangoon. As far as I was concerned, war meant good pictures, so I asked several times for permission to go to the front-line area and take pictures. Each time, the answer was 'no'.

In the end I thought, bugger this, and made my own way up to the front line. There was not much fighting going on: just a few Burmese troops taking cover. I asked where the other side was, and they pointed in a certain direction.

I simply walked up the road which had become a no-man's land until I came to the area occupied by the Karens. They didn't seem at all put out by my arrival: in fact they were very friendly, because they were quite pro-British. I moved around taking photographs, and then walked back again. As soon as I got back the Burmese troops were pressing me to tell them what I had seen: how many troops the Karens had, and so on. I suggested that they went to find out for themselves.

I came closer to a sticky end on the same trip when I went up the Irrawaddy on a naval patrol boat, and got interested in the great teak rafts that float down the river. We flew to Mandalay to do a story on them. The teak is felled in Mandalay, and all the logs pulled down the hillside by bullocks to the river, where they are lashed together to make a great raft at least the size of a tennis court, which has a crew of about two or three living in a hut built on top of it. They help to steer it clear of the banks during the year it takes to move down river from Mandalay to Rangoon.

I climbed on board one of these rafts, with my cameras slung round my neck, and we started moving slowly downstream. Suddenly the ropes holding the log I was standing on gave way, and the log began sinking beneath me.

Naturally, my first thought was to save my cameras. I was standing holding them clear of the water, when the thought struck me: if I didn't do something quickly, it wouldn't just be the cameras that were lost. If I fell right through the raft, the log would probably bob back into place, and I would be trapped beneath it.

It was the cameras or me, and I chose me. I put out my hands, and heaved myself up onto one side of the gap as quickly as possible, so the cameras only splashed in the water briefly. The crew told me afterwards that it was very common for the ropes to rot and give way like that, but I didn't find the information very reassuring. I was more pleased to discover that my cameras had hardly been affected by their quick dip.

From Rangoon, Woodrow and I flew on to Kuala Lumpur, where we stayed at the home of Sir Arthur Newbolt, the head of the Legislative Council. It was an extremely posh do, and we had to dress for dinner each night, which wasn't exactly a hobby of mine. I didn't even have my nice woollen sports jacket to wear: I had to borrow a dinner jacket, and rely on Woodrow to tie my bow-tie for me.

One evening he had another engagement, and I was forced

to tie my own tie. It was a difficult job, but after a half an hour or so I managed to produce something which looked almost right. I might not have appeared the best-dressed man in Kuala Lumpur, but I probably would have passed muster if, when we left the table to relax in armchairs for brandy and cigars, I hadn't crossed my legs and exposed my bright red socks!

It was a relief, after so much formality, to go on to Singapore, where we did a story on Malcolm MacDonald. I knew him slightly from the time, a couple of years earlier, when I had done a story on his installation as Governor-General of Malaya. MacDonald preferred a more relaxed style of living, and upset all the old colonial types by coming down to dinner in a short-sleeved shirt.

After meeting up with Gillie Potter and Rex Ebbetts, two old mates from the AFPU who had stayed on in Singapore, we flew back home.

Back in England, I was sent with Bobby Birch to a photo-call for Marlene Dietrich at the Savoy. Bobby was a reporter I liked working with, although he mostly worked with Kurt Hutton. He was tall and always wore very well-cut suits. He was in fact tremendously well dressed down to his ankles, but then the whole effect was spoilt by a pair of filthy shoes with the soles flapping loose. Perhaps he didn't think anyone would look that far down. Whatever his reason for not bothering about footwear, it didn't seem to affect his popularity with women. In all, he was married about seven times, once to a daughter of Tom Hopkinson; and when the marriages broke up, there never seemed to be any hard feelings.

Photocalls were really just an excuse to go and have a free lunchtime booze-up. But for once, here was a star who really did live up to her legend. You could see the hardened Fleet Street men going all soppy and falling for her, so instead of getting the usual pictures in the uninteresting surroundings of the Savoy River Room, I did a story showing the effect she had on the journalists.

If that story was intended as an excuse for a booze-up, my next one was an excuse for a holiday. I went down to Positano in Italy to photograph a starlet called Mercy Haystead. There was a tremendous beach enclosed by cliffs, and the sun shone all day. Since I didn't get on very well with my journalist, Derek Monsey, I soon forgot about him and found other ways to occupy the time.

I fell in love with Positano, and in particular with one of its young female inhabitants, a doctor's daughter. I hired a Lambretta, and when we weren't swimming, we went roaring off on it.

I don't like the sun – it doesn't agree with my skin. But although I didn't do any sunbathing, I still managed to get burnt on my back when I was swimming in the sea. Now I discovered another good reason to fall for a doctor's daughter: her dad was a skin specialist. While the daughter held my hand and comforted me, her father treated my back with some kind of surgical spirit and cotton wool. Each time he

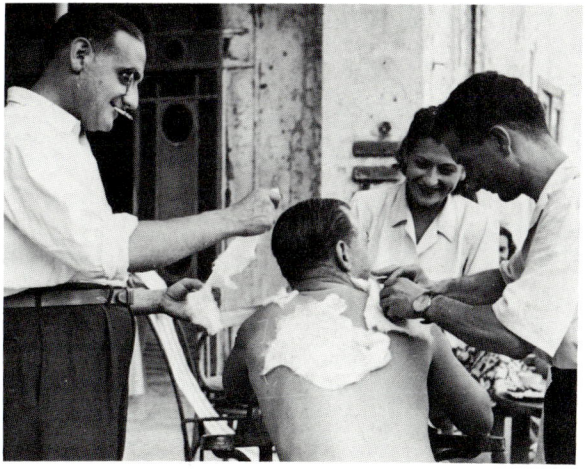

Marlene softens the hardened newsmen.

A pleasant operation in Positano. It didn't hurt a bit!

A chorus girl in Richmond Park, and then the same chorus girl in Paris with Fred Astaire. Coming downstairs is Diana Dors in her days as a Rank starlet. It was very windy.

removed the pads of cotton wool, the burnt skin came away, leaving my back as good as new. And although it didn't hurt a bit, I'm glad to say that at no stage did the girl consider it advisable to let go of my hand.

Quite a few of the starlets I photographed in those days went on to become famous. Soon after returning from Positano, I drove to Richmond Park with Derek Monsey and a chorus girl who seemed a bit different from the usual type of starlet.

I took some pictures of her in the park and down by the river. I liked her, and we sat around and talked a bit before setting off home. On the way back in the car, I discovered that I had lost my cigarette lighter. I was really fond of that lighter, so I turned round and drove all the way back to the park, where we retraced our steps and crawled about in the long grass looking for it.

The girl eventually found my lighter. She was very nice about it, and we all drove home. The next time I met her, years later, she wasn't quite so nice. She was famous now, and starring with Fred Astaire in a film being made in Paris. This was the first time he was dancing with a partner other than Ginger Rogers. She would have nothing to do with me when I asked her for the first pictures of her dancing with Fred Astaire. She had made an exclusive arrangement with an American photographer. In the end Astaire, who was very friendly and helpful, danced and posed for me, though she still didn't like being photographed with him.

Even so, I was still grateful to Audrey Hepburn for helping me to find my cigarette lighter.

Later in 1950, Bobby Birch and I took two young unknowns from the Rank 'Charm School' on a day trip to Boulogne. One was naughty and the other wasn't quite so naughty. The naughty one let me take a lot of pictures of the wind blowing her skirt up. We had a good lunch and good fun in the afternoon. We rounded off the day by buying them a bottle of perfume each. I sometimes wonder where

the naughtiness would have stopped if I had taken the saucy one out for the evening. She was to become very well known: her name was Diana Dors, and the other girl was Barbara Murray.

My all-time favourite 'saucy' personality was Gussie Moran, known as Gorgeous Gussie. Gorgeous was a tennis player famous for her short skirts and frilly knickers, which were always on view while she was playing.

Denzil Batchelor and I flew to Paris to do a story on her. We had a nice lunch, and took some good pictures of her kissing gendarmes and so on in the afternoon. By the end of the day, we were getting along so well that it seemed a shame to break up the party.

Queue up!

I offered to find the soap.

Unfortunately, Gorgeous had a date that evening with a rich Count who was driving all the way from Germany in his Mercedes to see her. We thought that with such a big fish turning up, we had better make ourselves scarce, but Gussie wasn't having any of that.

If the Count had been looking forward to a quiet evening discussing double faults, he was disappointed. She insisted that we must join them for dinner. We all drove to a restaurant just outside Paris (it was called the Coq Hardi) and continued our party.

One day after I had spent a night in town, I arrived at the offices of *Picture Post* at eight o'clock in the morning – an hour or so before anyone normally arrived. I was sitting in the office of Harry Deverson, the picture editor, when suddenly the phone rang. It was a strange hour for anyone to be calling *Picture Post*. When I answered, a business-like voice at the other end announced: 'Lord Beaverbrook is ready to be photographed. Send your man round right away.'

The job had obviously been set up for somebody else to do, but as I was the only one around, I had to go. I found out that he was based at Arlington House, overlooking Green Park behind the Ritz, and I took a taxi over there.

It was all very difficult, as I didn't have the usual journalist to keep him distracted while I got on with taking the pictures. I had to do all the talking myself.

Everything seemed to go all right. After a while, Beaverbrook abruptly said: 'Have you finished?' 'Yes, sir', I said, and it was time for me to leave.

While I was packing up my cameras, he walked over to a tall desk, where he used to work standing up, and stood with his back to me. There was something about the way he was standing which seemed to show what sort of man he was. I quickly took out my Leica again to photograph that posture. Because of the quietness of its shutter, Beaverbrook didn't hear any other noise than the door shutting when I left. It was to become one of my best-known pictures.

In March 1950 Tom sent me to Bechuanaland (now Botswana) with Fyfe Robertson. Fyfe was a comparatively new *Picture Post* journalist. He came down from Scotland and started work in the picture-editing department, but soon moved over into journalism. He was a very thorough man: he got hold of all the books he could about Bechuanaland and spent the long flight down to Rhodesia reading them.

The ruler of Bechuanaland, Seretse Khama, was returning to the country after being exiled for the 'crime' of anti-racialism – that is, marrying a white English girl, Ruth Williams, from Lewisham. Now he was planning to fly back into the country from Salisbury, Rhodesia, to a little air-strip where Ruth would be waiting to meet him. We found we were already at a disadvantage when we got to Salisbury: the men from the *Daily Mail* and the *Daily Express* had arranged to be on the same aeroplane as Seretse himself.

We searched round Salisbury, and eventually found a young Englishman who was willing to charter his plane to us for the journey. Although it only had one engine, and therefore it was (strictly speaking) illegal to fly across the jungle in it, we decided that the risk was worth taking. On the day, we flew out behind Seretse's plane, keeping it in sight and constantly zig-zagging through the air so that our little plane, which was much faster, didn't overtake theirs.

As we approached the airstrip where Ruth was waiting, I felt that even though we weren't on Seretse's plane, that needn't be a disadvantage. If we landed before he did, we would be able to scoop the *Mail* and the *Express* by getting pictures of Ruth waving to Seretse at the moment he stepped off the plane.

It was a good idea in theory, but things didn't work out like that. We got down quickly, but stood waiting. Seretse's plane was refused permission to land. I had to content myself with a picture of Ruth waving forlornly as her husband's plane flew low overhead.

The expected reunion between Seretse and Ruth didn't take place. Instead, Seretse was placed under house arrest, and Ruth returned to her tiny house with a corrugated tin roof in the village of Serowe. The men from the *Mail* and the *Express* stayed at a hotel in Palapye Road, about twenty miles from Serowe up a rough dirt track.

They commuted every day in a large American car they had hired. Fyfe and I decided that we would live in the village of Serowe, and were allowed to put up in the back room of the village store in Serowe, Williams Store, having got in supplies of food and beer. We were loaned a small truck, and while awaiting developments, did a nice story on the village itself.

We also kept on our chartered plane. The other photographers regularly needed to get to Johannesburg in order to wire their stories back to London. By sub-letting the plane to them, we managed to pay for the plane and make a slight profit on the side.

At last it became obvious that the reunion we were all waiting for wasn't going to take place. We arranged an interview with Seretse in prison in Labatsi, and smuggled him in a bottle of whisky – an anti-racialist crime for which we didn't get caught. Then we said goodbye to Ruth, with whom I had become quite friendly, and set out to return to Salisbury.

On the way back we stopped off at Mafeking to try to interview Tshekedi Khama, who was an uncle of Seretse. He was reluctant at first, but finally agreed to talk to us. He told us about a time when the British were annoyed with his countrymen, and wanted to make a show of strength in Serowe. They planned to position a large cannon in the town square to strike respect into the villagers. Unfortunately, it got bogged down in the muddy dirt road outside the town. Eventually Tshekedi had to come to the rescue, and organise a gang of men to go and pull the gun out. This was how the British made sure everyone knew who was in charge!

Over the years, I enjoyed an immense amount of travel working for *Picture Post*. For all that, some of my best work was to be done much nearer home.

A French Village – Mont

While we were there, the baker's son got married and I was able to photograph
the procession. Our host in Mont got his family to help with the winepress,
and overleaf he is also pictured as storyteller, which was his task
and pleasure while the pickers tasted the unmatured wine.

8: Life on the Poorer Side

The Gorbals: further pictures appear at the end of the chapter.

As a contrast to my more exotic jobs, I went to the gloom of the Gorbals, the slum area of Glasgow. Knowing Bill Brandt's feeling for atmosphere, Tom had sent him up to get a set of pictures of the slum. Bill returned with his usual contrasty pictures of the backs of policemen standing at the ends of streets, but nothing which really showed the human side of poverty. Tom decided to send me with Bert Lloyd, to see if we could do any better.

We stayed at a posh hotel in the centre of Glasgow, and took a tram over to the slums each day, where we just wandered around. Bert had a contact from the Communist Party who was supposed to help us, but we didn't seem to be able to find a way into the story.

The poverty was much worse than anything I had known around Blackfriars, and that was saying something. The long narrow streets were lined with high tenement blocks with grimy, uncleaned windows, and tattered rags for curtains. There was a tremendous amount of vandalism and drunkenness. Slowly, as we walked the streets, the misery of the place began to get to us.

There were few places for the children to play. One such place was the graveyard, where they played leapfrog over the tombstones. There was little for the men to do except go and drink away their cares and their money. But the people I felt most sorry for were the housewives. It was not their fault their flats were dirty: they were so rotten and damp that it was impossible to keep them clean. And it wasn't as easy for them to go and get drunk as it was for their husbands.

Each of the great blocks of flats had just one little lavatory at the bottom of the stairs, often with the door kicked off; and none had any proper washing facilities. I had to admire the spirit of the young girls, who still managed to look pretty and smart amid all the squalor.

One day, when we were walking around, a woman standing outside her home called out to us, 'If you want to see a bonny mess, come and look in here.' Outside the back window we could see children playing on piles of stinking refuse. Like everyone else, they had to leave their gas-jets burning at nights to keep the rats away. No one took much notice when I started taking photographs.

There were two rooms: in the front room, a girl aged about sixteen, obviously pregnant, sat at a table covered with dirty cups, and a Sifta salt packet, while her brother slept in a bunk bed behind her. In the next room the man who lived with the girl's mother lay drunkenly sleeping, at eleven in the morning, in a bed with filthy sheets.

When the story was used, the first page was made up of photographs taken by Bill Brandt, and the rest was my pictures. I entered my pictures for the 'sequence' section of the newly established Encyclopaedia Britannica Photographic Awards, and forgot all about it.

At the beginning of November, I went with Kurt Hutton, Lionel Birch and Hilda Marchant to do a silly story called 'The Pretty Girls of Leicester'. Kurt Hutton and Lionel Birch often used to work together on this kind of story.

Kurt and I were sharing a room in the Bell Hotel. It was easy enough for old hands like us to find plenty of pretty girls who were willing to have their pictures taken. And of course there were plenty more girls who thought they *should* be included. The word had even got round among the hotel chambermaids about what we were up to.

Kurt and I were in our room one day when a chambermaid came in to clean the grate. At first sight, she was not one of the pretty girls of Leicester, in fact she was rather ugly: she even had a funny eye. But she begged us to take her photograph for the story.

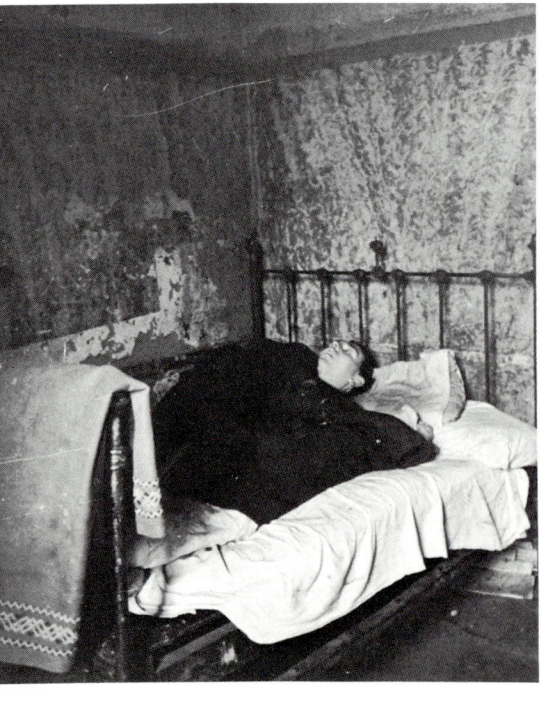

While someone sleeps off his hangover, for this girl breakfast means the start of another dismal day.

Kurt was being very diplomatic, and refusing politely, but she kept on insisting. In the end, just to please her, I took a picture of her bent over the grate looking back over her shoulder with her one good eye. Afterwards, Kurt said 'You silly fool. Why did you waste your film?' But when the story was used in *Picture Post*, the wall-eyed chambermaid duly appeared as one of Leicester's pretty girls.

If our stay in Leicester was a triumph for her, it was also good for me. While I was there, I received a telegram from Tom telling me that the pictures of the Gorbals I had entered for the first Encyclopaedia Britannica Photographic Awards had won the photo sequence section. Back in London, I collected my prize: a cheque for seventy-five guineas and a plaque, at a ceremony at the Savoy Hotel River Room on 16 November. Two days later, on 18 November 1948, Bert and I started work on a story about a poor area, this time a bit closer to home: it was the Elephant and Castle.

Like the Gorbals story, it was difficult to find a way to start. Bert and I didn't work on it every day. When we had time to spare, we used to take a tram across Blackfriars Bridge and wander around.

It was a dreary November, and in those days before smokeless fuels, the whole area was shrouded in a thick smog for most of the time. It wasn't long before Bert and I began to think we must be bloody mad: all we had were pictures of trams, smog, and trams *in* the smog.

We were walking round the back streets one day when I saw a young couple sitting on the steps of a house, obviously very much in love. They were totally absorbed in each other. I asked them if I could take some photographs, and they agreed. As I took my pictures I heard a voice from across the street calling out 'Ow about taking a picture of me, love?' Thinking that at last we had found a contact, I asked:

'What are these places like round the back?'

Without a second's hesitation, she replied:

'Bleedin' awful. Come and see for yourself.'

'What's your name?' I continued.

'Maisie'.

'Where do you work, then?'

'Piccadilly'.

'Whereabouts?'

She paused for a moment, looking thoughtful, and said, 'Lyons Corner House.' It took me a while to realise why she had been so vague: she was a prostitute.

Bert and I followed her down a narrow passageway to a tiny yard about ten feet square, where everyone hung out their washing. I looked around and saw, through a window, a young couple half-lying on a sofa just inside. I then said to Maisie, 'What's it like inside?' She said, 'Come and have a look.'

I went inside and asked if I could take a few pictures. They seemed totally unconcerned. When I set up my camera and tripod, they watched me blankly, without moving. In the end we discovered the reason: the girl was also a prostitute, and the man was a Canadian who had been released from

Maisie getting washed before going on duty.

Elephant and Castle: a sequence of pictures appears at the end of the chapter.

prison the day before; they had spent a hard night in bed celebrating his release.

Maisie's husband was in prison for robbery, and she lived in the basement flat with her friend. As I hoped, she acted as our contact and guide while we were doing the story, giving us ideas, and telling us where to find things we wanted. She could tell us where to find anything: bookmakers, for example, who were illegal at the time.

After our first meeting, Bert and I used to go round to her place whenever we went down to the Elephant to work on the story. When we arrived in the morning, Maisie would be sitting up in bed with a Woodbine in her mouth. Wherever she had been on the previous night, she always returned to her basement flat to sleep. One afternoon when Bert and I called, Maisie was getting ready to go out to work. She wasn't at all put out by us being there: she was stripped to the waist, and her friend was washing down her back with a bowl of water. I think Maisie had the most enormous pair of breasts I have ever seen. Her friend must have noticed me staring with disbelief: for a joke she took one of Maisie's breasts and flopped it back, clean over her shoulder.

Maisie used to tell us strange tales about her clients. There was a rich man who lived near Hendon who used to send his chauffeur to Soho to pick up a couple of prostitutes. Once he picked up Maisie and a colleague, and took them back to Hendon. There, they had to undress; one of them had to lie in a coffin, and the other kneel beside it with a lighted candle, while the rich man masturbated.

Not all cranks she encountered were so harmless. During the war, in the blackout, she was approached by an RAF man wearing the usual large bag containing his gas mask. Maisie had a room near Victoria Station where she used to take her clients, so they hailed a taxi to get there.

They hadn't been in the taxi very long when she noticed a revolting smell. She wondered what it was, but she knew that men going with a prostitute for the first time sometimes mucked themselves, so she didn't say anything.

When they got to her room, she finally had to ask the man what the horrible smell was. From being sheepish, he suddenly became aggressive. He opened up his gas mask case and showed her what was inside. Maisie felt sick. It was a woman's breast in an advanced state of decomposition.

'I cut that off a woman a few days ago', he said, 'and now I'm going to do the same to you.'

Maisie had to think fast. Somehow she managed to persuade him to grant her one last request before he killed her. She asked for a drink. She said that if he would take her to the pub over the road, she wouldn't make any attempt to escape. Amazingly, the man believed her.

When she got to the pub, Maisie saw some friends, and with their help was able to get away. The man immediately fled from the pub. Some time later, when she was once again on duty in Piccadilly Circus, she caught sight of him. Luckily, this time there was a policeman about, and the man was arrested and charged.

While we were still doing the story, Maisie said to us:

'I might not be here when you come tomorrow.'

We asked her wnat she meant, but she wouldn't say anything else. She just repeated what she had said. The next day, however, she was there as usual, so we asked her again what she had meant.

There was a butcher's shop in Soho where the owner did a roaring trade in black market meat (rationing was still in force in those days). Maisie had heard rumours that the butcher kept all the money he made in this way in the hollowed-out inside of his chopping block. So she and a friend planned to break into the butcher's shop and help themselves to his black-market profits.

At first, she told us, everything had gone according to plan: they got into the shop, they found the chopping block, and it was indeed hollow. But then their luck ran out. There was no money in it, or anywhere else in the shop. She had told us that she might not be at home in case she had been caught.

Bert and I covered just about every aspect of the Elephant and Castle with Maisie's help. When we had finished we wanted to give her something to show how grateful we were, but she wouldn't accept any money. Instead we bought her a bottle of port and a bottle of gin. In honour of the occasion, she took a night off from her work, and stayed at home drinking with her friend.

When I went back a few months later to look her up and see how she was getting on, she wasn't at home. This time something really had gone wrong on a job: she was in prison.

She had helped us to do what turned out to be a really wonderful story. The magazine was pleased, and I got a lot of strong pictures which subsequently won my second Encyclopaedia Britannica Award.

Back in England, I did a story with Bert Lloyd about the River Tyne. We traced it right back to its source at Deadwater, and followed it through the lovely market town of

A latter-day Pied Piper in Newcastle.

Hexham, which lay on its course, and along Hadrian's Wall.

It was now quite a few years since I had had a proper holiday with my family. Because the scenery around Hexham was so beautiful, I decided to go back there a month later with Dora, Michael and Terry, and Pierre, a French boy on an exchange visit to England.

We camped in a clearing in some woods outside Falstone. When I went into the village one day to collect some groceries and a newspaper, I saw that the war was hotting up in Korea, and that a *Picture Post* journalist, Stephen Schimanski, had been killed flying back to Korea from Japan.

I knew immediately that I wanted to go. I went straight to the telephone box outside the store and called *Picture Post*. When I got through to Tom, I told him that I would like to go. He was pleased to have a volunteer: after the death of Schimanski, he didn't want the responsibility of sending anybody to what looked like being a fairly nasty war. For the time being, he had made arrangements with Magnum, a large international photographic agency in Paris, but when he managed to sort that out, he would let me know.

A couple of days later we were all in our tents when we heard someone coming through the woods calling out, 'Is there anyone here called Hardy? You're wanted on the telephone.'

Tom had rung up the village telephone box, and someone had come to find me. I went back to the box, and Tom told me that he had managed to put off Magnum. As soon as I finished my holiday I would be going off to Korea with James Cameron.

Although I was excited, I didn't realise just how important my trip to Korea was going to be, not only for me, but for the future of *Picture Post* as well.

The Gorbals My favourite picture: this reminds me of what I was like when I was a kid. In this story I concentrated on the children, and how they kept their spirits up in conditions which were often dreadful.

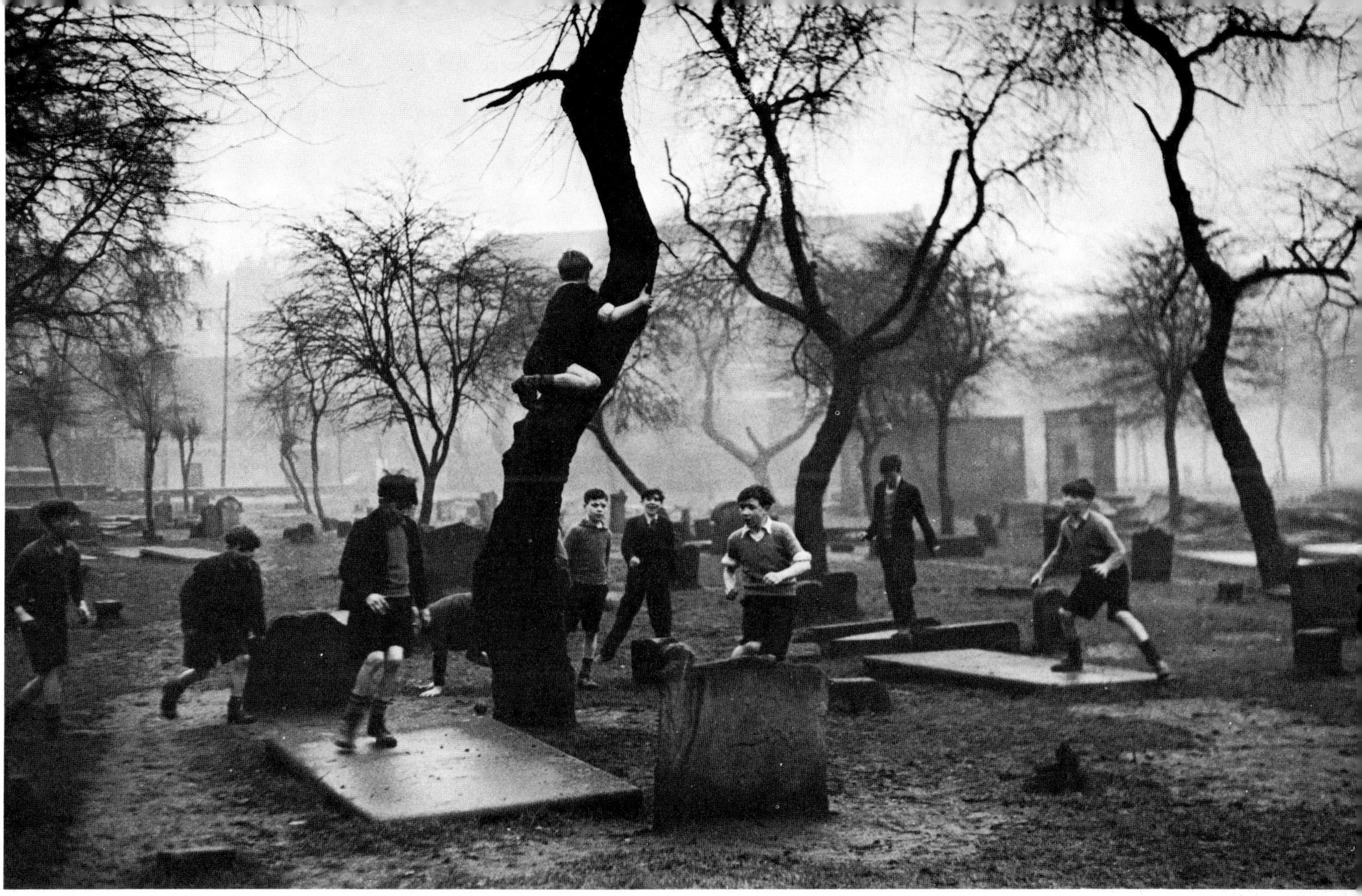

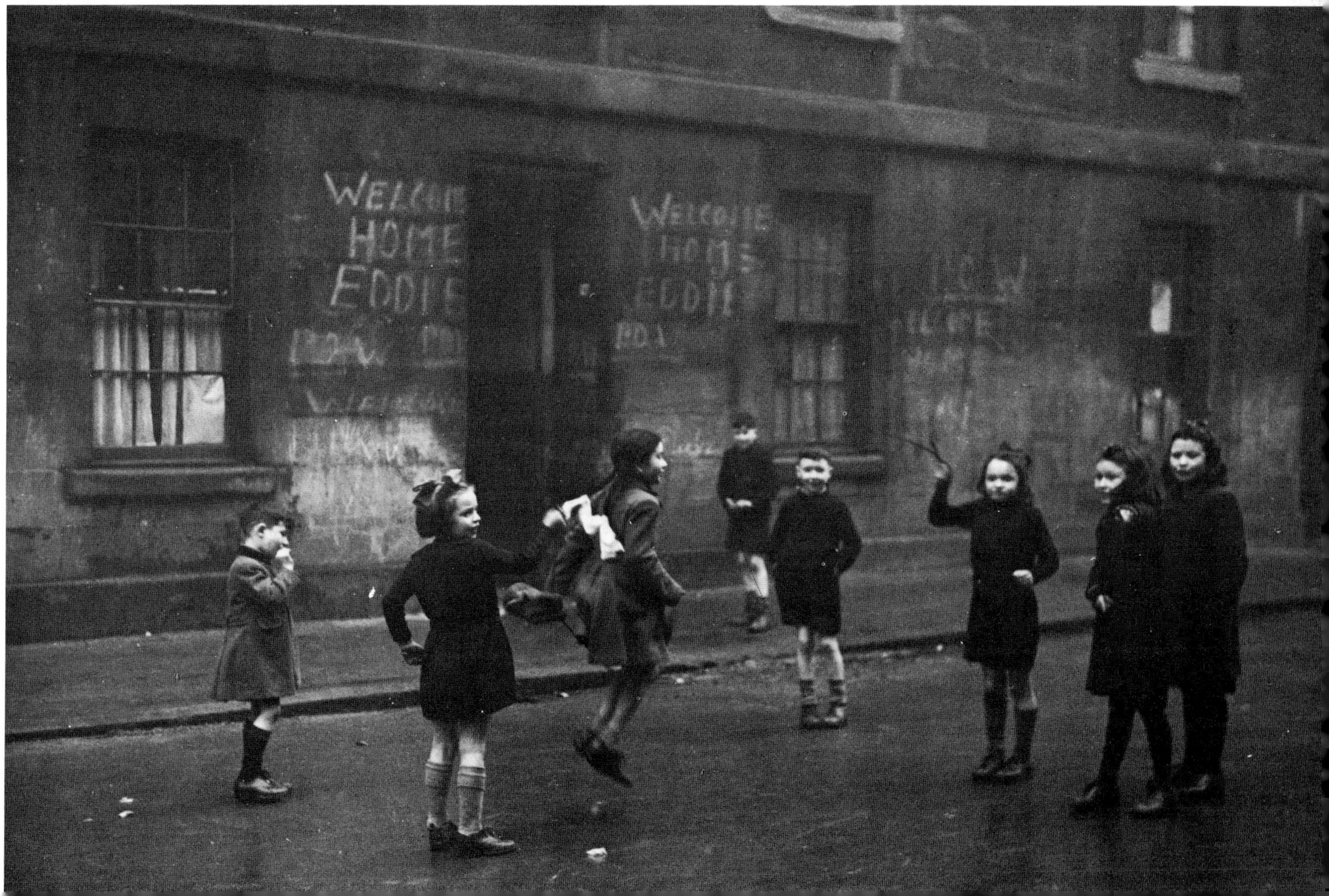
WELCOME
HOME
EDDIE
WELCOME
HOME
EDDIE

Elephant and Castle

This story took me back to my own part of London. There was still a blacksmith to shoe horses, and auctions to buy them, where I pictured the men with hats. The men with caps were enjoying themselves in an old folk's club.

Smog was unpleasant, and made noon seem like dusk, as in the picture overleaf. The men in the other picture are thinking hard before deciding to spend their shillings at an army surplus store in the London Road.

Cardiff

I did several stories on Cardiff, usually in the poor areas. There were youth clubs where you could listen to the latest hit records, but not much else for the young. As in London and Glasgow, they made their own fun. In Cardiff and London's Notting Hill, there were troubles with what we called the Colour Problem.

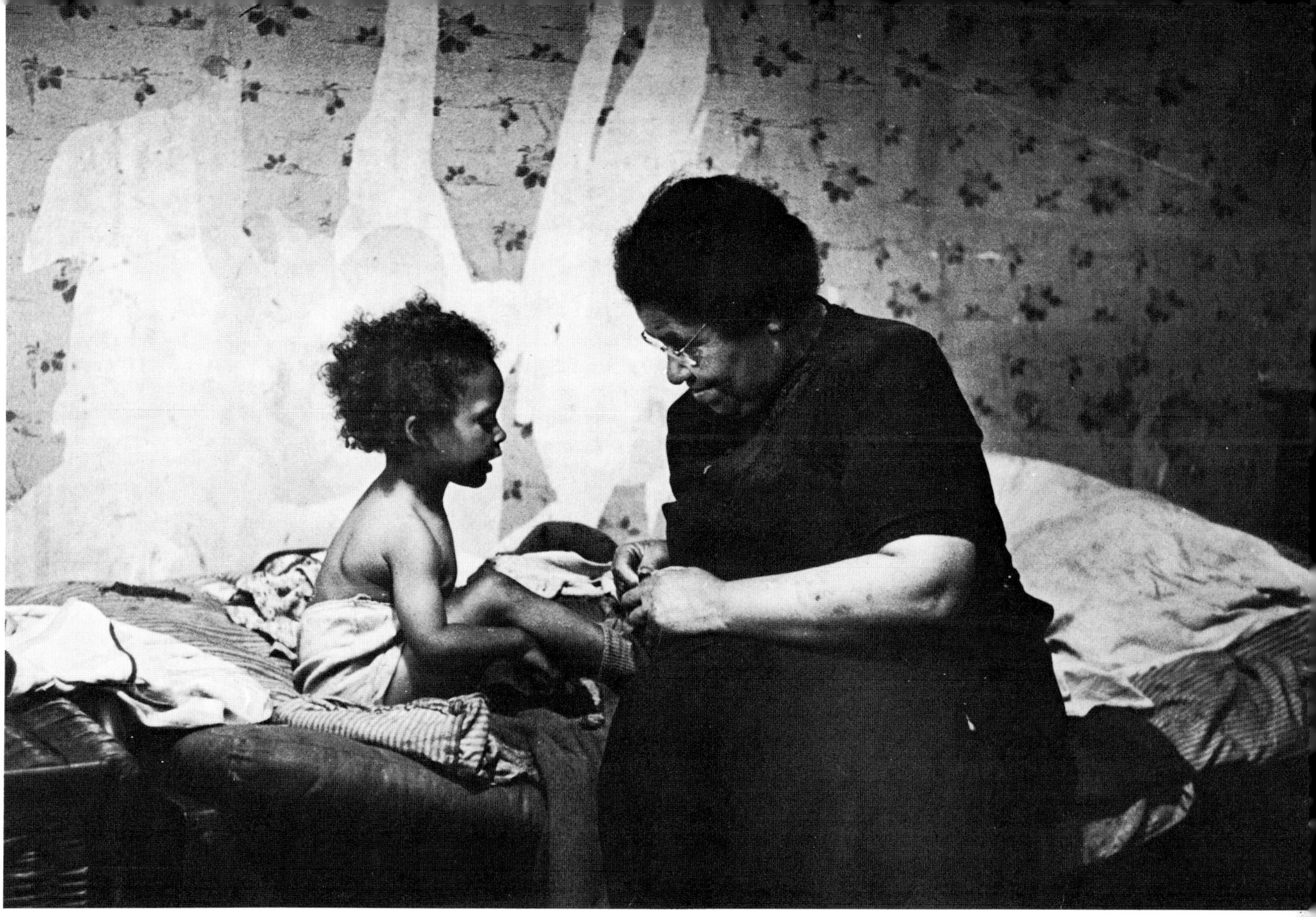

9: The Korean War

On 12 August 1950, Jimmy Cameron and I left London for Tokyo, where on our arrival three days later we put up at the Correspondents' Club, and got ourselves accredited. We were stuck in Tokyo for three days, and bumped into Haywood Magee, another *Picture Post* photographer, with whom I had worked during the war. He was having rather a good time in Japan, but was soon to return.

On 18 August, Jimmy and I flew in an American military aircraft to the airstrip at Taegu, where the US 25th Division was under heavy attack by the North Korean forces. Taegu was a dead-and-alive hole. It seemed to be in the process of being evacuated before the North Korean onslaught. Furniture and bedding had been cleared out, the cooks and all their equipment had gone, and so had most of the war correspondents; only one Public Relations man remained.

We were briefed in a Korean school house – probably because it was one of the few solid, brick-built buildings around. The PR man told us that the other correspondents had cleared out back to Pusan as quickly as they could, because they thought that Taegu was about to fall. While he was speaking, a general came in. He looked annoyed by what the PR man was telling us, and gave us his own ideas on the situation: 'Lot of Goddam nonsense', he said. 'They'll never take the town. My advice to you is to stay put!'

After a couple of days the other correspondents returned. Jimmy and I sat outside our quarters and shared a bottle of whisky with Randolph Churchill, who was working as a newspaper correspondent. When I say 'shared', I use the term loosely: I can remember watching the level of our precious whisky rapidly going down, while Jimmy and I hardly seemed to drink any of it.

The general who had corrected the PR man turned out to be none other than General Walker, who was the commanding officer of the 25th Division, so we thought he probably knew what he was talking about. The next day we got all our gear together, and hitched a lift to the front line, which was about twenty miles away. I reduced my equipment to the minimum: one Rolleiflex and one Contax, and a stock of fast film, which we carried round in two army shoulder-bags: I carried one, and Jimmy carried the other. As for clothing and personal things, I gradually whittled these down until I was carrying only a razor and washing things, and picked up a fresh issue of underclothing from the nearest US Army quartermaster whenever I needed it.

We quickly learned that one of the most important things to carry with you was a full water bottle. The heat was atrocious, and you couldn't drink untreated water: the fields were manured with human sewage.

The lorry bumped along a road littered with corpses and the burnt-out remains of trucks. The Americans had christened it 'The Bowling Alley', and it was under constant observation by the North Koreans. Finally we came upon the American front-line troops in action, and I took some pictures of the fighting.

After we had got what we needed, we walked some distance back along the hot dusty road, until we came to an old farmhouse with a gateway and a courtyard. There were a lot of American soldiers milling around the courtyard, but none of them seemed to notice an old Korean peasant lying on the ground in the blazing sun.

I decided to have a closer look. He must have collapsed from exhaustion, or heat, or both. There was a smear of blood, still wet, on the wall behind him, where he had hit his head in falling. His eyes flickered, so he was still alive, but his lips were parched. I thought I'd give him a drink of water to see if that did him any good, but then I had a better idea: one which would give me a good picture. I asked an American soldier if he would mind giving the old man some water while I took photographs. The American smiled: 'Sure', he said, 'Just so long as the water comes out of your bottle and not mine.' As far as I was concerned, it was a small price to pay. I took a few pictures and we carried him into the shade.

At this stage the Korean medical facilities were not good, and many Koreans were treated by the Americans. The Koreans seemed to have a sort of indifference to their own condition, and to that of their fellow countrymen, which I found hard to stomach. I will never forget the sight of one man, a soldier, who had been shot by a bullet which had passed in through his back, up through his neck and out of his cheek. He was standing, not even lying down, without any kind of expression of pain or distress on his face.

A GI kindly parts with my precious water.

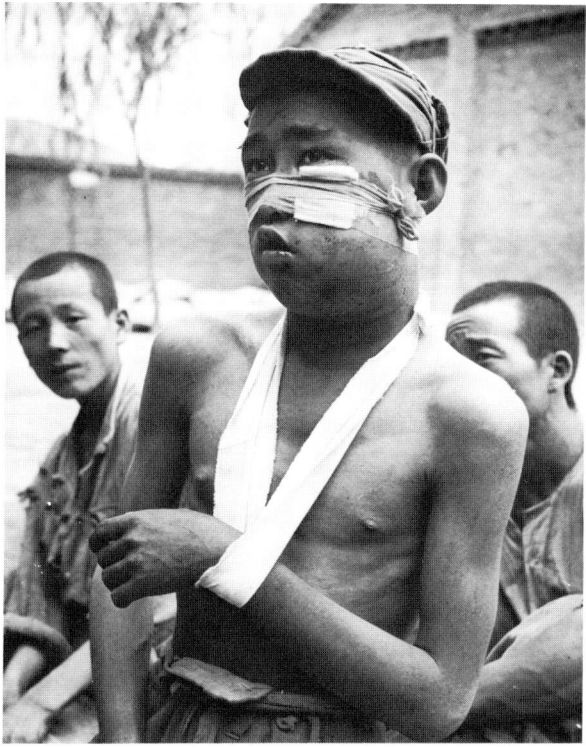

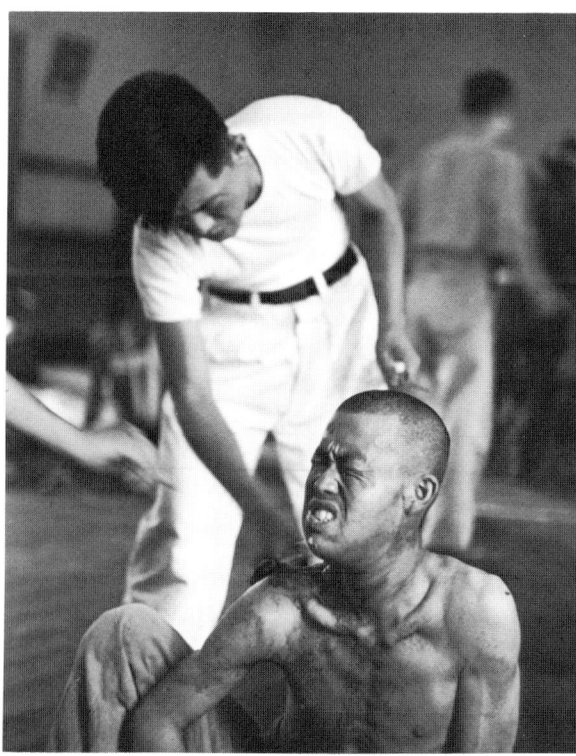

Far left: The wound on his cheek is the bullet's exit hole.

Left: A North Korean prisoner treated by a South Korean doctor.

Jimmy decided that he needed to get away from it all to write his article, so he flew back to Tokyo. He took my films with him, and sent them back on a BOAC aircraft from Tokyo to London. Altogether he was away for a weekend. When he came back he showed me a copy of his story. It was so good, I just hoped that my pictures would do it credit.

We came to feel quite at home in the tented area at Pusan. It was the nearest thing to a base we managed to establish. We quickly teamed up with Ralph Izzard, the foreign correspondent of the *Daily Mail*, whom I used to run into all over the world. He always seemed a lonely man – perhaps because he spent most of his professional life roaming the world's trouble spots alone, but he was marvellous company. We soon managed to set up a supply of beer – warm and explosive at first, until someone with contacts in the US Army mortuary managed to get hold of a supply of ice.

Ralph was experienced in the ways of the army, and his knowledge of military things sometimes came in handy. Jimmy, Ralph and I used to hitch everywhere. When we wanted to travel long distances we used to go to the nearest airstrip and hitch a lift on an aircraft: the Americans were very relaxed about it. Once, the three of us hitched a lift from Taegu to another part of the front. At that early stage of the hostilities, the Americans never seemed to bother with reconnoitring a road before they advanced along it, so they were always driving into North Korean ambushes. To make up for this, the drivers just used to go as fast as they could, with the idea of reducing the amount of time in which they were exposed to danger.

On this particular occasion we were sitting in the back of a truck being driven particularly hard and fast along a bumpy track. Suddenly Ralph noticed what was loaded in the wooden boxes we were sitting on: live shells and ammunition. We didn't panic. Instead Ralph hammered on the roof of the cab with all his strength until the driver allowed himself to be distracted from his reckless progress.

The driver didn't want to stop. He told us we were sure to be shot up if we got out and walked. As calmly as possible, we informed him that we would rather risk being shot at, than be blown sky high by a mobile ammunition dump. In the end he agreed to let us off.

We walked some of the way, but soon got a lift in an ambulance, which seemed a much better way to travel.

A contingent of British troops arrived in Pusan at the end of August. They were immediately sent up to Kyongsun, and Jimmy and I followed them in an American plane by way of Taegu. There were two regiments: the Argyll and Sutherland Highlanders, and the Middlesex regiment. We first tried to make contact with the Middlesex regiment, but there was an immediate contrast with the free and easy attitude of the Americans. The Colonel-in-Chief was a short man, bristling with rage. He seemed angry that we were there at all. He certainly didn't want anything to do with us, and told us that he had responsibility for our lives in the event of an enemy attack. We would have to sleep outside the camp perimeter, where, if attacked, our lives would be our own responsibility.

Bloody but unbowed, we pitched our tents outside the perimeter, then went along to visit the Argyll and Sutherland Highlanders. Here the reception was a complete con-

An American tank commander approaching Taegu.

Opposite: One of the faces of war.

Political Prisoners: these pictures appear at the end of the chapter.

trast. We were greeted in a friendly way, and taken at once to the officers' tent, where the whisky flowed freely. Later, when we had become very jolly, we were left the problem of putting up our tent. This we managed surprisingly well. I pinned a little sign saying '43 Shoe Lane' (the *Picture Post* address in London) over the flap of our tent, and Ralph took a picture of Jimmy and me sitting in front of it.

By now, the fighting was very heavy. On our last ride back from Taegu to Pusan, Jimmy and I travelled on a hospital train filled with wounded Americans and South Koreans. As the train jerked and clattered through the night, we could hear their cries and moans.

At Pusan Station, the wounded were unloaded through the doors and windows of the train, and laid out on the platform on their stretchers. As I was going round taking pictures, an American boy called out to me. He seemed to want to talk badly. He told me that he had only just got married before he was sent to Korea. Now, he said, he had been wounded 'down there'. I didn't realise what he meant at first; I thought he meant his leg. Then I read the tag on his stretcher, and discovered that he had been severely wounded in the groin. I began to feel very ill.

The next day Jimmy and I went back to Pusan Station to get more pictures of the wounded arriving on hospital trains. But as we were leaving the station we were stopped in our tracks by the sight of another type of human cargo which had come down from the North, and was now filling the square outside.

About sixty of them – from boys of no more than fourteen to old men – were squatting miserably, dressed in rags and tied together with ropes, in the square. It had rained that day, and there were a few puddles on the ground. The prisoners were being closely watched by armed guards, but the intense heat must have made them very thirsty. Whenever they thought that no one was looking, they would try to scoop up the rainwater from the ground and drink it. If one of the guards noticed them doing this, he immediately set on them and beat them mercilessly with his rifle butt. These guards were in the army of our allies.

The human degradation reminded me of the scenes I had witnessed at Belsen. Our enquiries drew the answer that these were 'political prisoners' – not North Koreans, but people suspected of having the Wrong Views. We wondered how young boys of fourteen could possibly be 'political' prisoners, but since none of them had been tried anyway, it probably didn't make much difference how old they were or what they thought.

At intervals, a batch of them would be separated from the rest and herded into the back of a lorry which then drove off. Our impression was that they were being taken off to be shot. We were appalled, and decided that we must try to do something about it.

We went to the United Nations Office, and they didn't want to know; they wouldn't do anything about it. Then we walked across town in the sweltering heat to the Red Cross offices. They told us that nothing could be done, and suggested that we should try the United Nations. We said we had already tried them, but just to be sure, we went back again and pestered them a bit longer. Once again, they didn't want anything to do with it. What the South Korean Government got up to was entirely its own concern: it was not their business to interfere in these matters.

Jimmy and I were pretty steamed up, and when we finished the story, and I had been through the usual desperate hunt for paper and string to parcel everything up so it could be put on a plane home, we knew that what we had produced was highly controversial. It would look bad for the United Nations to be associated with such unsavoury allies, but that was not our business. We just felt that people in the world outside should know that these things were going on; then perhaps they could be stopped. We didn't realise how drastic the consequences of the story would be for the future of *Picture Post*.

With the help of an interpreter I did a story on the recruitment of a young Korean into the army. He pleaded with me to get him released, but there was nothing I could do. I felt really sorry for him. New recruits were given six days' training, and then sent to the front. Usually there were not enough rifles to go round, so the procedure was for an unarmed man to advance behind an armed one until he was shot, when he could pick up the rifle and carry on fighting.

Tom sent us a telegram saying that he had more than enough material in what we had sent back, and we could come home whenever we liked. But while Jimmy and I were hanging around Pusan, we noticed that there was a lot of ac-

The morning of Inchon's 'liberation'. As the pictures show, no one could feel safe.

Inchon Landing: a sequence of pictures can be found at the end of the chapter.

tivity going on: landing craft and other ships were arriving, and there was a general air of expectation.

We asked what was happening, and could get no real information.

Luckily, an American naval officer happened to overhear our conversation. Although he wouldn't tell us what was going on, he did tell us who to contact to get a ride on the armada which was assembling off-shore. Our contact was the captain of a small transport ship, the *USS Seminole*. On 11 September, at 10 a.m., we sailed from Pusan. A few hours out to sea, he opened his sealed orders and discovered our destination: we were bound for Inchon, where a massive landing was going to take place. We hoped to go ashore with the first soldiers in the first wave of the assault.

We arrived off Inchon on 15 September at 1.30 in the afternoon. The sea around us was filled with craft of every shape and size bobbing up and down on the water. The assault was timed for 5.30, and we knew that it got dark not long after that, which left us with a pretty tight schedule for taking photographs. By about 5 o'clock there was no sign of our lift, and we were getting really worried. But then a landing craft with the word PRESS painted in large letters came alongside our ship, and someone with a loudhailer called out, 'Hardy & Cameron!' We clambered down some rope rigging at the side of the ship with all our equipment swinging

from our necks, and fell into the bottom of the launch.

All the landing craft were now lined up, like horses under starter's orders. Our craft was slightly in front of the others, and we wondered if the Press boys were going to be used to test the sort of reception the North Koreans had in store for us. At last the signal was given, and all the landing craft, with ours still out in front, made for the shore as fast as they could. Not surprisingly, we were the first to reach the beach. The air overhead was full of everything from rockets to mortar shells. We now made the discovery that the 'beach' was a high sea wall. Although we felt safe enough from North Korean fire while on our side of it, we were reluctant to poke our heads up above it and see what was on the other side.

The light was fading fast. It began to look like a case of now or never as far as taking photographs was concerned. Wearing a tin hat for the first time in my life (it was something I superstitiously avoided during my time in the army), I put my head up. Nothing hit me, so I pulled myself up onto the top of the wall and quickly started taking photographs. As soon as the others saw that I hadn't been shot, they followed me.

By now I had to work with my Contax at speeds as slow as 1/25th second at f1·4 to get pictures. The American photographers couldn't really take anything at all with their Speed Graphics, whose largest aperture was f4·5. I was the only one

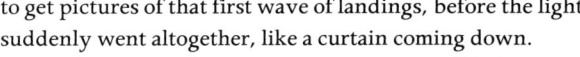

to get pictures of that first wave of landings, before the light suddenly went altogether, like a curtain coming down.

There wasn't much more Jimmy and I could do in the darkness, so we found an empty landing craft and headed back for the mother ship, where General MacArthur was directing operations. On our way, we passed a number of empty landing craft heading towards the beach. They waved desperately to us, signalling us to go back, but we told them what to do with themselves, and carried on. When we got to the ship, we found why we had encountered so many difficulties: our landing had taken place on the wrong beach, one which was still being 'softened up' by the Americans. No wonder things had felt a bit hectic. And all the landing craft we had passed on our way back had been going to get the soldiers off before they were hit by fire from their own ships!

The next day, Jimmy and I went back ashore. I was wandering around with my Contax and Rolleiflex, using the open-frame viewfinder for quick, spontaneous stuff. The South Korean troops were wandering round Inchon settling old scores, smashing windows and kicking in doors. I passed a shop which had been smashed in and looted, and where a couple of old Korean men were sitting. When I came back half an hour later, they were both lying on the ground dead. They had been shot. On the same day, I took one of my best pictures ever, of an old Korean peasant walking along with

A North Korean prisoner: I wonder what his chances are.

Opposite: The uncertainty of liberation.

cause the ship was flat-bottomed. When we were all safely tucked in, one of the officers switched off the light, and we all fell asleep. I don't know how long it was before we were suddenly awoken by a crashing noise and terrifying screaming. When we switched the light on we saw Jimmy, sitting bolt upright, while his bed skidded violently backwards and forwards across the floor.

We tied his bed to a desk which was bolted to the floor, then tucked him in and put the lights out again. After a while we all fell asleep. All of us, that is, except Jimmy. Again, it would be difficult to say how long passed before we were once more woken by screaming, even louder than before. This time Jimmy had been rolled over the edge of his camp bed, and was skidding and crashing across the room wrapped in his blankets. I can't remember how we coped with the problem this time, but the rest of the night passed uneventfully.

From Sasebo, we flew to Tokyo in a Catalina amphibian craft full of wounded men, which was so heavily loaded that it couldn't take off. The pilot finally managed by using the choppiness of the waves created by his own wake to bounce the plane into the air for take-off. As we landed in Tokyo at Hanada airport, I saw a BOAC aircraft standing on the tarmac with its propellers turning, ready to taxi along the runway and take off. I asked our pilot to land as near as possible to it. As soon as we were down, I jumped out and ran over to the BOAC plane. The stairs were just being wheeled away, so I shouted up to the steward, and threw him my packet of films, asking him to telephone *Picture Post* when he arrived at London Airport. It was a bit of a risk, but by then the deadline was very close. Thanks to that unknown BOAC steward, my films arrived safely and in time for the next edition of the magazine.

In Tokyo, Jimmy and I at long last were able to get down to some serious relaxation. We left the stuffy, cramped Press Club, and booked into the Sudaiso Hotel. I hired a car with some other correspondents, and we did a comprehensive tour of Tokyo's bars and night-clubs, losing both the car and ourselves in the process. Then Jimmy and I went up country to the famous sulphur springs at Atami, where we were massaged into submission, and served with dinner, by a geisha girl. After living under canvas in Pusan, and days and days of sea voyages, it was a good feeling to get the last of the Korean dust out of our skins.

At last we returned home (by way of Delhi, where we did a story on Nehru). We were hoping for some relaxation, and little suspected the shocks that were in store for us back in England.

his hands up among the rubble and destruction. Being liberated didn't seem to mean much to him at that moment.

When we got back to the ship that night, I had the feeeling that I had taken some pretty good pictures, and Jimmy felt he had seen enough. We decided that we were now free to take Tom's advice, and go back home. The only difficulty was how to get there. We wanted to make sure that my films and Jimmy's story on the Inchon Landing reached London by 25 September, when *Picture Post* went to press. The only way back was aboard a rocket ship, the *USS Mount Mackinley*, which had used up all its rockets the night before. It was headed for the port of Sasebo in Japan. We decided that it sounded like a good bet, and hitched a ride.

The trip back to Japan took three days. The *Mount Mackinley* had three officers who shared a cabin. Since there was nowhere else to sleep, Jimmy and I shared the cabin with them. As one of the officers always had to be on duty, one of the bunks was free each night, so we tossed a coin to see who would have it. I won, so Jimmy had to try to make himself comfortable in a camp bed on the floor.

It was a very rough sea that night, made worse for us be-

Inchon Landing

These pictures show the Americans preparing for the attack. The rocket ship (below right) softens up the enemy (and then us!). All hell was going on around us when I photographed the actual landing (overleaf), but my chief worry was to get my pictures before the last light went.

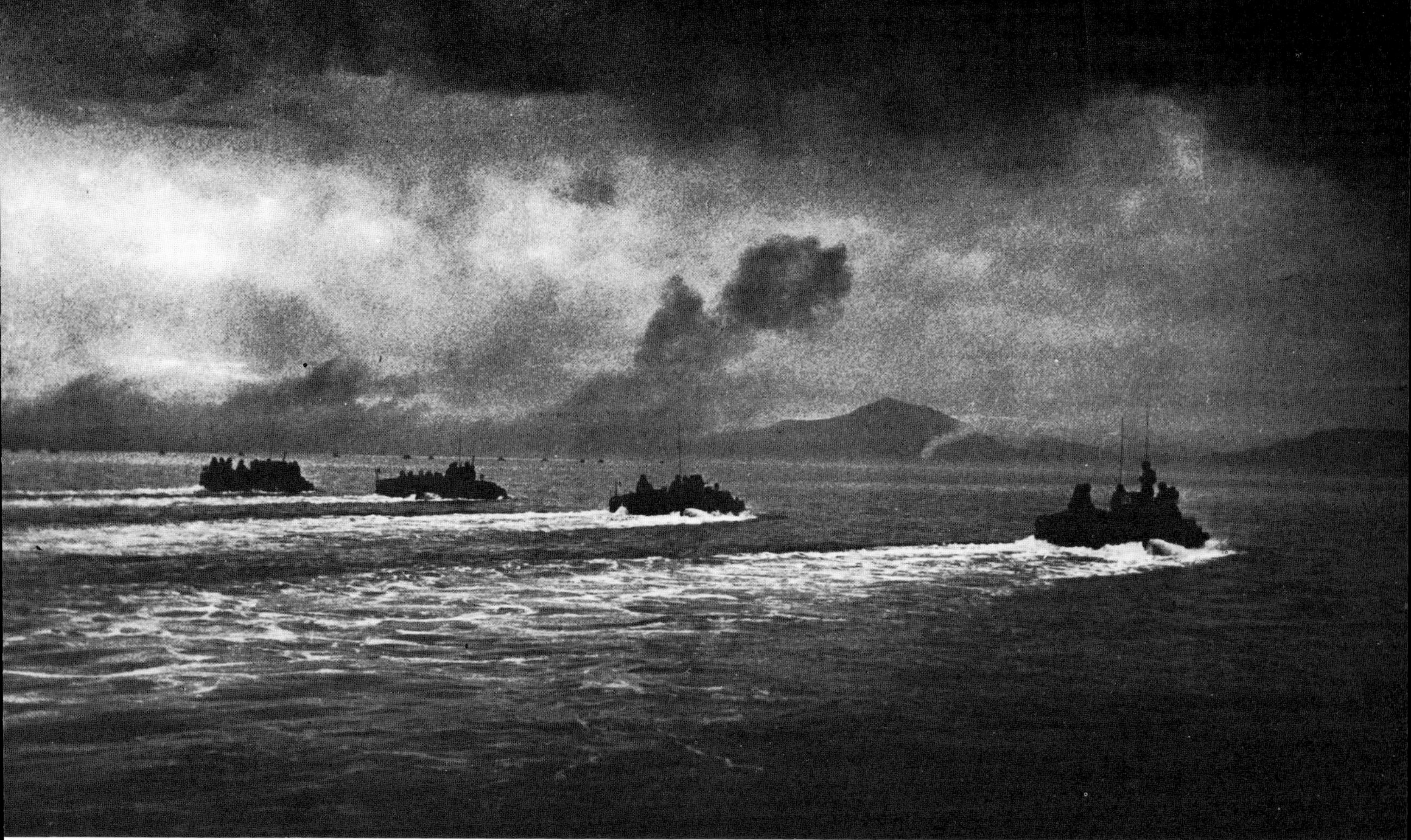

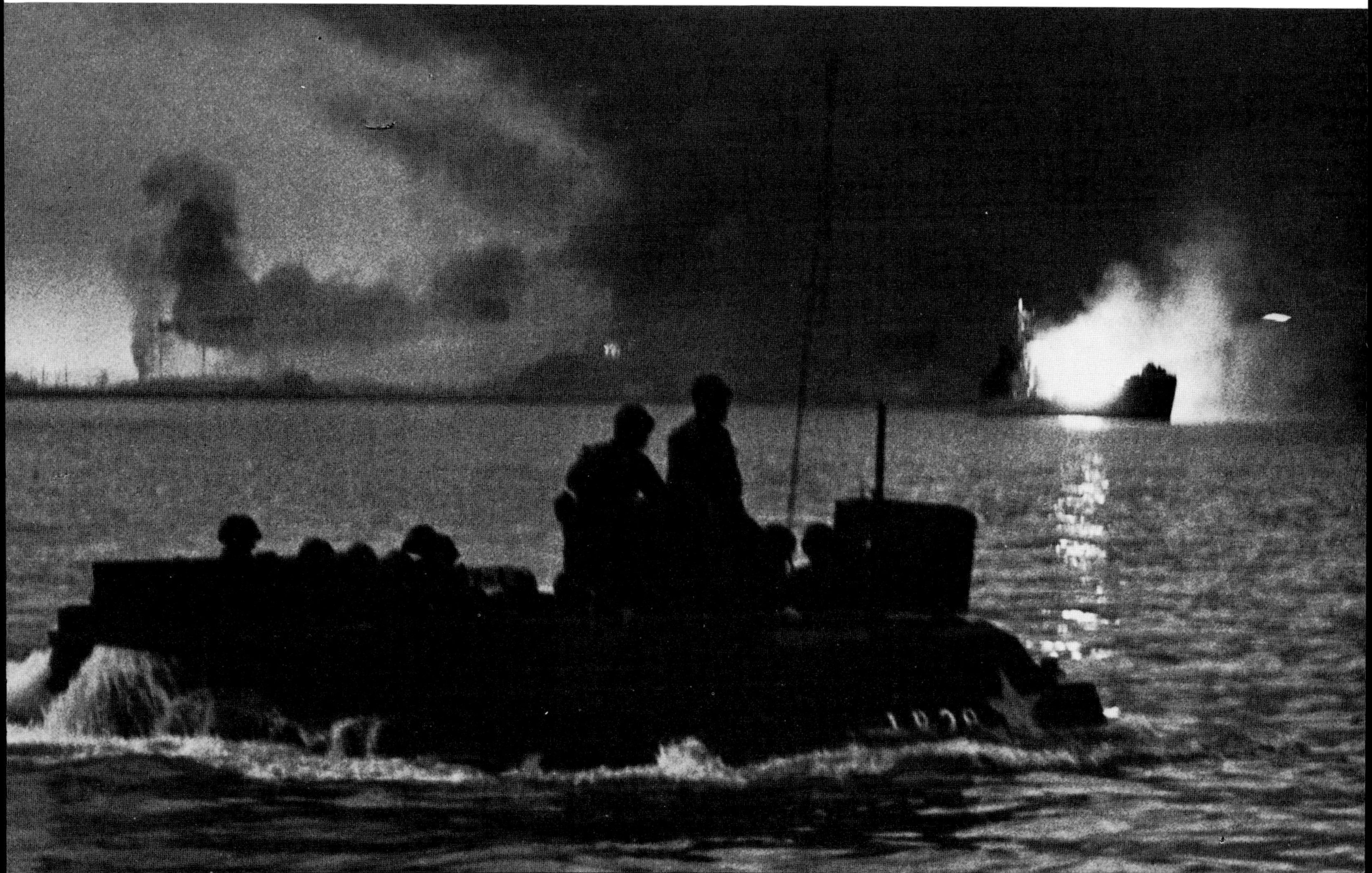

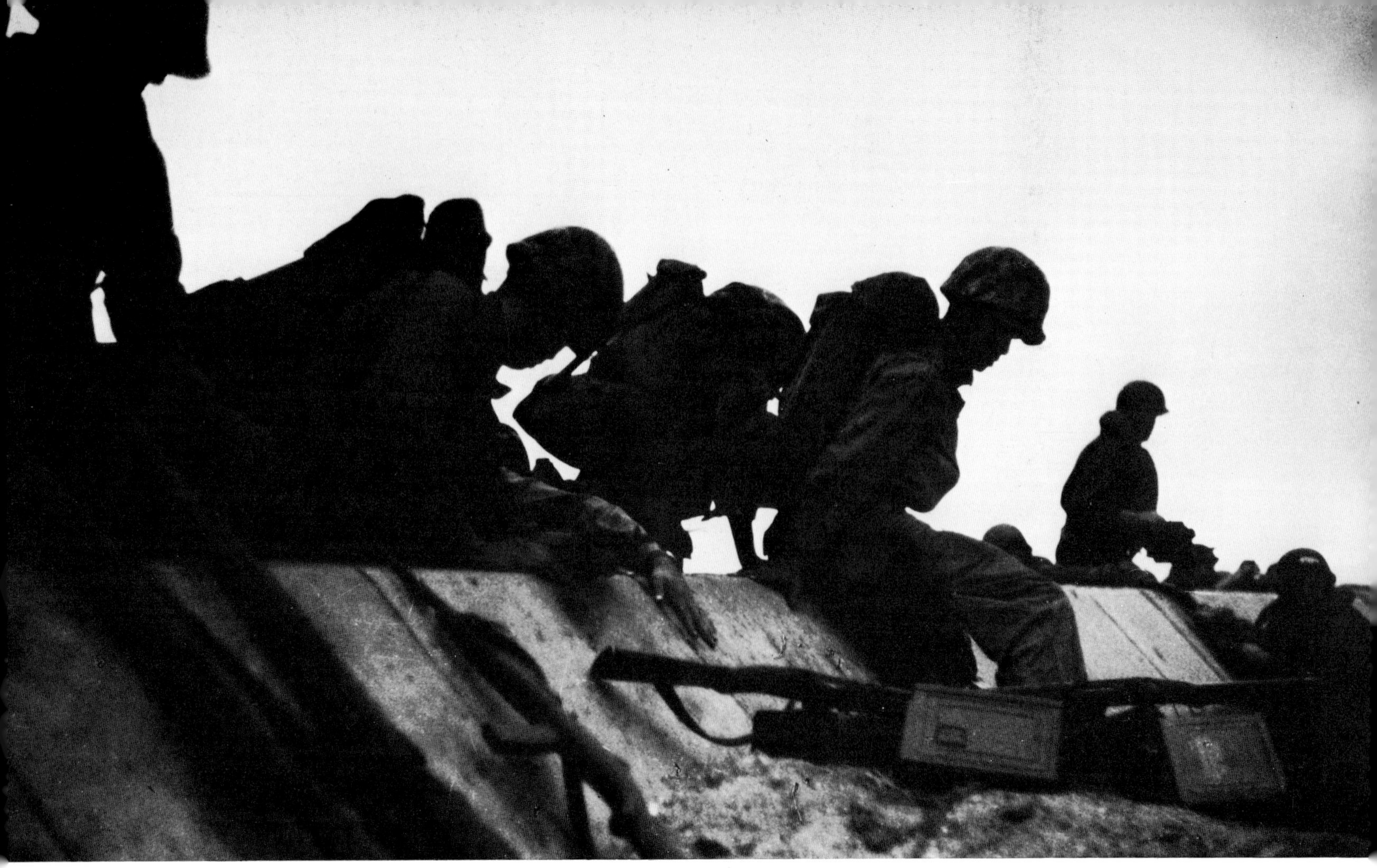

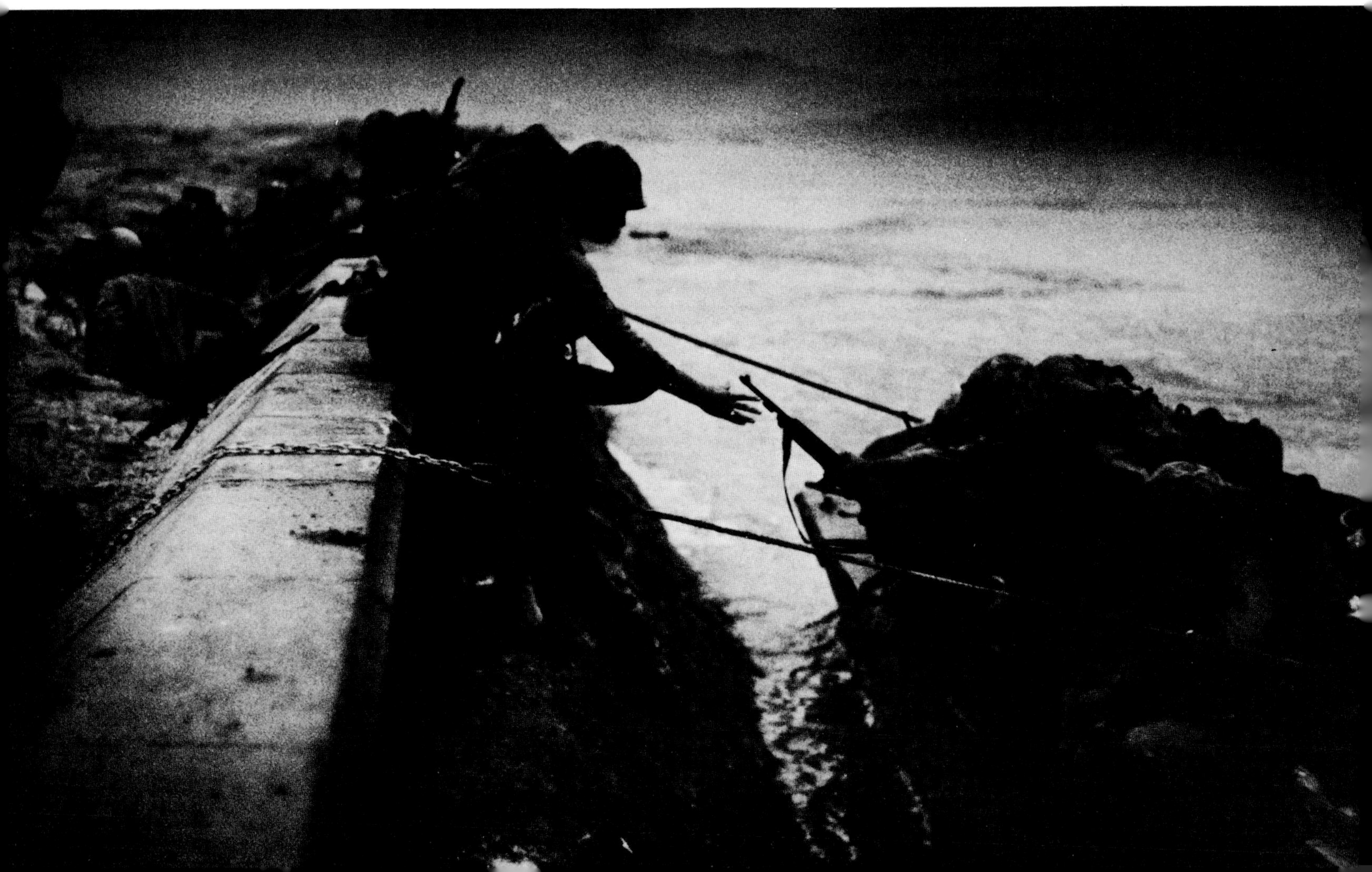

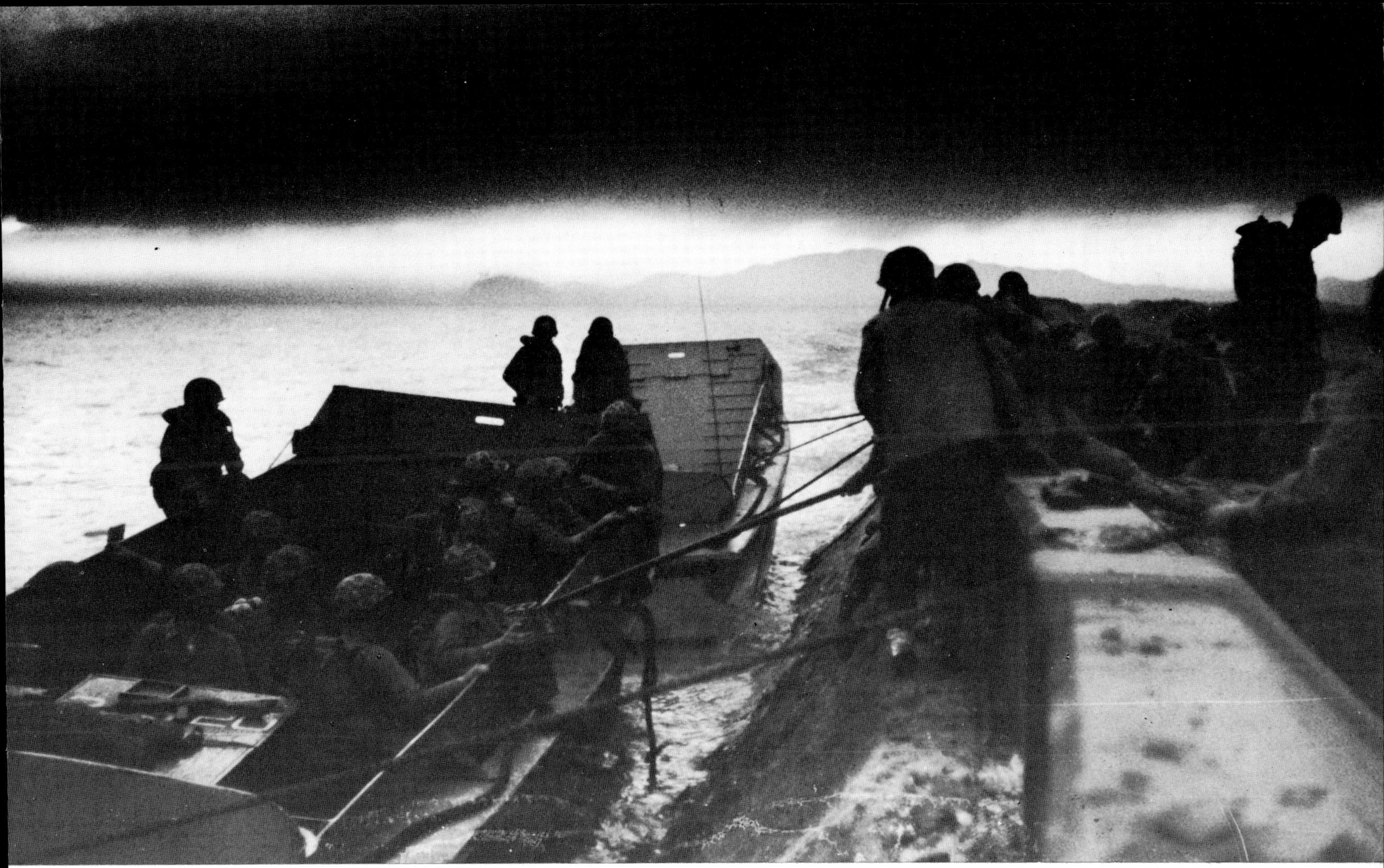

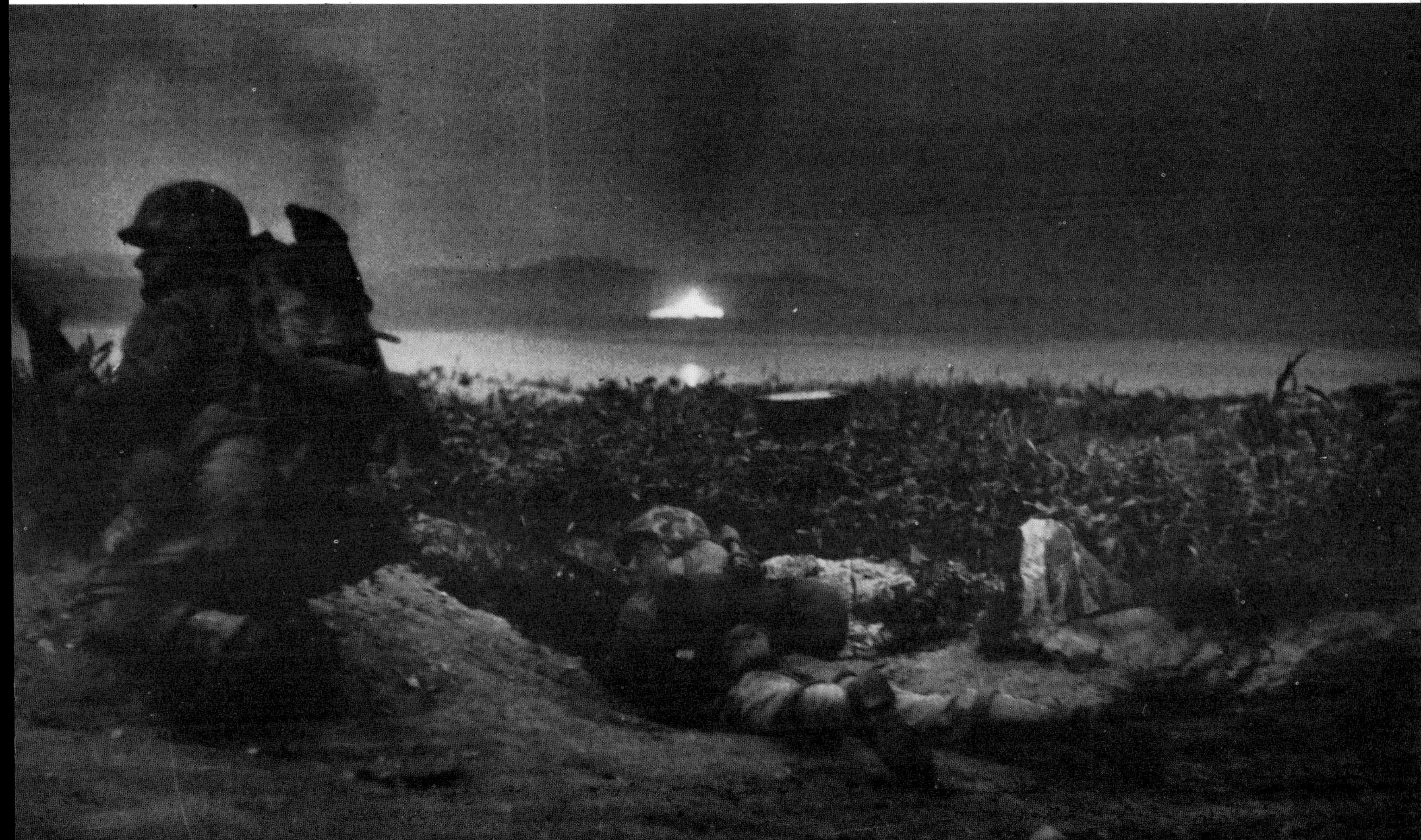

Political Prisoners

Jimmy Cameron and I were horrified by what we saw, and checked very carefully before sending back our story. We knew it would cause trouble, but not that it would also change *Picture Post* for ever.

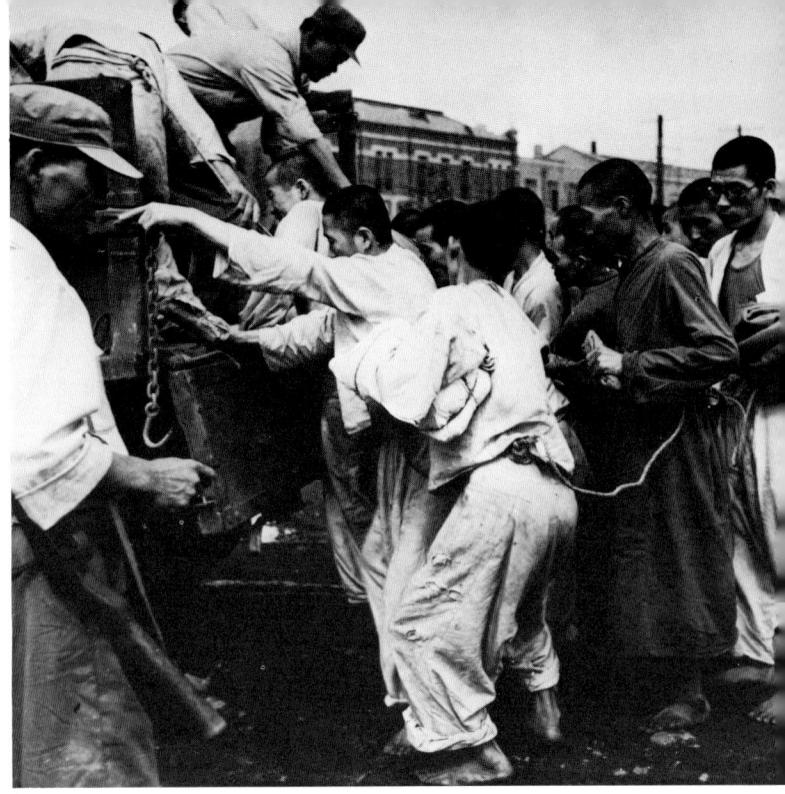

10: *Picture Post*'s Decline

Three generations of Indian Prime Ministers pictured together in a relaxed moment.

Jimmy Cameron loved India, and seized any chance to return. He got on well with Pandit Nehru, and our time with Mr Nehru was very relaxed. At one stage we were joined by his daughter and her child, Rajiv. I decided to photograph them together by a lily pond. It seems remarkable now that I was picturing, in Mrs Ghandi and her son, the next two Prime Ministers of the country.

When we reached London, we found that Tom had been holding over our story on the North Korean political prisoners until we returned, just to make sure that everything about the story was quite right, and that we hadn't distorted or missed out anything. In fact a story about the incident had already appeared in *The Times*, but Tom was still worried. The combination of Jimmy's writing and my pictures would really bring what was going on home to people. Because of its implied criticism of the United Nations, it was bound to create a controversy. Tom was concerned because Edward Hulton, the proprietor of the paper, was known to dislike controversy. He wanted to be absolutely sure about the story before he printed it.

Bert Lloyd and I were wandering around London looking for the best Guy Fawkes we could find for a story on Bonfire night, when we heard that Hulton had personally ordered the presses to be stopped at Sun Engraving in Watford, and

the issue of *Picture Post* to be made up again without the story of the political prisoners.

Rumblings and noises of dissent began to be heard. There was talk of mass resignations if this sort of interference in editorial policy happened again. The following week, when the paper went to press, Bert and I were up in Birmingham starting work on a story about a day in the life of a typical shop girl, which ended up as 'Millions Like Her'. As the most left-wing of all the reporters on *Picture Post,* Bert was the most upset by the business. On 30 October he telephoned from Birmingham to see if the paper had been allowed to go to press without any interference from Hulton. When he found out that exactly the same thing had happened again, and Tom had been sacked for refusing to comply with Hulton's requests, we drove straight back to London, where Bert handed in his resignation.

In spite of all the talk of mass resignation, most of the others stayed put. By sacking Tom, Hulton was forced to make him a payment. But anyone who resigned would not get anything except the salary they were owed. Even for Jimmy and me, who had done the story, resignation was not a luxury we could afford. Tom called a meeting and advised us all to stay on. For the photographers particularly there were no other magazines to compare with *Picture Post* as out-

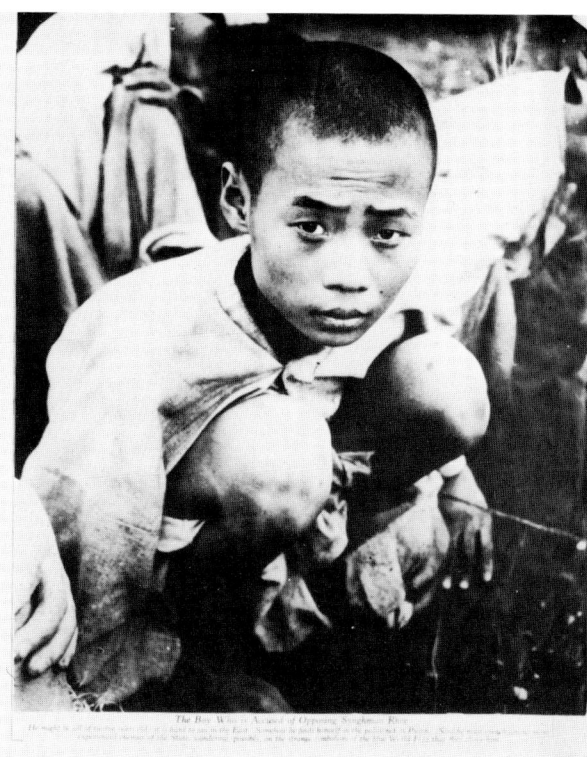

The layout for the story that was never published, for which Tom Hopkinson was sacked.

lets for their work, so they really would find themselves in trouble. Ted Castle, Tom's assistant editor, was promoted to Tom's job, and we tried to carry on. I went back to Birmingham with Hilda Marchant to continue the story I had started with Bert.

Although things quietened down after Tom's sacking, they were still not back to normal. At that stage it was impossible to guess just how much the paper had lost when he went. Looking back on it, it seems quite clear that without Tom's social commitment, *Picture Post* lost its edge and its

Above: On the long road from Lhasa to Kalimpong.
Below: The wool train approaches Kalimpong.

popularity. Contrary to the opinion still held in Fleet Street, people aren't only interested in pictures of pretty girls when they buy magazines. Meanwhile, Jimmy seemed to spend most of his time sitting around the office looking miserable and hoping to be sacked.

At Christmas Jimmy and I did a silly story at Bertram Mills Circus about a little boy who wanted to be a clown. Then, at the beginning of January, somebody had the bright idea of sending Cameron and Hardy, the two trouble-makers, off to Tibet, where the Dalai Lama was fleeing from the Chinese invasion. There was not much chance of us finding anything controversial in the Himalayas, and they had the added charm of being 28,000 feet high and 6,000 miles away.

We equipped ourselves with tents and stoves and everything else we thought we might need for mountain trekking at a shop in the Grays Inn Road. On a Monday morning we caught the plane from London Airport, and by tea-time on Wednesday we were booked in at the Mount Everest Hotel in Darjeeling (only 10,000 feet above sea level despite the name). From here we had a wonderful view of Kangchenjunga, the second highest mountain in the world.

We tried to get visas from the Indian authorities to cross over into Sikkim, but they weren't very interested.

The nights were cold, and rather than sit alone in our rooms with our ration of one bucket of coal each, we sat together in my room, pooled our coal ration, and topped up on warmth with brandy.

After waiting for a few days, we decided to move to Kalimpong. Although it wasn't in Tibet, at least it was a bit closer to the border. I hired a car at tremendous expense; the driver assured me that if by any chance a landslide should block the road – which frequently happened – there would be a driver on the other side of the landslide to take us the rest of the way, all included in his price.

As predicted, the road was blocked by a landslide. We got out and had to climb above and round it, and engaged some people who were conveniently standing by the fall to carry our baggage. To one side of us there was a sheer rock face, while on the other side there was a sickening drop. The rarified air made us short of breath, but we scrambled on; the climb took us an hour. When we finally got to the other side there was a car waiting to take us the rest of the way to Kalimpong all right, but the driver said he didn't know anything about our arrangement with the driver from Darjeeling. After a discussion, we agreed to pay an extra huge sum.

We stayed at the Himalaya Hotel in Kalimpong, which was run by a Tibetan woman. Jimmy and I continued our attempts to get a visa for Sikkim. Just in case nothing else came of the trip, we started to do a story on the caravans of Tibetan traders which were arriving in Kalimpong, bringing tea and wool in exchange for kerosene and cigarettes.

In their layered costumes of leather and cloth, with daggers shoved in their belts, the Tibetan traders were a colourful sight. The caravans were always accompanied by dogs like huskies, wearing flowers around their necks to keep the evil spirits at bay, and barking happily in the road. They seemed quite harmless – you could even stroke them. What we didn't realise was, that as soon as their owners made a camp, and they were tied up, they underwent a personality change. One day Jimmy and I went into a little camp at Kalimpong to get some pictures and pass some baksheesh. We didn't take much notice of their barking until Jimmy went too close.

The dogs were on Jimmy in a flash. Before he could pull himself away, they had torn his sleeve and ripped open the leg of his trousers. Somehow it was typical of Jimmy's luck. I suppose we were grateful that their teeth didn't actually break his skin, otherwise we would have been faced with paying for another car ride back to Darjeeling, and a desperate scramble to the nearest hospital in Calcutta in case Jimmy started frothing at the mouth and biting people.

In the evenings at the Himalaya Hotel everyone sat around a charcoal fire in the centre of the main room, passing round their bottles, and dancing the Charleston to records on the old wind-up gramophone. There were a lot of rather upper-class Tibetan refugees there, some of whom spoke English with posh Oxford accents, and the highlight of one evening's merrymaking was when one of them, a Tibetan lady, gave us her interpretation of 'Buttons and Bows'.

But we couldn't wait for ever. I knew that the Dalai Lama was only just across the border, and I was determined to get to him, with or without the approval of the authorities. After making discreet enquiries (we couldn't be sure that we weren't being watched by government agents), we managed to arrange for a jeep to take us as far as the border, where we would be met by an interpreter.

We packed all our equipment (including an eighteen-inch frying pan, the only thing we had forgotten to buy in the Gray's Inn Road, and unfortunately made of cast iron) and set off. Everything went according to plan: we drove in the jeep as far as Algara, where the road ended, then got out to walk. The track was incredibly hard going underfoot. Originally it had been made of cobbles packed tightly together, but these had been worn into points by the hooves of the pack ponies, and you had to look down at your feet all the time when you were walking.

Near the border, as arranged, the interpreter came down a mountainside, and started to walk in front of us. By this time, to add to our troubles, the rain was pouring down steadily. Late in the afternoon, we decided to call a halt, and pitch our tents for the night.

I managed to get the tents up (I don't think Jimmy had ever been a boy scout). After a few experiments, I realised that the primus stove we had bought was never going to work at that altitude. If we were going to dry out and cook something to eat, the only thing to do was to collect some wood and make a fire. We turned to the interpreter, who hadn't spoken up to that point and explained: 'We'd better get some wood so we can make a fire'. He looked at us.

'Get wood. Make fire.' I repeated. He looked puzzled

Above: It meant a lot to get a shot used as a *Picture Post* cover.
Below: On arrival, the wool is sorted from the yaks' tails (supplied exclusively for America's Santa Claus beards).

Barcelona: a group of pictures can be seen at the end of the chapter.

again, and shrugged his shoulders. It was only then that we realised that although he spoke Bengali perfectly, and had very good Tibetan, he didn't speak a word of English.

We eventually got a fire going. We opened a couple of tins – one of biscuits, and one of skinless sausages, which Jimmy immediately left out in the rain. I made some attempt to cook them in our cast-iron frying pan, but without much success, and in the end we decided to eat them as they were. After eating this rain-washed mess, we retreated to our tent, and the interpreter retreated to his (neither of us wanted to share with him). To keep our spirits up, we took out a couple of bottles of brandy we had brought with us, and got drinking. We managed to finish both of them: it seemed like fun at the time, and we slept like tops.

The next morning, the combination of brandy and altitude had given me the worst hangover I have ever had. Jimmy was the same as me. We couldn't bear the sight of each other. My head rang with the least noise, and our rucksacks seemed doubly heavy. For the first half of the day, we struggled along on the pointed stones of the road.

In the evening we were feeling somewhat better. We had arrived at the monastery of Pedong. The corridor leading to the monastery had rows of small brass bells hanging on ropes. As you passed along ringing them it was as if you were saying a prayer. I signed the visitors' book (the last entry was eight years old). Although there was no sign of the Dalai Lama, at least we could do a story on the monks and their daily duties. I was most impressed by the monks and their way of life, and for a while I had serious thoughts of becoming a Buddhist.

After leaving Pedong we pressed on for a couple of days. The Tibetans with their caravans of heavily-laden mules looked at us strangely whenever we passed them. We both began to think that perhaps we might never find the Dalai Lama in this great mountain wilderness: instead we might end up being shot at by the invading forces. Although neither of us was willing to admit defeat, we were only too willing to accept retreat if the other one suggested it. When in the end we did break, it happened to both of us at once. We turned back with a new spring in our steps.

Back in Darjeeling once more, we did a story about the native Indians carrying the goods from a goods train across a landslip which had blocked the track between there and Baghdoda. Everything was carried on packs on their backs, held in place only by a cloth band which passed round their foreheads. Everyone helped, including the women and children. I even saw a nine-year-old girl carrying a five-gallon can of petrol in this way.

We returned to Delhi, and to make our trip a bit more worthwhile, we went up to Kashmir to do a story on the Prime Minister. At a hotel in Jammu, I received a telegram from *Picture Post* telling me that I had won first prize in the Encyclopaedia Britannica Photographic Awards for my pictures of the Inchon landings.

Hardly had Jimmy and I got back to England, than we were sent off to Spain. A wave of strikes happened while we were there, and we had to be very careful when we were working because taking pictures was absolutely forbidden. We stayed in an expensive hotel in Barcelona, but the beauty of the city was spoilt for us by the obvious poverty of the people. Jimmy made contacts with the underground movements through the dwarfish page boy at our hotel, and even met one of them by being given a ticket for the next seat at a bull-fight.

Cloak-and-dagger activities were not confined to Spain: back in England, on the First of May, Ted Castle was sacked from his job as editor, and the Managing Director of Hulton Press, John Pearce, called a meeting of the staff to explain the situation. The new editor appointed to replace Ted Castle was Frank Dowling. Frank Dowling had once run a small advertising agency; a tall man, with a shock of fair hair, he liked to live well. He had a house in the country and a flat in town, and had a chauffeur-driven car to take him about. Although he was in a completely different mould from Tom Hopkinson, I got on well with him. I got on still better when, not long after he got the job, he gave me a rise in salary of £500 per year, backdated to the day he started.

If I liked Frank, I liked his son Brian even better. Brian was already working for the paper when his father became editor. He didn't allow the fact that his dad was the editor to affect him in any way: I think he recognised that the paper was going a bit soft, and he used to criticise his dad for it. Just to show that the old spirit lived on, he used to encourage me to sing 'Maybe it's because I'm a Londoner' whenever we walked past the door of the editor's office.

For me, Brian soon took over from Bert Lloyd as the person I liked working with best, and with whom I did the best stories, although he was quite different to Bert. Bert had come up the hard way, whereas Brian had been educated at Marlborough and showed it. He was tall and elegant, with the same fair hair as his father. His suits were always immaculately cut, and every day he sported a fresh carnation in his button hole. Silly sod.

Beneath his posh appearance, he always enjoyed a joke, and as a boozer he was in world championship class, so he was always good fun to go on a job with. When we were staying in particularly tough areas in places like Liverpool or Manchester, we used to play a trick in pubs. We'd find a really tough looking pub, and walk up to the bar. Brian would be in his smart suit with his button-hole, and you'd see all the regular drinkers thinking 'what have we got here?'. Then we'd get into conversation with them about who could drink a pint of beer the quickest. Eventually a challenge would be made: a contest between Brian and the toughest drinker in the place, the loser to stand a round for everyone.

They obviously thought they'd got it made. But then Brian would pick up his glass and tip the beer down his throat in three seconds flat. No one ever beat him, and we got many a free drink that way. It's amazing what they teach you at public school.

Brian and I soon became every bit as good at enjoying our-selves when we worked together as Bert and I had been in the good old days. When, slightly later on, we worked to-gether on a special Northern edition of *Picture Post*, we used to stay at the Adelphi Hotel in Liverpool and go out on the razzle-dazzle every night. The next morning we would rise at about ten-thirty and make our way unsteadily to the magnificent hotel lounge for a late breakfast. As soon as we had taken our seats, the head waiter would appear with a tray which had two pint glasses of beer on it, and announce: 'Your breakfast, sir'.

We also became adept at making ourselves thoroughly at home in Paris. We had our favourite hotels and restaurants, and we often used to go to a certain bar in the Pigalle area, where we were particular friends with a prostitute. She used to break off from her evening's work just simply to have a talk and a drink with us. Seeing two men with one girl, other tarts would sometimes approach us, but she simply waved them away. She was working to save up money quickly: her boyfriend was a sergeant in the Foreign Legion, and she hoped that by the time he was demobbed she would have saved enough for them to get married.

In May 1951, Brian and I were in Paris doing a story on a night-club called the Bal Tabarin. We worked on it for a few days, but by then I had a pretty good instinct for knowing whether something was going to 'make', and I had a strong feeling that this story wasn't going to. I never liked to return from a trip without at least one story. We had a day and a half left in which to think of something. Then I thought, why not Sunday morning in the Champs Elysées?

In summer all the cafés have tables with large parasols out-side on the pavement. I wanted to capture the feeling of Sun-days with everyone looking natural, so I didn't want anyone to know I was taking photographs. Brian and I sat down at a table with a drink, and I set my Rollei at a distance of about six feet, and kept my eyes open. Whenever I saw a good sub-ject, I would start to explain to Brian how the Rollei worked: 'This is how you wind the film on. You look down here for the viewfinder. And you press this button to take the picture.' Because of the reflex viewfinder it was easy to aim the camera without looking as if that was what I was doing. And the shutter action was so quiet that nobody noticed what we were doing. This was how I managed to make one of my best-ever stories out of an idea forced on me by the des-peration of a pressing deadline.

Later in the year, with the magazine's circulation declin-

Sunday at their favourite café, and a reminder that it is the Lord's day.

Sunday morning pleasure: a glass of grenadine sucked through a straw.

One day's news seems much like another, but he'll read the lot.

Blackpool: the pictures appear at the end of the chapter.

ing, and some fairly startling stunt needed to boost sales, Frank decided to run a £10,000 competition for amateur photographers (with a huge first prize of £1000). I was to launch the competition with an article on how to take a picture. Somewhere in my article I made the statement that it doesn't matter what sort of camera you've got: even if the man standing next to you has a flashy chromium-plated job, and you have a box camera, it's the person behind the camera that matters, not the camera.

Having printed my article, Frank now said I was going to have to prove it. He arranged for me to travel up to Blackpool, where I would be presented with a Box Brownie by the Lord Mayor. I would then have to try to make a really good story.

As per instructions, I travelled up to Blackpool with Brian, and was presented with a Box Brownie. But no sooner had we booked in to our hotel than Harry Deverson, the picture editor, phoned: he wanted me to get to Manchester Airport as soon as possible and fly to Ireland to do a story with Derek Wragge-Morley on an island off the West Coast. I had only time left for one trip up the beach and one trip back before leaving. With a standard-issue Box Brownie and a close-up lens plus yellow filter and an improvised cardboard viewfinder, I roamed the Golden Mile looking for suitable subjects. In the end I got a couple of showgirls from the pier theatre to help me. The picture I eventually took of the two girls sitting on the railings with their skirts blowing up has been one of my most popular photographs. People who have hardly even heard of me will suddenly remember that picture: 'You're the man who took the picture of the two girls on the sea-front at Blackpool!'

I can't think why I was sent to Ireland with Derek Wragge-Morley, since, as far as I can remember, he was a science writer. Of course, science didn't necessarily have to mean test-tubes. One very interesting story I did with him was by way of being an experiment: a scientific one, but a branch of science in which I was rather interested. We wanted to see just how much a man could drink before he passed out, recording the event in pictures. For a guinea-pig, we chose my old friend Sid Smith.

Sid lived up the road from me in Eltham. He worked nights at Woolwich Arsenal, which seemed to mean that he spent every evening until closing time at a pub in Eltham before making his way to work, where he spent the rest of the night sleeping it off.

You meet a lot of boozers in Fleet Street, but I have never known anyone to match Sid. He seemed like the ideal man for our experiment. Derek, Brian, a lady artist and I met him at the Black Dog in Shoe Lane at seven o'clock one evening. We started well, and just kept going. For every one drink I had (I can't talk about the others) Sid had two. By ten-thirty, the rest of us were feeling slightly queasy. The lady artist had given up and gone home when she found she couldn't hold her pencil any more. But Sid seemed quite happy: it was the kind of employment he had always dreamed about.

After the pubs closed, since Sid seemed none the worse for wear, we decided that we had better continue the experiment at Derek's house in Hampstead. Luckily he had laid on a plentiful supply of drink, and pausing only to get our second wind, we started up again. At two in the morning Derek's supplies finally ran out. In one last attempt, I staggered round tipping the slops from our glasses into Sid's, then made him knock it back. There was a short pause, then Sid looked at me with a funny half smile: 'I think you've done it', he said. And with that he passed out – leaving us without one picture of him looking the worse for wear.

There was no chance of us getting back home at that time of night in our condition, so we all bedded down with blankets on Derek's living room floor. The next morning we were awoken by a cheerful whistling and the tinkling of tea-cups. Sid had already been out to get himself some cigarettes, and now he was making us a cup of tea.

The summer found me back in France with old friends from my pre-war days on *The Bicycle*, Bill Mills and Jock Wadley, to cover the Tour de France.

On the Tour, the Press follow the competitors in special cars with identity number plates. In the mornings they usu-

ally start slowly, and it's only later on that somebody makes a break and the pace hots up. One morning, Bill Mills and I got a bit tired of this, so we got our driver to speed up a bit, figuring that if we could get a couple of hours ahead we would have time to enjoy a good lunch before catching them up again in the afternoon in time for the most interesting part of the race.

After driving fast for a while, we came to a beautiful hotel in the Alps. We had a glass of wine and were just sitting down to what promised to be an excellent meal, when there was a sudden commotion outside, and the leading riders in the race went shooting past. They had made a break early on before we had even had time to eat.

It seemed a shame to let good food go to waste, so we decided to enjoy our meal. We knew we could catch them. In any case, having thought about the problem, I decided I could produce a laid-on picture which might work. As soon as we had finished eating, we persuaded the chef and the bell-boy to stand outside the door of the hotel and wave as if the race was passing by. This photograph proved to be a great success: *Picture Post* used it, and it was syndicated to many continental magazines.

Cheering on the ghost riders.

Candlelight gives pictures great atmosphere. In the centre, there's a very odd glance for the Cardinal.

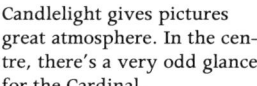

Hop Picking, The Port Harvest, Sudan: these sets of pictures can be found at the end of the chapter.

Thanks to the £500 increase in salary Frank Dowling had given me, I was now fairly well off. In September I moved from Eltham to Blackheath — an area which I knew from visiting Bert Lloyd. But although my greater prosperity meant that in some ways I was moving up in the world, it didn't mean that the rest of my life got any happier. From about the time of this move, my marriage to Dora went into a sharp decline, largely as a result of my life-style.

Although I had probably changed because of my job and the sort of people I met, the fact that I was hardly ever at home was no doubt as much to blame as anything for the fact that Dora and I stopped getting on. By now, I was working on several stories each week. Almost immediately after moving to Blackheath, I went off to Kent with Brian to do a story on hop-picking (Brian had done it as a student: he had discovered that a lot of other things besides hop-picking went on in the hot summer nights). Soon after, we went off to the Douro outside Oporto in Portugal to do a similar story on the Port wine harvest.

It was like the story I did with Bert on the wine harvest at Mont, except that we lived far more luxuriously at a *quinta*. Every day was so much of a party that it was a struggle to do any work at all.

As we were finishing, we heard about a festival for the end of the Holy Year which was taking place nearby at Fatima. We decided to drive on there before returning home. Fatima was the place where the Virgin Mary appeared to three girls in 1917, and hundreds of thousands of pilgrims were making their way there along the dusty roads in motor coaches and

on foot. Mass was being said continually but the high point of the celebrations was a great ceremony which took place at night. Thousands of people watched as a statue of the Virgin surrounded by fantastic gold lanterns was carried to the sanctuary in the Chapel of Apparitions. It was a dramatic scene I liked: candle-lit and full of atmosphere. I used a flash bulb to freeze the faces in the foreground, and the slow speed of about one-tenth of a second picked up the light of the candles of the pilgrims in the background and blur the candles, and added an extra feeling of energy to the picture.

A week or two after my return from Portugal, I was off again, this time to Egypt and the Sudan. My first stop was at Khartoum, where I met my journalist for the trip, Kenneth Allsop. I was also able to perform another little errand for *Picture Post*: a certain Doctor Bloss, winner of the *Picture Post* amateur photography competition, lived in Khartoum. He had won with a picture of a boy jumping into a swimming pool. I presented him with a cheque for his prize.

The situation in the Sudan was pretty tense at that time, and anti-British feeling was running high.

The British authorities had banned meetings of more than three of four people, but meetings were being held all the same. We got to hear of an illegal meeting of the anti-British Ashigga party being held at night at a place outside the city, so we hired a car and drove there.

The meeting was held in a courtyard. There were certainly more than two or three people there — more like two or three hundred. To get a better view, Ken and I stood up on the platform where the speakers were, and I began taking

pictures. There was virtually no light and I was forced to use flash bulbs. Once again, the scene had dramatic ingredients: darkness, atmosphere, and movement; but the darkness simply drew attention to the flashing of my camera, the atmosphere was distinctly hostile, and the movement changed into fists being waved in our direction. Ken and I suddenly had the feeling that if we didn't want to be beaten up by the mob, we had better make ourselves scarce.

We rushed to our car. As we climbed in, the crowd surrounded it and began rocking it from side to side to turn it

over. I asked the driver to ease the car slowly forward, and at the right moment got him to accelerate fast. We shot clear, and didn't slow till we got home. Ken and I then decided to do a story on a Kenyan village and see some of the less hazardous sides of African life. We took a plane down to a place called Juba, where we hired a jeep, a cook, and all the equipment we needed for trekking, and set off for a place called Torit, near the Ugandan border.

We immediately struck up a warm friendship with the British District Commissioner in Torit, John Owen. I did stories on native rain dances, which involved the purchase of a sacrificial goat; and the local prison, which was a sort of open compound where the prisoners were quite happy to stay because they were guaranteed at least one good square meal a day. Then John Owen told us that an elephant had been running wild and damaging the patches of land where the local people grew food crops. It would have to be hunted down and shot before it did any more damage.

A hunt was arranged for the rogue elephant. The trail was easy to follow: as elephants move through the tall elephant grass – which is at least six feet high – they trample it into a sort of corridor in the direction in which they're travelling, and all you have to do is walk along the trail after them. The only trouble is that, because the grass is so high, you can't see what else is lurking around: I must admit I felt pretty edgy. Ken wasn't half so worried: because of his artificial leg (he lost a leg in the war) he didn't have to sweat it out like the rest of us. Wearing a pith helmet, and looking every inch the white hunter, he was being carried shoulder-high by native

Left: Waiting for food in a Kenyan prison.

bearers in stately procession, sitting in a chair on poles.

I hadn't had much experience of elephants, but my Baroda experience meant that I didn't think of them as man's best friends. Suddenly we heard a terrific rumbling noise, and the District Commissioner signalled us all to stop. A large herd of elephants was nearby: the noise was the rumbling of their stomachs. We had to be careful that they didn't get our scent, because they would have charged at us. The D.C. might be able to drop one with his gun, but for the rest of us, the safest course would be to climb a tree. The only problem was that there were no trees to climb. It was a truly frightening moment.

On this occasion, we were lucky. The wind was blowing away from the elephants, and we were able to retreat without disturbing them. Now our only problem was getting back: walking against the direction of the spear-like blades of elephant grass was a painful experience. The only way to avoid getting stabbed where it hurts most was to tread most carefully and lift your feet terribly high.

The next day we went out again. But this time the elephants weren't so considerate as to give us an early warning with their tummies. One minute we were walking along through the tall grass, and the next we were out in a clearing, and a bloody great elephant was charging straight at us. There was nowhere to go, no trees to climb. The only obstacle between us and the elephant was the D.C. with his gun.

Keeping his nerve, John Owen lifted his rifle and took careful aim. Not until the beast was about seven or eight yards away did he fire. The elephant fell down dead. I practically collapsed with relief. I don't think I have ever been so scared in my life, not even during the Inchon landings. I was so scared that I didn't even manage to take a photograph.

After doing another story on Latoka tribesmen shooting fish with bows and arrows in the Fala Rapids – I thought fly-fishing was hard enough – Ken and I headed back up north to Khartoum. At our hotel there, we received a telephone call from Brian Dowling and Thurston Hopkins, who were, I seem to remember, nearby in Egypt. They had also been working on African stories, and now they were going to have a bit of a holiday before going back to London with all their stuff. I wished them a good time, and when they had rung off told Ken that we'd better get back to London as quickly as possible. *Picture Post* could only print a certain number of African stories, and I wanted them to be *ours*!

Back in London, not long before Christmas of 1951, I was at the Empress Club in Piccadilly. The Duke of Edinburgh was the host at a party given in aid of the National Playing Fields Association, and among the guests were Frank Sinatra and Ava Gardner. For some reason, I was the only photographer allowed in. Naturally I wanted to get pictures of the husband of our future queen, while, just as naturally, he tried to avoid being photographed. In the end it almost turned into a sort of game, with me dodging from pillar to pillar while he tried to keep out of my viewfinder. However, I did manage to get some interesting pictures of him dancing rather closely with Ava Gardner. To my disappointment, when Edith Kaye in the *Picture Post* darkroom developed the pictures, she said there was only one thing to do with them, and destroyed the negatives.

At about this time, the new editor, Frank Dowling, came under a cloud at *Picture Post*, and went off on a long holiday. After the Korean affair, life on the paper, and the future of the paper itself, were still looking far from secure.

Guess who told the funny story.

Right: Getting to know you: the Duke with Sinatra and Ava Gardner.

Barcelona   It is a Sunday morning in Barcelona. In the well-to-do areas, you can see a uniform for every occasion, but on the other side of the city there are none — except the uniform of poverty.

The Port Harvest

I loved working on this story. The weather, the people and the place itself were all marvellous. I took the portrait in the hope of making the cover, but it wasn't used. There was plenty of opportunity for backlighting, and I got the old fellow with the donkey (overleaf) to kick up the dust to improve the effect. The chicken appeared to be wondering whether it was next in the pot. Brian Dowling and I trod the grapes, and when we emerged from the vat our legs were washed in brandy!

Blackpool

Having accepted the challenge, I knew I had to produce something special with my Brownie. I set out from the pier in my search for pictures, walking along the beach. After a four-mile walk, we still had no shots of pretty girls. There was a rehearsal of the pier show going on, and we asked a couple of the girls to pose for us. The girls on the rail became one of my best-known pictures. The shot of the sailor was taken with a close-up attachment on the Box Brownie.

Sudan   The powerful sunlight made for contrasty shots, and I had to avoid making pictures look too static. The fishing net was ideal for the purpose. The men playing a Tsolo game were sitting down, but the picture still seems active, somehow. I photographed the village women at sunset to get a strong silhouette.

11: The Last Years of *Picture Post*

While Frank Dowling was facing difficulties with the management of *Picture Post*, I was off travelling in Italy with a journalist. A part of the journey took us from Milan to Trieste on the Orient Express. We had a magnificent carriage to ourselves, but my colleague was not a man to be put off by such surroundings: he opened a small travelling case, took out his travelling clock and other bits and pieces, and spread them all out on the table between us. I was so embarrassed that I told him to bloody well put them away again.

Because it was the frontier with Yugoslavia, Trieste was still filled with army personnel. There were a lot of officers and their wives staying at the same hotel as us, The Excelsior. I think they were mostly rather bored, and looked on us to provide a bit of interest in their lives.

Somehow, we got to hear about a brothel, which was supposed to be very special. One evening after we had had a few drinks, the journalist suggested we went along there to see what it was like.

It was a large house in a tree-lined avenue, just like all the other houses from the outside. The door was opened for us by a maid, and we were shown into a magnificent room in old-fashioned style, all plush and velvet. After a short wait, the Madam appeared, and asked us what we would like to drink. By now, I was beginning to feel uneasy.

We ordered our drinks, and then we were shown into another magnificent room. This time we were confronted by two of the most beautiful girls possible, in a tempting state of undress. I was sorely tempted, but I had my principles. The girls performed a bit for us. I was even more sorely tempted, but I just couldn't go through with it. I suggested to my mate that we should bugger off.

He wasn't exactly happy about it, but we left together. Back at the hotel, all the officers' wives moved in for a report on our adventures and were duly disappointed.

The journalist suggested that to make up for it we should go back to England via Venice, but once again I was forced to let him down. I think I had probably had enough of travelling for a while: since returning from Tibet, I had been to France three times, to Spain, Ireland, Portugal, Egypt, Kenya, Sudan, Greece and Turkey, not to mention Lancashire and Kent. I just wanted to go home.

Once we got back to London, I started a new story called 'The Life of a Chorus Girl', with Brian Dowling.

We based ourselves at a classy little club next to Simpson's in Piccadilly, called The Pigalle, after our favourite part of Paris. We picked a couple of girls who worked in the club and based our story on them. The job involved a lot of intensive background research: staying up to the small hours every night, and consuming free drinks provided by the management of the club. It was hard work.

After one such exhausting night of research, we staggered out into Piccadilly in the early hours of the morning. I looked around me, and suddenly had a flash of inspiration. 'What are we looking for?' I asked Brian. 'We've got one of the greatest stories right under our noses.'

The next day we put up the idea at the editorial conference, and it was accepted. We got down to work straight away. The story was so full of possibilities it was endless. It could involve any aspect of daily life in the area around Piccadilly Circus, which was not only a symbol of London, but a centre for American troops and for the Chinese. For outdoor shots, I relied on the candid camera technique I had developed over the years; for indoor work, such as in Lock's the hat makers, or Madam Ve-ara's, 'Society Clairvoyante and Palmiste', I relied more on some posed shots.

The story took us a long time to complete. By the end, we had hundreds of photographs. There were fewer pages in the magazine now that *Picture Post*'s circulation was falling. This meant that there wasn't enough space to do the story properly, and it was therefore decided not to use it at all. However, I entered it for the Encyclopaedia Britannica Award anyway, because I knew the pictures were some of my best.

By now, many of *Picture Post*'s most talented journalists, like Jimmy Cameron, had left the magazine. On 23 September 1952 Harry Deverson, long-time picture editor, whom I had known from my AFPU days, was sacked. Soon after his removal, I was sent off to Cairo with an agency journalist, a Miss E. Thompson, to cover the overthrow of King Farouk by General Neguib. On my arrival I was very pleased to find not only Ralph Izzard, but also Jimmy Cameron there, covering the same story for different papers. It began to seem a bit like old times.

While we were there, we heard that the house of Nahas Pasha, Farouk's last Prime Minister, had been surrounded by army tanks and that he was about to be arrested at any moment. I hired a car and drove in past a cordon of tanks.

We were shown to a waiting room lined with chairs, where twenty or so Egyptian journalists were sitting waiting for an interview with him. They looked as if they had been there a long time, but an official told me not to worry. If I took a seat, Nahas Pasha would see me soon.

Presently coffee arrived. A long time passed. The official returned, and we asked again when we could see him.

'Just wait a little', he said, 'then you may see him.'

More time passed. More coffee arrived. We went and found the official: 'When can we see Nahas Pasha?' 'Soon, just wait a little while.'

I had some more coffee, sat around for another couple of hours, talked to the Egyptian journalists. They had long ago given up demanding to see him, and were now resigned to sitting and waiting until the unbelievable happened. When the official returned, we pounced on him:

'We must see Nahas Pasha.'

The official looked slightly taken aback:

'But he is ill.' So I left.

I came back early the next day. Once again I was shown to the room. The same journalists were sitting around waiting. When the inevitable coffee arrived, we sprang from our seats:

Chorus Girl, Piccadilly: these two photo-stories can be found at the end of the chapter.

'When can we see Nahas Pasha?'

The official was as helpful as ever:

'This afternoon.'

When I went back that afternoon, I didn't waste any time: I asked to see Nahas's secretary. When I got to him, I told him that I had come all the way from Great Britain to do a story on Nahas Pasha, and had a private plane standing by to rush the results of the interview back home. That worked like a charm: within five minutes I was admitted into his presence, and Nahas apologised for having kept me waiting.

I got my photographs, and Jimmy Cameron took my films back to London with him that night. But after all the fuss, *Picture Post* only used one of the pictures, very small.

Later Miss Thompson and I heard that General Neguib was going on a private tour of Egypt. We asked if we could go with him. It was all very sudden: we were told to report to the army barracks and stand by. A long line of trucks and cars were waiting, and we all piled into them, and took off at high speed.

Nobody told us that the tour would last three or four days, and we were completely unprepared. On the tour, we stopped with local Pashas, and consumed enormous banquets. If the Pashas had intended to butter up the General, they failed. Each night the General placed myself and Miss Thompson next to him at table in order to keep the Pashas at a distance.

On the last day of the tour as we neared Cairo, our car pushed on ahead of the rest of the procession. Towards dark, we came to a village where the crowds awaiting Neguib were so large that we had to stop.

Something had made them angry, for they began banging violently on the roof of our car. Our Egyptian driver responded by revving the engine and driving at them. This really annoyed them. They began manhandling the car violently; luckily the driver managed to force his way into a dark side street.

We had left the crowd well behind: or at least most of them. There were still a few hanging onto the car when we stopped. The two Egyptian army officers who were travelling with us got out and beat them with their canes until they fell. We drove the rest of the way to Cairo at great speed.

When I got back to London after this story, I found that the situation at *Picture Post* was getting even worse: two photographers and four more journalists had been sacked. And now, although I had narrowly escaped death at the hands of angry African mobs twice within the space of a year, somebody had obviously decided that my luck must run out some time, and I was sent to Kenya with Warwick Charlton to do a story on the Mau-Mau.

The Mau-Mau were a secret society of black Kenyans who were attempting to get rid of the British colonialists by vicious terrorism. Warwick Charlton had fixed up to do the story by claiming that he had contacts with the Mau-Mau (though he didn't). I was pleased to find on my arrival in Nairobi that Ralph Izzard was there. Ralph and Warwick

and I decided that the only way to get to grips with the story was to go to Nyeri, in the heart of Mau-Mau country, where the British Army was involved in a drive to flush out the Mau-Mau. We hired a front-wheel-drive Citroën, and with me driving and two native Kenyan soldiers in the back, we set out.

The roads were just broad red bands of unmetalled red dust. As soon as it rained they changed into skid-pans. On the first day's driving, I discovered that it was easy to get the Citroën into a skid, though I managed to avoid any serious incident. We spent that night in the Outspan Hotel. The next day, we were deeper into Kikuyu country, Mau-Mau territory. There were three British army camps arranged in a rough triangle, and we were driving between them.

It was late afternoon, and it was raining. I had my foot down fairly hard so that we would make the next camp before nightfall. We had just driven through a village. The natives had stared at us with expressions which left us in no doubt of their feelings. I decided to speed up, when we hit a left-hand bend too fast. The car skidded across the road, and came to a halt teetering on the brink of a sharp drop on the right-hand side.

The car was literally balanced over the edge. Warwick and Ralph inched themselves carefully out of the door. The soldiers stayed put while I slid across from the driving seat and climbed out of the left-hand door. Then I helped out the soldiers. We could see that there wasn't any hope of getting the car back on the road on our own. The only way on was on foot.

I took charge: I made one of the native soldiers walk in front, and the other behind, although I can't say that I thought they would make much difference to our chances of survival if we did run into trouble. We were still miles from the nearest camp. In an hour or so, it would get dark. As we walked along the road, we could hear people moving about in the jungle which ran beside the road. Ralph was as calm as

Our crashed car (you can see the skid marks). The slope was steeper than it appears in the picture. Here I am with one of our two African guards.

Opposite: Picking up Mau-Mau suspects for questioning.

always; Warwick was getting nervous; I felt as scared as I had ever been.

After walking for about a mile, we came to a crossroads. If we took the right road, we might make it to the camp before nightfall, but if we didn't, the Mau-Mau would get us. Pretending I knew what I was doing, I chose a road and we started walking along it. I glanced at my watch: it was about the time when my friends in London would be enjoying a nice cool glass of beer.

After we had gone some way, we heard the sound of an engine. A jeep appeared in front of us, loaded with soldiers. They were ours. To say we were pleased to see them would be something of an understatement. We jumped in and drove back to the camp with them, where we had a very, very stiff brandy to settle our nerves.

As soon as the brandy had done its work, I went out again in the jeep with some soldiers, and found the car and got it back on the road. The next night we went out with the soldiers on a tour of the surrounding villages, picking up Mau-Mau suspects.

When I got back to the Outspan Hotel in Nyeri, I found a telegram telling me that I had won an Encyclopaedia Britannica Award for my Piccadilly photographs. As a result, *Picture Post* were finally forced to publish some.

During a break in rehearsals for the Memorial Concert, I hopped into an empty seat among the violins. When Barbirolli returned, he was now facing (and conducting) me. The strain seems to show on the bassist's face.

One of my first assignments on my return to England was to go up to Sheffield and take pictures of the Hallé Orchestra with their conductor Sir John Barbirolli. It was a bad time to have chosen: when I arrived on the scene, he had just come back from London, where he had taken the singer Kathleen Ferrier to see a medical specialist. The specialist had confirmed that she had leukaemia, and had only a short time to live. Barbirolli asked me not to take any photographs at the time, and I was sadly forced to finish the story a couple of months later in January 1953, when the orchestra was in London, rehearsing for the Kathleen Ferrier Memorial Concert.

At about this time, John Pearce, the Managing Director of Hulton Press, who had tried to calm everyone down at the time when Ted Castle was sacked and Frank Dowling appointed, was sacked himself.

I was soon off out of the country again: this time to Italy with Zoë Bernstein, a journalist and the former wife of an impresario. She used her contacts to get an interview with Ingrid Bergman and her husband (the film director Roberto Rossellini). Ingrid Bergman had been the victim of a lot of unpleasant publicity after she left her first husband in America and went to live with Rossellini. We wanted to photograph her with her baby twin girls. I found her a very nice woman, but it took a couple of days to win the confidence of her husband. He made films about poverty, and drove to work each day in a Rolls-Royce. However, he was not all that impressed by the Rolls.

From Naples, I travelled via Rome to Belgrade, where I met another *Picture Post* journalist I got on well with, Sylvain Mangeot. Belgrade was a dreary place and at that time thick with snow. The only redeeming feature was that the smart

hotel where we were staying was opposite the Press Club which had a bar that attracted some very smart and friendly professional women. Once again, my natural inclinations were stopped by my phobia about paying for such things. And anyway, how do you describe them on an expenses sheet?

Sylvain and I were told that we would be allowed to photograph President Tito. There were a few Yugoslavian photographers there, and I thought that something special must be happening. I had taken several pictures of him, when, halfway through the session, his wife came in. This was the first time he had ever allowed himself to be photographed with his wife, who hadn't been seen in public before. I had to work quickly. Within the space of ten minutes, I got one set of black-and-white and one set of colour pictures.

Coronation Day, 2 June 1953, found me back in London standing on the roof of the Lodge Gate in East Carriage Drive, Hyde Park. I had come a long way since standing on a sand bin in the Blackfriars Bridge Road twenty years earlier, using my sister's head as a tripod, but this didn't seem any more glamorous. I had needed to get up at three a.m. to get in position by seven, so I could take my one picture as the carriage came past nine hours later, at four p.m. In addition, I was supposed to be taking a colour picture of the Coronation Coach. Colour films were so slow in those days, and the light was so bad, that it was touch and go whether I would get any sort of picture at all when the vital moment came.

I'm pleased to say that my wait was rewarded: my picture did come out. It was used as a full-page spread, having been rushed up to Sun Engraving at Watford, where the presses had been especially held up for the picture. Only after the first editions were out did somebody notice that they had printed my photograph in reverse, with the coach apparently heading in the wrong direction!

Unfortunately, the rain that summer didn't stop, even for my first family holiday since the fateful one I took before the Korean War. This time I took Dora and the boys on a camping trip to Gairloch, where I had arranged to meet a friend from Keystone Press with his wife at a map reference point, in order to spend two weeks enjoying the outdoor life.

Incredibly we both arrived at that isolated spot at exactly the same moment, but from then on, our luck was out. It rained non-stop. There wasn't the faintest hope of camping, so we had to find a boarding house to stay in. It rained so hard that there wasn't even much hope of going for walks. Instead, each day we used to go along to the bar of a nearby hotel and drink our sorrows away.

Towards the end of the holiday, I realised that it had been costing me a lot of money. I reckoned that I had to make some money to pay for it – but what hope was there of finding any sort of story in such a remote place? Then my mind went back to the beginning of the war, when I went to Wales to do a story on B. L. Coombes, the miner. On that occasion I had also done a story about rescuing a sheep, which the paper had used. There seemed to be plenty of sheep around here, and plenty of awkward rocks. In that case, I thought, the sheep must often get stuck and need to be rescued. I had my story.

I fixed the whole thing up and produced a story. When I got back to London, I showed it to Frank Dowling. He said he couldn't pay me anything for it, because I was a full-time employee of the paper. I pointed out that I had been on holiday at the time. He said that it didn't change anything, although I could claim expenses for the story if I liked. Without giving him time to reconsider, I immediately presented my claim for two weeks' stay for the family in a bed-and-breakfast, plus liquid refreshment and mileage. There must have been a few raised eyebrows in the accounts department, but it was passed. It was my greatest-ever expenses coup.

Around then *Life* magazine must have got wind of what was happening at *Picture Post*. In August 1952 they had approached me and offered me a job as a photographer on their staff. But even though the salary they were offering was three or four times what I was receiving at *Picture Post*, I didn't fancy it. At that time I didn't have any thought that *Picture Post* might pack up. I had been with the paper for most of my career as a photographer, and they used practically every story I did. I knew that on *Life*, even the best photographers only got about one in three or four stories used, and that they often spent up to three months working on a story. I liked to work under pressure: I didn't think I could work properly in that sort of vacuum, so I turned down the offer. When I let this be known to the management of *Picture Post*, they rewarded my loyalty by giving me a new and bigger company car.

After I came back from my holiday, I decided to have

Ingrid Bergman in Naples with her twin baby girls.

Jovanka Budisavljevic was an army major when she married Marshal Tito. When I asked Tito to move closer to her for my picture, he asked 'Why do Englishmen always want wives and husbands to appear so closely united when we are told that British wives wear the trousers and beat their husbands?'

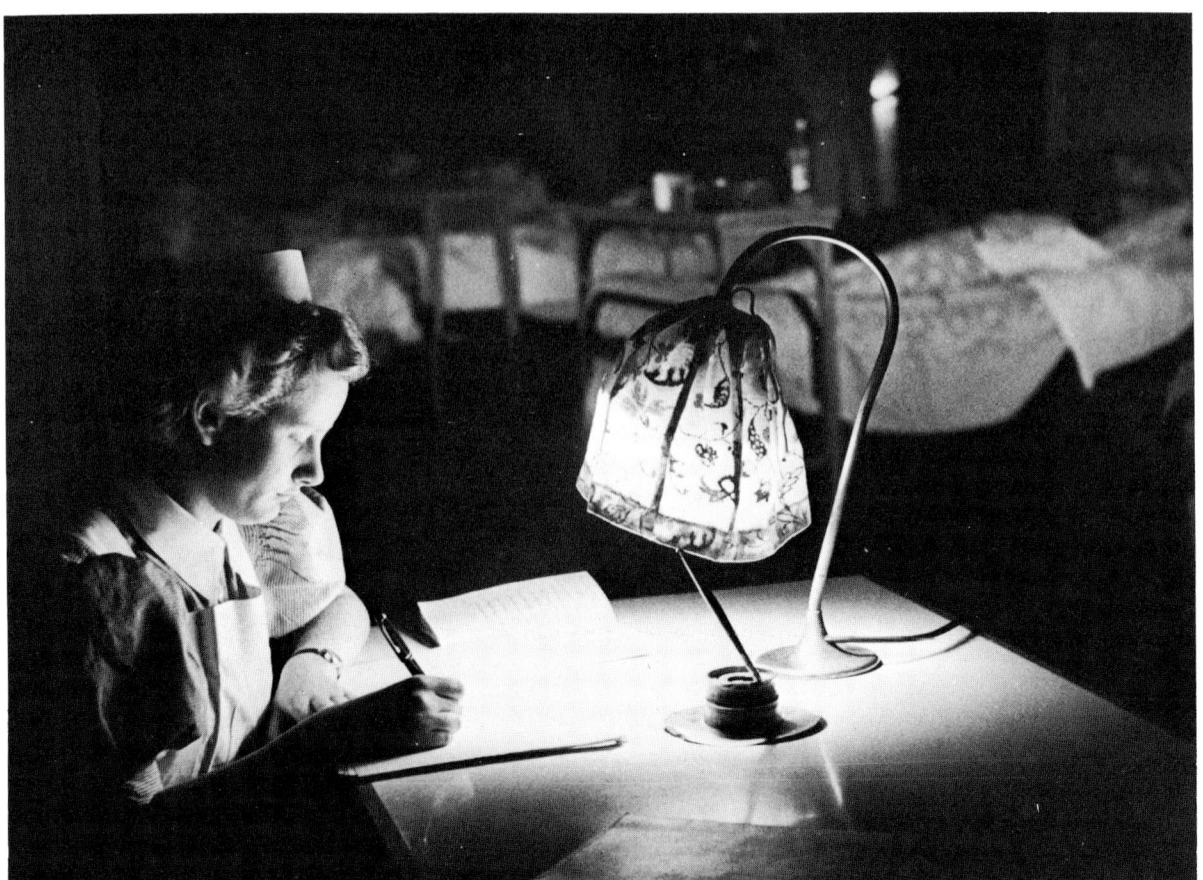

The night nurse on duty in Rachel Ward writes a letter home. In the morning, Sister Clarke prays for help in the 'holy calling' and for the patients and their families.

Opposite: Sister Doris Bulley MBE looks after an emergency patient.

something done about my right eye. It was the eye I used for looking through my viewfinder, and I had been having trouble with it for some time. To this day it is a lot weaker than my left eye – but the only explanation my doctor could think of was that so much squinting through a viewfinder had weakened it. On the advice of my doctor I was admitted to the London Hospital in Whitechapel.

Dr Henson, whom I had been seeing privately, told me not to bother with a private bed: treatment in the public ward was just as good. I arrived one afternoon, and duly got undressed and into bed. By the time I was ready, Dr Henson was just finishing his rounds for the day. I called to the Sister and told her I was ready to be looked at. She looked at me very frostily. It was too late for Dr Henson to look at any more patients. I would have to wait until the next morning.

I felt a bit sour. After all, I was lying there in bed when I could be out working. But then, after a short while, Dr Henson came back especially to see me. From then on the Sister's attitude changed: if he was prepared to make a special trip just to see me, I must be more worthwhile than she had thought.

After that I settled into hospital life. The treatment I received in Rachel Ward made a strong impression on me. I decided that as soon as I was out, I'd come back with Brian and do a story about the hospital.

In October, we went and spent ten days covering every

aspect of life in that hospital, from prayers first thing in the morning to lights-out at night. Brian and I even took the rather severe Sister out to lunch one day. She was not as hard as I had thought at first. When we picked her up by taxi she unbent, and insisted that we call her by her christian name.

Although some of the doctors were not all that keen on our presence, we got on extremely well with most nurses and patients. On the last night, Brian and I smuggled a couple of bottles into Rachel Ward and, in a small room at the end of the Ward, we had what can only be described as a fairly wild party with the nurses and a couple of patients who had been in with me.

In November 1953, Frank Dowling was sacked for the second time and replaced by Hulton himself. Len Spooner, formerly editor of *Illustrated*, became his assistant. The decline of *Picture Post* went into top gear.

The new year, and the last phase of the magazine, started well for me. I did a promotional story about the monastery where Green Chartreuse liqueur is made. The story itself wasn't much fun to do, but we were given plenty of free samples. The plane on which I was travelling back with some other newsmen was held up for a couple of days by fog. It's amazing what a good time a small party of people can have with a half a dozen bottles of Green Chartreuse: but all good things have to come to an end. When the fog still hadn't lifted by the third day, I decided it was time to go home anyway, and caught the boat train instead.

Looking back on it, serious stories were becoming few and far between. I started doing a lot of colour pictures of football matches. The film was so slow (8 ASA) that this was a very difficult job. I also began to have to set up stories again, just like in the old days when I was working for GPA – such as a story on Spivs I did with the help of an underworld contact called Jimmy O'Connor, a thoroughly nice chap who had served time for murder.

My trip to Berlin to cover the Berlin Conference was an exception rather than the rule. It was serious all right, but it was a bread-and-butter story, and not really interesting to do. Apart from the Coronation, I don't think I had then seen so many photographers concentrated in one place in my life. There must have been about thirty or so Press men there, and a fair number of those were photographers. Security arrangements were very tight. Every one of us was thoroughly frisked (even our fountain pens were opened) before we were marched to the conference room by security guards. We were all crammed along one side of a vast, poorly lit room, with our elbows in each others' ribs, jostling for the best place. When the ministers from the various countries came in, they stayed on the other side of the room, like shy girls at a dance, and we had to do all our shooting from forty feet away. Once again, thanks to my Leica and 135 mm lens, I was the only one present to get Eden and Molotov shaking hands.

The next day, for a bit of light relief, Paul Anderson (the journalist) and I crossed over into the Eastern Sector of Berlin. There was no wall yet, but the atmosphere wasn't easy. Cameras were not allowed in, so I hid my Rolleiflex under my coat. The place looked grim: there were police everywhere, on foot and in cars. It was so appallingly cold that the shutter oil on my camera froze: my shutter speeds were all over the place. I was set on 1/250th second, but whenever I pressed the shutter release, there was a slow whirring and a click, and the results show that it was probably working at more like 1/50th second. What was worse, whenever I held the camera up to my eye the metal felt as if it was burning a hole in my forehead.

Then, at a road junction, I saw an incident which seemed to me to sum up the feeling of the place: a policeman was fining a pedestrian on the spot for jay-walking. I set my focus for a distance of four yards, and then wandered in their direction, and with the camera slung round my neck and half invisible beneath my coat, I took a couple of pictures.

The policeman must have heard the suspicious slow shutter sound. He stopped writing in his notebook and began to stare at me angrily. 'Cold, isn't it, mate?' I remarked, and blew in my hands. But he was not to be fooled: he had seen the camera, and now he was pointing at it and shouting at me. I nodded at him.

'Yes, yes. Very cold. Brrr, cold, Chilly.'

Then, as I didn't have time to stand around talking all day, I looked about for my friends. They were all walking very

I was lucky not to be fined too (or worse!).

fast in the opposite direction, so I quickly walked after them. A glance over my shoulder revealed that the policeman was still waving his arms in the air. I waved back, like an old friend. Without slackening our pace, we headed back for West Berlin, and a good hot rum toddy.

Back in England I used Jimmy O'Connor again, to do a serialised story with Brian Dowling about what happens when a prisoner leaves jail. We invented a situation, in which Jimmy's 'wife' was played by a rather attractive model I happened to know, and another model played 'the other woman' with whom Jimmy was supposed to be carrying on. It was fun to do, like directing a film, but, like the picture sequences I used to have to think up before the war, it all had to be set up. We took pictures in a café and in private rooms, but the highlight of the story was set in a pub, where the convict's wife confronts his girl-friend and has beer thrown over her.

We had the pub cleared, and the staging of the fight went very well. Afterwards the 'other woman' had to go upstairs to change her beer-soaked blouse. For some reason I went up with her and the landlady of the pub. As I say, she was an attractive model, for whom I could have fallen rather heavily if only she would have let me. My one regret is that I was not quick enough with my camera to record the expression of disgust on the landlady's face (or anything else for that matter) when the model, without a second thought, took off her blouse and revealed a beautiful pair of oojahs. This story, which was entirely fictional, ran as a serial over three issues.

In March, Trevor Philpot and I went on naval manoeuvres off Malta. The exercise involved one half of the ships 'fighting' the other half. The ships of our opponents were commanded by none other than Earl Mountbatten. Towards the end of the exercise, while his vessel was being refuelled at sea, he got to hear of our presence, and invited us to come over to visit him.

Trevor and I, dirty by now from several days at sea, were winched across the choppy waters in a breeches buoy (not an experience I recommend). We took a few pictures of Mountbatten on the bridge, and he warmed to us. He always liked publicity. Finally, he invited us to dine with him and one other officer that night.

It was the old story of the dinner jacket. Even if I had brought one with me, I could hardly expect to have it winched across for me to wear that night. Trevor and I decided that our only hope was to persuade a couple of junior officers to lend us theirs, so we found their Mess and set about persuading them at the bar.

We borrowed the dinner jackets, and even managed to use somebody's razor to scrape off the stubble of several days. But they do know how to enjoy themselves in the navy, and I'm afraid to say that, when we finally staggered into dinner in our ill-fitting jackets that evening, we were unpardonably late. But we were allowed to sleep in Mountbatten's spare cabin that night.

Under Hulton's editorship, I now found myself doing stories with titles like 'Frankie Howerd Rescues Three Pretty Girls', or photographing Eva Gabor, Zsa-Zsa Gabor's sister. One of Hulton's ideas was a series called 'Personality Girl'. A different girl was featured each month, and it wasn't normally her personality that distinguished her. They were usually bright young things, and often seemed to have double-barrelled names. I had a bit of fun with Miss Jocelyn Wardrop-Moore by getting her to scrub the steps of her Kensington mews cottage for the picture. I think she enjoyed it too, and I'm sure it was a novel experience for her.

I began doing outside work: I flew to Knoxville, Tennessee to do a promotional booklet for Bowaters, and I was doing a lot of work for a magazine put out by Ford Motors, called *Ford Family*.

One compensation for staying on at *Picture Post* was that by this time I knew the Hultons well, and was friendly with them – particularly Lady Hulton. At the end of the year, Len Spooner and I were invited to go with them on a ski-ing holiday in Switzerland. I bought all the latest clothing and equipment on expenses at Simpson's in Piccadilly, but I never actually learnt to ski. The funniest moment came when Lady Hulton persuaded Len and me to go to the top of the slopes on a ski lift, and then had us brought down again on accident stretchers.

Early in 1954 I was back in Germany doing a story on a factory which specialised in the production of artificial limbs. I went with Ken Allsop and Jack Garnham, a Hulton Press colour printer who, like Ken, had lost a leg in the war. It was a strange experience to share a hotel room with the two of them, especially when they both sat down on their beds and unstrapped their legs each night.

Jack Garnham stayed on a while and fell in love with a German girl who was there to have an artificial arm and leg fitted after having fallen under a railway train. I think they got married in the end.

A man in Belfast who kept lions in a filthy cage in his back-yard; the training of a Bluebell girl by Madam Bluebell; a trip to Nice with Fred Mullaley and five models; and the laying of the foundation stone of Hulton House in Fleet Street by Sir Edward Hulton; all took up my time in the early part of 1955. In July I was pleased to get away to cover the Tour de France which I always enjoyed doing, with my old friends Bill Mills and Jock Wadley.

We were driving through the Alps in our chauffeur-driven car, descending a steep road full of hairpin bends. I was sitting in the front next to the driver, and Jock and Bill were in the back. Most of the time, the driver had to keep the brake-pedal jammed down, just to stop the car running away. The brakes were the old-fashioned type, and as they heated with the constant friction, they began to fade. There was a vertical cliff wall on one side of us, and a sheer drop on the other. Suddenly, the brakes faded altogether: the car began to run out of control, and the driver panicked.

I never liked letting other people drive very much anyway. As soon as I realised what was happening, I reached across and grabbed the steering wheel. Then I gradually steered against the rock-face, to slow the car down. When we finally came to a halt, the driver got out and sat by the road and burst into tears. The side of the car was knocked about a bit, but I don't think that was what was bothering him. The brakes eventually cooled down and we started off again, though the driver was still too upset to drive. I didn't mind too much: it gave me a good excuse to take over.

Kenneth Allsop left *Picture Post* in August. More staff were sacked in November (at the time I was photographing girls in coloured night-shirts in the boardroom). Although it was getting more difficult to do good stories, it wasn't impossible. A story I did about an unemployed man in Londonderry just before Christmas was so touching that it brought in a record number of donations from readers.

For a photograph which was supposed to demonstrate the effectiveness of a new stain-resistant fabric, I had models in dresses made of this fabric throwing coloured paint at each other while dangling on the end of ropes. When I had to take photographs with the slow old colour films of the film star Pier Angeli doing a song-and-dance routine on the set of the film *Port Afrique*, I decided to use the movement of the dancers in the background to give an expressive blur of colour. It was much the same sort of thing that I had done in my pictures of the Princess and her bridesmaids at the Royal wedding, only more extreme. Later, in my advertising work, I took it even further.

At the end of November 1955, my dad was admitted to St Francis's Hospital in East Dulwich. He was still there when, three weeks later, my mother also had to be admitted with what turned out to be leukaemia. Only two days later, she was dead.

In recent years, they had been moved by the council from Blackfriars to Crystal Palace, but I don't think they felt so happy there. My dad didn't like having to commute by train to the place where he used to work on the other side of the bridge where he had earned his nickname, 'Seagull'.

Early in 1956 I did another story which could have come straight from my early days at GPA: 'Loneliness in London'. I used a model, just as I would have done if Bertram Collins had been around, but this model was slightly different. I took photographs of her sitting by the fire at home and so on. She was a lowly sub-editor on the staff of a women's magazine, and she was obviously bright. I was very impressed with her, and had a word with the editor of *Picture Post*, who arranged to meet her, and then gave her a job: her name was Katherine Whitehorn.

At last, in March 1956, I decided to call it a day with Dora. Sheila and I had been leading an awkward double life for some time, as was usual then because of the difficult divorce laws in those days. We now eagerly accepted the only possibility open to us, which was to live in the front room of my brother Sid's house, in Brockley, South London.

When I telephoned Sheila to say that I had made up my mind, she thought for a bit, then asked me to make sure to buy a bottle of milk on my way to our new address. No sooner had we moved in than I was sent off to Cyprus to cover the civil war there.

I went with Timothy Raison, the son of one of the Directors of Hulton Press, Maxwell Raison. He was a pleasant young man, but very reserved. The war in Cyprus was a dirty war. It didn't have the photographic interest for me of the Korean War. Whatever action there was was quick guerrilla action, and you never actually knew who the enemy

was – it might even be the old peasant with a donkey who seemed to make such a good subject for a picture.

My only brush with danger was at a distance – far more comfortable than in Korea. After we had been out with the 4/15 Commandoes raiding a village called Milekouri, we had to get back to Limasol. We were all for hitching a lift in an army vehicle if possible, because we thought that at least we would be safer with army protection. The officer in charge of the unit we were with disagreed: he said we'd be far safer if we took a taxi. In an army vehicle we'd just be sitting ducks for snipers. Somewhat reluctantly, we took his advice and got a taxi. A day or two later, we heard that he had been killed when the army truck in which he was travelling was caught in an ambush and blown up.

I didn't manage to spend much time in Sid's front room. Almost immediately on my return, the Hultons wanted me to go and join them in Rhodesia, where they were engaged in buying property in what was then still seen as a safe area for investment. They also brought with them their private doctor, their lawyer and his secretary.

I took some pictures of Hulton in a topee and below-knee-length khaki shorts on his farm outside Salisbury. Then he asked me to go and inspect a tea plantation which he owned in Nyasaland. He had never been there personally, but the manager was claiming that he needed a lot of new machinery, and Hulton wanted me to check that this was really true. I flew out and inspected the old machinery. I didn't have the faintest idea whether it needed replacing or not, but since I liked the manager and got on rather well with him, I decided to recommend that the machinery be replaced. While I was at the plantation, the tea dust brought on my first-ever attack of asthma. This was to affect me much more in the future. A doctor had to be sent for, and I was pumped full of drugs so that I recovered enough to carry on as normal.

After flying over the Victoria Falls in a private plane with Lady Hulton, and taking some pictures of them (which made a two-page colour spread in *Picture Post*), I flew back home with her and some others from the party.

Six months after my mum, my dad also died in East Dulwich Hospital. In my diary, I wrote 'now they are together'. In fact he had improved enough to come out of hospital to attend my mum's funeral. We had even begun to make arrangements for him to live with one of my sisters if he got well enough, but this never happened.

While I was getting over this second loss, I was approached by the organiser of the 'Family of Man' photographic exhibition, Edward Steichen. He happened to be in London, and asked me to contribute a few pictures for the exhibition. Since he only had a few minutes to select my entries, and because I was still based in Sid's front room, it wasn't possible to show him the pictures which I regarded as my all-time best. I still regret that.

The next month, I was off with the Hultons again, this time to America, where Hulton had decided to cover the American Presidential Election campaign. The whole thing

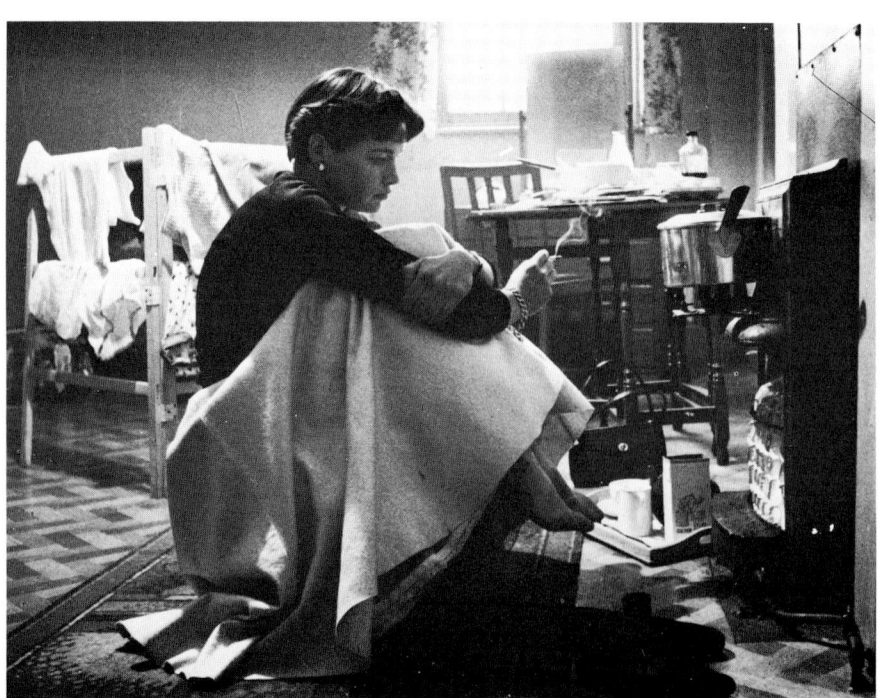

Katherine Whitehorne was an excellent model, with more common sense than most.

Above: A Milekouri villager is searched for arms.

Left: Grading tea on Sir Edward Hulton's tea plantation in Nyasaland (which I don't think he had ever seen).

Below: Sir Edward with farm manager outside Salisbury.

was extremely relaxed: each morning I was given a large whisky, and briefed by Lady Hulton clad only in her bath towel.

Hulton himself was rather ill on this trip. Drink seemed to have a funny effect on him. When we were on an airplane flying down to San Francisco, he had a couple of cocktails, then suddenly began to say a number of extremely rude things about the Americans. In San Francisco, he retired to his hotel room to recover from his illness. Lady Hulton hired a nurse to look after him, but one morning she couldn't come, so I was asked to look after him instead, and keep him company.

It was a difficult job. Hulton liked a drink, even though it had such an unfortunate effect on him in his unwell state. He immediately began to look round the hotel suite for something. I wasn't his nurse, I was his employee, so I couldn't tell him what to do. When we had emptied the bottle, he wanted to go out and find somewhere where we could buy another drink. As I followed him out of the hotel, protesting weakly, the nurse loomed up on the horizon, and I was pleased to hand him over to her tender mercies.

She soon got him over the worst. Hulton made a good recovery, and we began following Eisenhower's whistle-stop tour. But I don't think he could get used to the idea that he was just an ordinary journalist with the other journalists. As the train was pulling out of the station at Salt Lake City, we couldn't get back on. At least, I could have hopped aboard, but Hulton was far too plump. Instead, he ran along holding the rail of the observation car, shouting 'Stop the train, I want to get on!'

The train took no notice, and we were forced to take a taxi to the next stop on the tour.

When I was at home in London, Sheila and I were still having to lead a bit of a double life. With the exception of Sid, a lot of my family didn't approve of me leaving Dora. We kept where we lived a secret from them in order to avoid unpleasant scenes.

Then, one evening in our little front room, Sheila suddenly began to feel very unwell, and had pains in her stomach. I toured the streets of Brockley trying to get a doctor to come out, and found one at last. When I got back, Sheila looked so bad that he sent for an ambulance. As I did so, I had a funny feeling: one of my brothers-in-law was an ambulance man in South London. Given the luck of the Hardys, he would be sure to turn up.

When the ambulance arrived, I took refuge in another room. Sure enough, the ambulance man was indeed my brother-in-law. He must have thought that something odd was going on: what was Sid doing with a strange woman living in his front room? I stayed out of sight, and followed the ambulance to the hospital in my car. I thought that as soon as he had cleared off, I would be able to see Sheila. But his curiosity was not so easily satisfied. He hung around and hung around. In the end I was forced to break my cover and explain everything. Shortly afterwards, *Picture Post* sent me

to do a story on the emergency doctor service. I wasn't amused!

Sheila made a good recovery from her mysterious illness, which turned out to be appendicitis. Shortly before Christmas we were able to put an end to our refugee life-style by moving to a new home in Bromley. It was a brand new house, built in the open-plan style, with picture windows. The only place where you could kiss and cuddle during the day, without drawing the curtains and letting the neighbours know what you were doing anyway, was in the hallway, under the stairs.

We planted a Victoria plum tree when we moved in, to celebrate our success in at last getting together, and I christened the house 'The Priory' after the Priory Buildings, where I was born. I expect everyone still wonders why such a modern-looking house has such an old-fashioned name. However, we weren't able to celebrate our first New Year together there: the Hultons asked me to join them in Norway, where they were going to ensure a white Christmas for themselves, so I had to go.

In January 1957, I was in Rome with one of the few *Picture Post* journalists I have ever actively disliked, Bill Richardson, when news came through of the fighting in Aden, so I rang through to London and got permission to go. It was to be the last war I covered for *Picture Post*.

After waiting around for ten days in Aden, we finally got permission to go into the interior of the Yemen from King Ahmed. The only money recognised there was the heavy Marie Therese silver dollar (worth about five shillings), so, carrying all our cash in a sack, we set off in jeeps for the capital, Taizz.

The journey took three days. The roads were so rough that at one stage the leaf springs of the Land Rover snapped; but it must have been a common occurrence, because our driver carried spares, and changed them over while we sat and ate our sandwiches. We spent the night in Taizz in a government guest house, and the next day drove on to the fort of Akaba. It was a beautiful journey through a wild landscape dominated by rock fortresses. On the road we passed groups of wild looking tribesmen armed to the teeth, and the occasional elderly looking gent on a donkey, with a rifle slung across his back, and holding an umbrella to keep off the sun. Any women we saw were shy, and scampered for cover rather than let themselves be photographed.

In Akaba, we were opposite the British lines in the village of Sona, in the Dhala area of the British Protectorate. After spending a night in the fortress, we set out with a party of local tribesmen who were engaged in skirmishes with the Cameron Highlanders.

It didn't take me long to work out which side I would rather be on. After squabbling amongst themselves for a while about who had the most bullets, a group of about fifty tribesmen got down to the serious business, loosing off their rifles at some British troops about a mile or so away on a ridge, where I had been standing a few days before. It was fine just as long as the British Army took no notice.

The tribesmen carried on popping away for some time. At last their efforts were rewarded: there was a burst of machine-gun fire, and then a couple of mortar shells landed nearby. One of the tribesmen was hit in the chest by a piece of mortar shrapnel, and pandemonium broke out. In no time, the fighting was called off for the day, and we all returned to Akaba.

We drove back to Taizz that afternoon, arriving there at one a.m. the following morning. After a day's sightseeing, we were told that we had been granted a photographic interview with King Ahmed. We would fly to his palace at Sukhne by Yemen airlines: two aeroplanes manned by Swedish crews, strictly for use by the King and his officials only.

As soon as we landed, our party of journalists was surrounded by a band of tough-looking tribesmen, who were the King's bodyguard. We were given refreshments at a small guest house, then escorted to the palace a quarter of a mile away. When we got there, we passed through another group of fierce-looking tribesmen and into a small, dark room. I was the first in, and found myself shaking hands with a bearded gentleman in a black cloak: this was the King of Yemen.

Although it wasn't much of a war as far as wars go, I came back from Aden with some pretty good pictures, especially my series of pictures of King Ahmed.

Getting to photograph the Queen of England on her visit to Paris a month later should not have been quite so difficult: she was not usually surrounded by bunches of fierce-looking tribesmen (unless you count the Household Cavalry), but there were other obstacles: like the tiresome thing called the rota system, which meant that, as a Press photographer, you could only take pictures of her when and where you were told to.

The Queen was due to visit the Paris Opéra, and I wanted to be there to take some pictures, although officially I wasn't supposed to be. The French Press had been cheating like mad, I knew. I decided that it was about time the British Press did a bit of cheating.

I had my usual difficulty getting hold of a dinner jacket. The only one I was able to borrow was several sizes too big, but that suited me: I was able to hide my Leica inside it. As for my brown shoes, I just hoped that no one would look down that far. The next little difficulty was getting into the Opéra. I didn't have a permit, so I waited outside on the pavement until a group of French dignitaries wearing grand plumed hats, who had got out of various cars, came towards the entrance. I sidled up and joined them. I was appearing to get on fairly well with my few words of French, when they all moved to go inside. I moved with them. The police saluted, and everybody bowed (I hoped they didn't notice my shoes), and I was in.

I quickly looked for the best vantage point to get a good picture of the Queen coming in. I went up the magnificent staircase, and found a little box by the side where the occupants made room for me, thinking I was an official Press man. It was a fabulous panorama, and I began to realise that the scene was just too large for a standard lens to take in. The only thing to do was make a massive 'join-up'. Before the Queen actually entered, I started taking shots of the vast entrance hall, working slowly from left to right, and from top to bottom, and making sure that the edges of each shot coincided as far as possible with some feature like the edge of a balcony or a pillar. In all I took about twenty separate shots, and the last shot of all showed the Queen climbing the stairs. After I sent the film back, I telephoned Sheila to explain to her what I had done, so she could tell the make-up man how to piece the jigsaw together. The finished picture was the most ambitious example ever of the technique I had learned from William Davis, and was published on 20 April 1957.

It also turned out to be the last interesting picture I took for *Picture Post*. A month or so later in June, suddenly and without warning, Hulton decided to close the magazine. I suppose we had all realised that the quality of the paper wasn't what it had been, but the details of the declining circulation figures had been kept from us. A letter went up on the notice board, and with a sense of shock the staff sat round and watched the announcement on the television news.

Years later, when I attended an auction to bid for some bound volumes of *Picture Post*, the bidding kept going up and up, and I began to feel a bit out of my depth. As it reached the thousand pounds mark, I decided that I would have to let the set go. I turned round to the people behind me who had out-bidded me and said: 'You've just bought twenty years of my life.'

A voice called out 'Bert Hardy!' It was Hulton's daughter, whose husband had just won the bidding. But what I had said was true. Although the news of the closure took a bit of time to sink in, the best part of my life as a photographer had come to an end with the death of the magazine which had helped me to become the type of photographer I am.

Overleaf: The biggest join-up ever done. No lens could take in this scene without distortion. You can see that the guards on the right have not yet drawn their swords, as they were pictured before the Queen entered. The technique is explained on p. 188, in the technical notes.

In the kitchen of the Ritz Hotel in Paris, where I accidentally broke one of these icing ships.

Chorus Girl

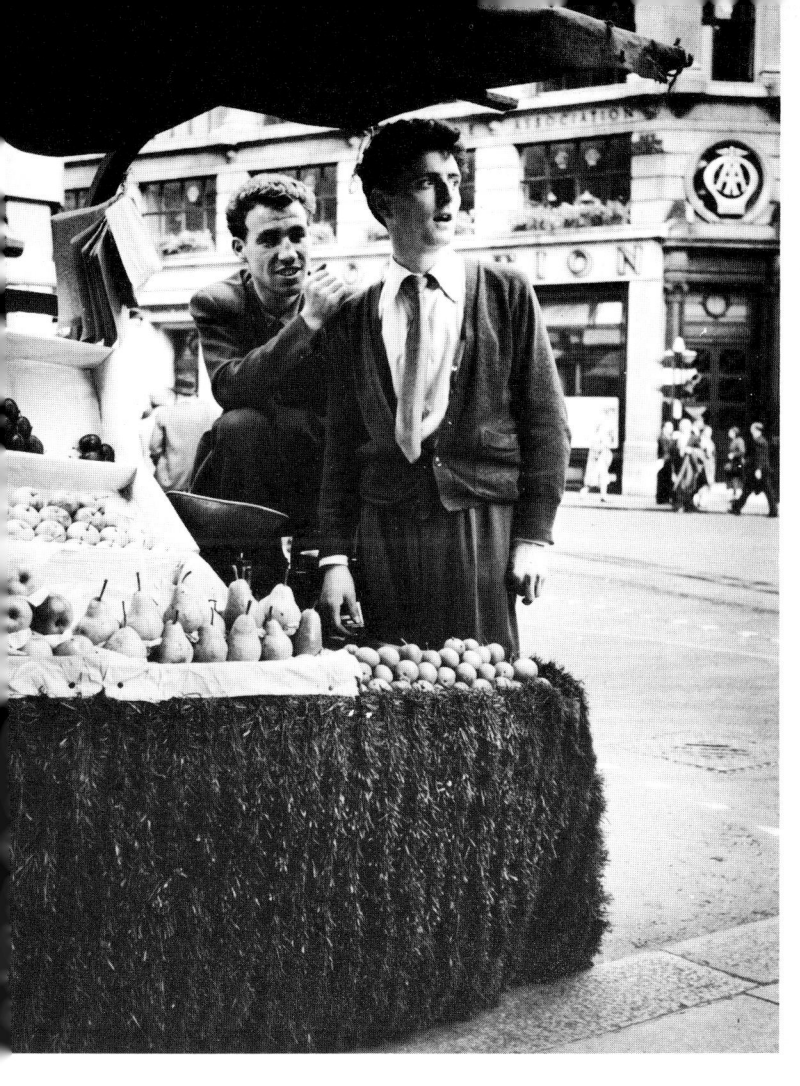

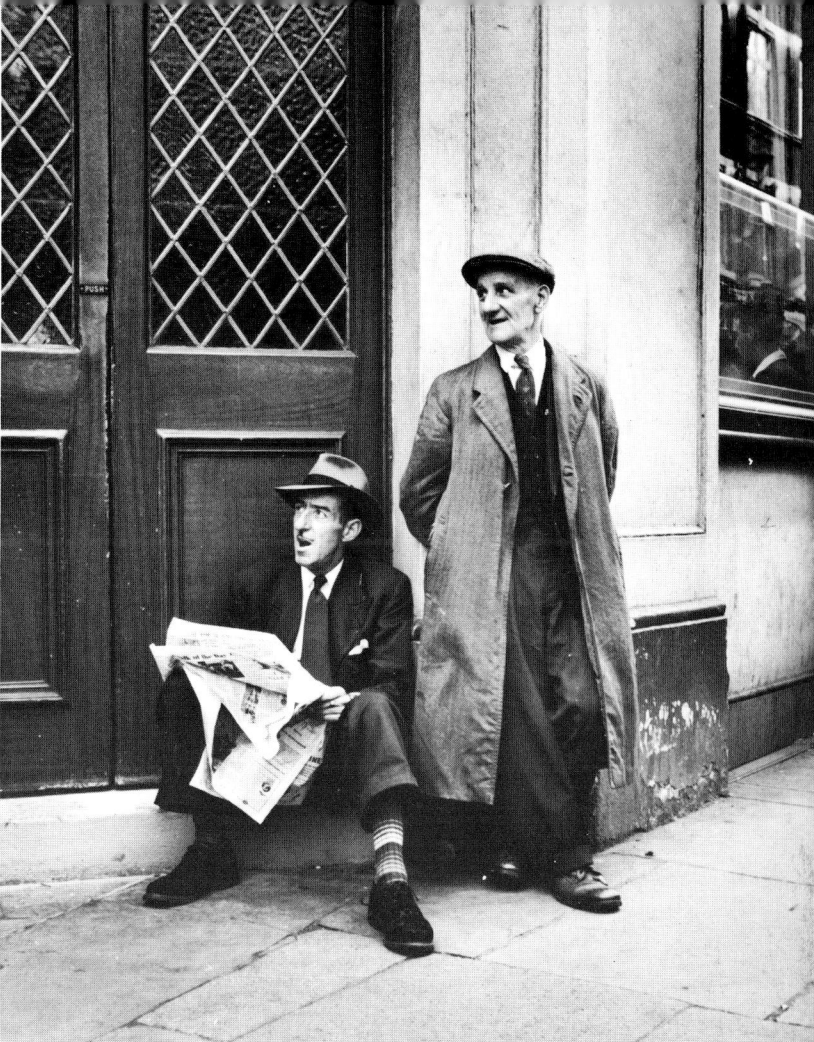

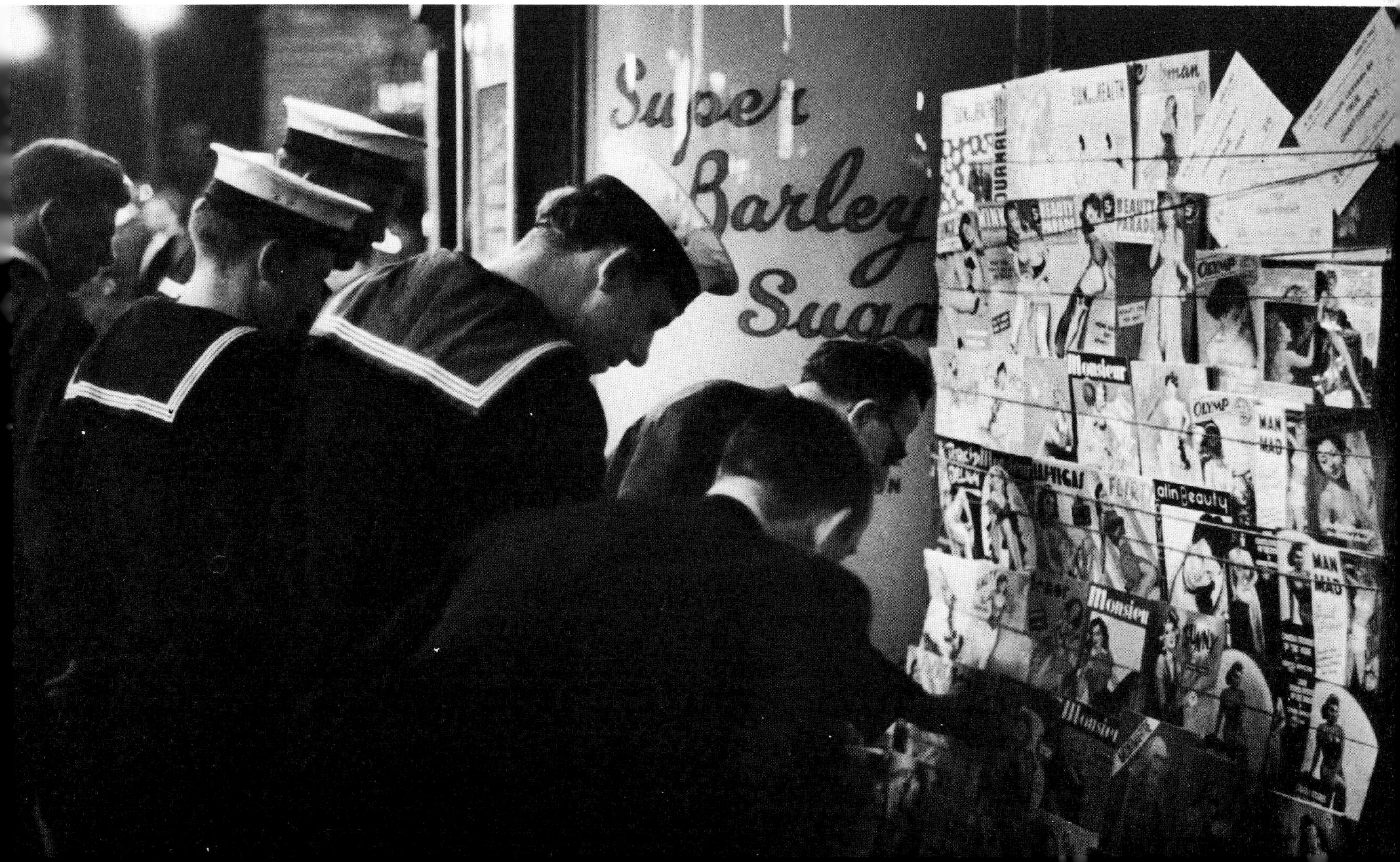
Barley
BEAUTY PARADE
Monsieur
OLYMP
MAN MAD

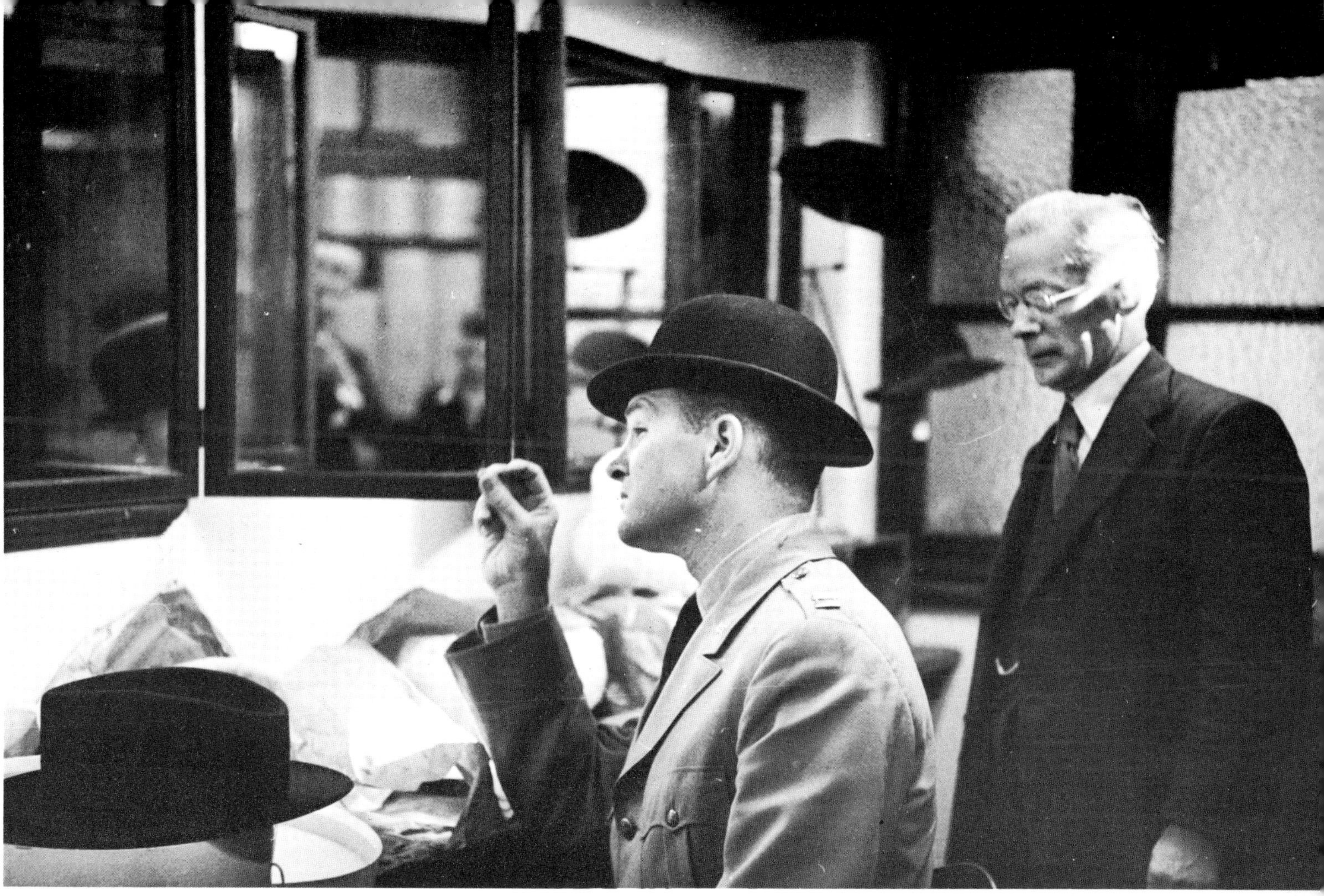

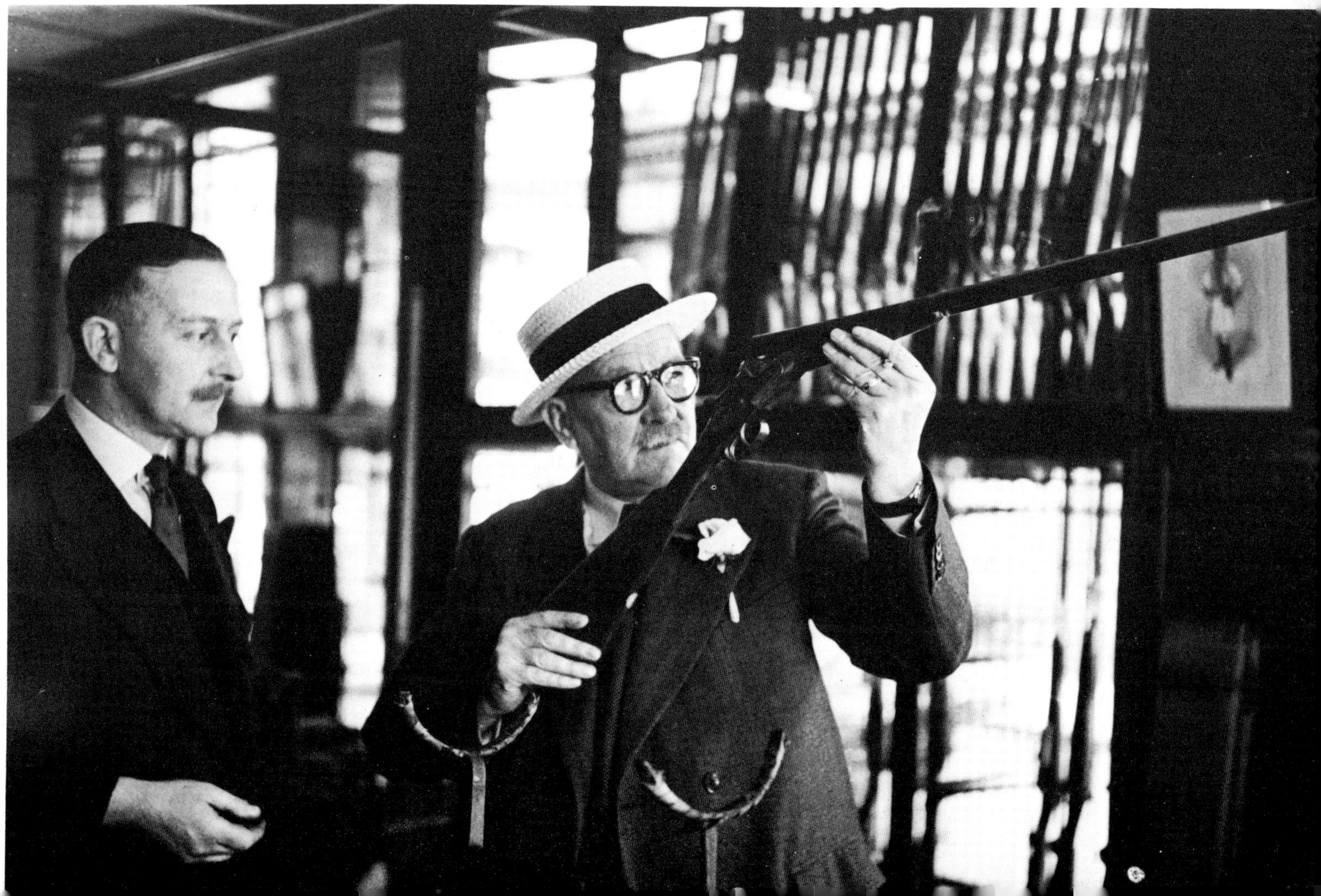

12: Advertising and Farming

Most of the staff of *Picture Post* were sacked. But as a good-will gesture Lady Hulton told me that I could stay on. I had already done a bit of work for the other magazine started by Stephan Lorant, *Lilliput*; now I could also do odd pictures for all the other magazines, from *Farmers' Weekly* to *Housewife*, including the children's magazines, *Eagle*, *Girl* and *Robin*.

I would have liked to have left, but I needed my salary. I had to make payments to my ex-wife, as well as keep up the payments for my new house, and I simply could not afford to take any risks. The editor of *Lilliput* was now none other than Bill Richardson, the journalist with whom I had been to the Yemen. One of his first actions on being appointed was to order himself a large, impressive-looking glass-topped desk. I still didn't like him, but there wasn't much I could do about it if I wanted to keep working.

This state of limbo continued for two years. I hardly took any interesting photographs, just pictures of farmers' wives, and boys' hobbies. On one occasion I had to go and take pictures of John Dankworth and Cleo Laine at home for *Housewife* magazine. I arrived at their flat over a shop in the Edgware Road on a Sunday afternoon to find them and their guests resting after what must have been an extremely good lunch. The place was not looking its best. I knew that the readers of *Housewife* would not appreciate seeing it like this, but at the same time I couldn't really ask them to clear it up. Finally I compromised by taking them up onto the roof and photographing them there.

At this time I was occasionally working for *Esso Magazine*, an in-house magazine run by the petrol company. I also did some work for Bowaters. Then I began to make contacts in advertising, and began a series for Lucozade. For one of the pictures I wanted to show a tired-looking girl sitting by a fire drinking Lucozade, but I couldn't seem to find the right model. In the end I had to use the pictures of Katherine Whitehorn I had taken for the *Picture Post* story 'Loneliness in London', and this proved to be a success.

In June 1959, Hulton Press was taken over by Odhams, and my salary came to the attention of the managing director. Odhams, he said, was run by its accountants. He was very nice about it, but what he was saying was that I would have to go. I could choose my time, but I would have to go. I had been thinking of starting up on my own, but never quite had the guts to do it. This now decided things for me.

By now I had built up a number of contacts in advertising, and had the feeling that I could make a go of it, so I wasn't too worried. I could still carry on doing freelance work for Odhams, but just wouldn't receive a fixed salary. As a condition of leaving I negotiated that I should receive a year's salary plus the continued use of office space at Hulton House until I managed to find somewhere for myself. As I got more and more busy with advertising work, I handed over a lot of my freelance work for Odhams to my younger son Terry, who was now working for me. The funny thing was that, while I was a permanent employee I had been earning £3,000 a year; in the first year as a freelance, our work for Odhams

alone brought us in £4,000.

My older son, Michael, had started working in the darkrooms of *Picture Post* with the intention of becoming a photographer on the magazine. However, National Service intervened, and by the time he came out of the army, *Picture Post* had packed up. He got a job instead working as the Paris photographer for the *Daily Express*.

Advertising jobs began to flood in; when I arrived on the scene advertising photography tended to be rather formal. I introduced the 35mm camera and the inventive story-telling approach which had been so popular in *Picture Post*, to give a fresher, more candid look.

One of my most successful advertising campaigns was the famous 'You're Never Alone With a Strand' series for Strand cigarettes. Even now people remember the slogan and the pictures, though not the cigarettes.

Bruce Hobbs the art director, and John May, the copywriter at Benson's Advertising Agency had only a vague idea of what they wanted when we met them with a male and a female model, at seven o'clock one October night. It had been raining, and they had in mind a drizzly sort of shot, with street lights reflected in the wet cobblestones. We had a drink, then set out for the Tower Bridge area, where we started taking pictures around the warehouses.

As the evening wore on, we gradually worked our way westwards. By now I was taking some pictures of the models in an alleyway off St Martin's Lane, when suddenly I realised what was wrong: the woman looked like a pick-up, so I suggested we got rid of her. The scene looked much more dramatic and effective with the man on his own.

From then on it was plain sailing. At about midnight, we were on the Albert Bridge, with some final shots of the model leaning against the parapet. Terry was holding a strong torch to get just enough light on the man's face to look like lamplight without losing by contrast the streetlights in the background, many of which were now being turned off. We ended up at about six o'clock at a coffee stall in Sloane Square just as it was getting light. From that night's work we got eight national Press advertisements, for which I was paid 80 guineas each, and two 48-sheet posters, for which I was paid 250 guineas each. It was a very good night's work, and as a result I was asked to shoot the whole campaign, which lasted over a year.

But not all advertising work was so straightforward. At the end of the same year (1959), I was hired by Nestlés to go with a party of schoolchildren to Iceland. The idea was that they were visiting Father Christmas (I always thought he lived in Greenland). The pictures I took would not be used as advertisements, but would be sent back to the daily Press to be used as news photographs, which would just happen to mention that the whole trip was sponsored by Nestlés.

It came as a bit of a shock to us all, I think, when we found out that there were only three or four hours of daylight at that time of year in Iceland. We spent most of our time cooped up in a hotel trying to make the children behave

The Strand picture above was the first 35mm photograph to be made into a 48-sheet poster. It became very well known, and was imitated by 'Monsewer' Eddie Gray of the Crazy Gang (left).

themselves. The nanny who had been brought along to look after the children was very friendly with the publicity man, so I often ended up looking after the children. And anyway no one in England was interested in the photographs we were sending back after the first few.

I carried on using my office space at Hulton House for as long as possible. In April 1960 I was asked by an agency to do some work for Heineken beer. They asked me to hire a couple of models for the job, and then sent over two art directors from Holland to approve my choice. I had a desk on the floor where a Mrs Starke supervised a typing-pool of girls who were answering readers' letters. When I knew the Heineken men were coming, I arranged with *Lilliput's* make-up man, Henry Fuller, to use his office beside the typing-pool. The art directors looked extremely impressed throughout my interview with them. It was only afterwards that it occurred to me that they had looked at the row of offices, and Henry Fuller's office, and the pool of typists typing away, and assumed that they were all part of a huge Bert Hardy organisation.

For the Heineken job I had to travel all round Holland with two models and a silly little stuffed bird. This was because for some odd reason each picture had to show a girl and a man with a bird perched on his shoulder.

For KLM, the Dutch airline, I flew across the Atlantic in a DC8, one of the very earliest jet airliners, taking on average a picture a minute throughout the whole flight. It turned out to be a very successful campaign, and was used worldwide, both in the Press and as small exhibitions in all the KLM offices. At this time I was working hard, doing three or four times as much work as the average advertising photographer, and still travelling a lot. I didn't mind too much: I wanted the money, and at the beginning I was still allowed to use my own ideas.

A job for BP simply specified that they wanted something different (in colour) for a full-sized poster. I started to think of using movement, as I had done in some of my work for *Picture Post*.

I wanted to show a road overhung with branches with the sun shining through them, as it would appear from a car travelling at speed. It was quite difficult to find the right place, but eventually we discovered it on the borders of Kent and Surrey near Westerham. (I had no idea that one day I would be living just down the road.) I sat in the boot of my car with my Rolleiflex, and Terry drove. I soon found that it was a good idea to wear a wet handkerchief round my mouth and nose because the exhaust fumes were being sucked up straight into my face. Terry drove along the road until he saw a bit where there were good overhanging branches and plenty of potholes, then he yelled out of the window and accelerated. I was working at a slow shutter speed of about a tenth of a second, and the bumping of the potholes gave that extra bit of movement I wanted which made the pictures a success.

By July 1960, the end of my first full year in advertising, I

A blur of speed for BP.

had done a great deal of work. To the utter surprise of me and my accountant, I had earned about twenty-five thousand guineas. When I realised this, I decided to get myself something I had always wanted, and the next day I telephoned a Mercedes dealer and ordered my very own Mercedes 205. I also bought Sheila a blue Carmen Ghia, a sporty version of a Volkswagen.

Advertising was beginning to take over our lives. Even our house at Bickley had become a studio. I had always liked to take pictures of people and places that really existed, rather than using models and studios. Now whenever we had to do an advertisement for Kelloggs, or Lucozade, or Oxo, we would run through the list of our neighbours and simply select who we thought most looked the part. We even used the children: they loved it, and especially the two pounds per hour modelling fee they were given (the standard fee at the time). On one occasion, when I had been trying out an idea with them for which I hadn't actually got paid, I told them that I would pay them when I did the actual job. Their response was instant: they organised a strike. I collapsed under their pressure. From then on, trial runs would be paid at half the full rate.

We probably livened up the neighbourhood quite a bit. When I did an advertisement for Nivea Cream, I decided to disguise my back garden as a swimming pool. Of course there was no pool and no water, but that didn't matter. My brother Sid got hold of a thick plank of wood and tacked a piece of rope round the edge so that it looked like a diving board, and we set that up. Then I got hold of half a dozen beautiful models and got them to drape themselves around the place in the skimpiest possible bathing costumes. So long as I took pictures against the sky, no one need ever know that the nearest swimming pool was several miles away.

We were doing quite well until the girls began to complain: the house was on a corner, and anyone who walked round it could see into the back garden. An old man had

"A Freshly cooked meal at 6 a.m.!"

At 6 a.m. this morning, for the first time since I went on shift work, I came home and sat down to a piping hot meal. Yet my wife was still asleep.

The new, fully-automatic electric cooker was only installed last Saturday. Mind you, I had to talk my wife into getting it — she thought she'd never be able to understand those dials.

I told her it was as simple as an alarm clock. Just set it to the time the meal is wanted and Bob's your uncle. She knows how long everything takes to cook, so she didn't have any trouble working out when it was to *start* cooking.

And now, instead of my having to heat up something left over from the family supper, I get a good meal, all freshly cooked. *Perhaps you don't want hot meals at 6 a.m. but you can get the breakfast*

ready overnight and find it ready for you at 8 a.m. Or you can go out for a day's shopping knowing that your dinner will be freshly cooked and waiting for you on your return. Expensive to buy? Not at all — easy terms are really easy.

Go to your Electricity Service Centre to choose your new cooker; they are all tested and approved and there is a good selection for you to see. They will also tell you about easy terms.

Get up to date 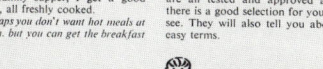 go electric!

Issued by the Electrical Development Association   9618-2

We can't promise you a smile that will chase the clouds away...

...**but we can promise you this:** for really sensible care of your teeth—and your children's—WISDOM is the wisest toothbrush you can buy.

Wisdom is the only toothbrush with the curve in the handle that lets the head reach every tooth correctly (and between the teeth too!) right back to your wisdom teeth. That's how Wisdom keeps your teeth so healthy, your mouth so fresh.

With natural bristle 2 6, Flextron tufts 2 3, nylon 1 8. All types come in extra-hard, hard or medium textures, with a variety of brightly coloured handles.

BRUSH UP YOUR SMILE WITH WISDOM

THE CORRECT-SHAPE TOOTHBRUSH   *Wisdom*

ADDIS LIMITED BRUSHWORKS HERTFORD

My brother Sid opens a bogus gate while the milk float draws up. I used friends and neighbours as well as my family to model for me, and the Wisdom tooth lady had been in charge of the correspondence department at *Picture Post*. She's as happy and friendly as she looks.

spent the last half-hour standing on the pavement with his tongue hanging out. They refused to carry on until I went and asked him if he would mind moving on. This he did, and we got back to work. Later we noticed where he had gone: he had moved round the corner, where he was pressed up to the fence with his eye glued to a knot-hole.

Sid often used to help me in various ways. Occasionally he even used to model for me. In one advertisement I did for the Electricity Council, he was supposed to be a night worker, coming home in the early hours of the morning to a hot dinner which, thanks to an electric timer, was ready and waiting for him in his electric oven.

I knew the type of light I wanted: dawn breaking, with the streetlights still on. We found the right sort of street near Sid's house in Brockley. I wanted the night worker to be coming through his front gate, with a view of the street behind him, as if his house was at the end of a cul-de-sac. To get exactly the right shot, Sid had to build a false fence with a wooden gate. We painted it green, and set it up right across the road. Everything worked fine: just when the light was how I wanted it, the milkman came along in his float, and added an extra bit of realism to the picture. But then along came a real night worker on his bike, cycling home. As he slowed up, I opened the gate of the little fence and the man pedalled straight through, grinning all over his face.

In June 1961 the German magazine *Stern* selected the top photographer and journalist from several different coun-

tries, and gave them as long as they wanted to do the story of their choice on a German subject. I was chosen as the British photographer, and Malcolm Muggeridge as the British journalist.

Because of the pressure of my other work, I was only able to set aside a week for the job. We were given a chauffeur-driven car, and decided to drive down the full length of Germany from north to south to see what we could find for a general story on the country.

Early on our journey, we stopped off at Belsen, where I told Malcolm Muggeridge the story of the time I threw a plate of food at the face of a German guard. All the great open mass graves I had seen had been marked by huge rectangular monuments like giant slabs, six feet high. As we stood looking at them, I noticed that Muggeridge was weeping, so I left him alone for a while.

One Sunday morning I was walking around Munich, looking for possible pictures. I saw a small bakers with the windows crammed with delicious cream cakes. There were a lot of people out in their Sunday best, staring in cake shop windows. I asked permission in one shop, and was allowed to stand inside behind the counter and take pictures out of the window. On cue, along came a smartly dressed family – all rather on the fat side – who started staring in at the cakes. The look on their faces with their mouths watering told the whole story.

I took a lot of pictures in that week – if anything I had actually started to work faster since I had gone into advertising. One of the other photographers who had been selected took a couple of months over the job, and got three or four pages in one edition for his pains. My pictures were spread over two editions.

In 1962, Odhams finally decided that I couldn't use their offices any more. I didn't have long to find somewhere else, and there was nowhere that exactly suited my needs until Sid noticed a little building up for sale in Burrows Mews, off Blackfriars Road. It was opposite a bomb-site which had once been a school where, as a boy, I had listened to the saucy stories of the instructor who was supposed to be teaching us all about petrol engines; and it was only a few hundred yards up the road from Friar Street and the Priory Buildings.

Sid did the conversion work in record time. Within three or four weeks I had a new office with a proper developing and printing laboratory downstairs. I now managed to persuade Gerry Grove, who had worked for Hulton's and Odhams for years, and was without a doubt the best printer in London, to join me. The partnership of Grove Hardy was set up.

I continued my advertising work, but it was never as enjoyable as my work for *Picture Post*. I would almost say it was done purely for money. When I was driving off in the morning to a particular location, I would just be thinking that, in a certain number of hours, I would be coming back along the same road, having finished the job. Advertising meant hard work and money, but it never meant anything more than that to me, although I was touched to learn that a picture of Lewes High Street I took for BP had been requested by a prisoner in Lewes Jail, to put up on his cell wall.

When I first took the plunge into advertising, I said to Sheila that I reckoned I would last about five years. What I meant was that after that, the novelty of what I was doing would go out of fashion, and I would be left high and dry. But, at the same time, I was determined that I would never go touting for trade. As soon as commissions stopped coming to me, it would be time to pack up.

By 1964, the work started slowing down as I had felt it would do. I was tired and fed up with advertising. There was never any sense, as there had been at *Picture Post*, that you could actually do any good with your pictures. Because we used The Priory, our Bromley house, as a studio, it was impossible to get away from work even at home. For the past two years Sheila and I had been looking for a country cottage where we could escape to and relax, without finding what we wanted. Then Sheila read an advertisement in the Sunday papers for a small farm near where I had done the BP advertisement a few years earlier. It seemed like a ridiculous idea: after all I knew next to nothing about farming, but I was tempted. We viewed the farm on 21 February 1964. There was a lot of work to do on it, and it would be a big commitment. Four days later, we signed the agreement to buy it. To celebrate, we drove down to visit Mr Phipps, the owner, with a big bottle of champagne. The next Sunday I was immediately thrown into farming the hard way: while Mr Phipps sat on the terrace and sipped, I tried my hand at chain harrowing. It was the first time I had driven a tractor since the war, when I was doing a story on Land Girls for *Picture Post*, and showed off by driving it up near-vertical banks.

We moved in at the end of April. We had to learn everything about farming from scratch. Our bible was *Primrose McConnell's Agricultural Notebook*. There were pigs which had to be weighed every week (until they reached the ideal weight for sausages), and half a dozen calves which broke out occasionally through the rotting fences. Sheila had to learn how to use the milking machine, though she eventually found that she preferred to milk the cows by hand. We also had sheep and horses, and meadows to look after.

It was back to the land with a vengeance, so I did the only sensible thing in the circumstances: I took off with Lionel Birch on the *Queen Elizabeth* to do a promotional book on the great liner for Cunard. Sheila, the farmer's wife, was left with only Primrose McConnell to aid her.

It was an enjoyable trip. When we reached New York, Lionel stayed on and joined his wife at the World Fair.

On my return trip, when we berthed at Southampton, most of the passengers were going on to Cherbourg, so I joined a party given by the purser and some of the ship's officers. Sheila was waiting on the quayside in the Mercedes to take me home, but I didn't want to go for the time being. We smuggled her on board, and carried on with the party.

At last, in the early hours of the morning, the party broke up. An angry customs man, who had been waiting half the night for me to disembark, irritably waved me through while Sheila was sneaked off the ship. At last he could go home to bed. Sheila and I got into the Mercedes, and we began to drive home.

After we had got hopelessly lost a couple of times and our speed had dropped to about five m.p.h., I handed the driving over to Sheila. We arrived back at the farm just as it was dawn. It was a beautiful morning and I felt restless, ready to start my new life as a farmer. Instead of going in to bed, we climbed the haystack. It was very ticklish, but of all the uncomfortable places I have slept, that was the best.

I was back home.

On the Farm   Now I have become a farmer, and live in beautiful countryside, where I like to ride. The picture overleaf, taken in 1978, shows my two grand-daughters, Rachel and Anna, in the lane leading to my house. Sometimes when I am in the mood. I get my camera out, still preferring to take black-and-white pictures. It is something that I have seldom found boring, and it has never seemed difficult or unnatural to me. Everywhere I look, and most of the time I look, I see photographs.

Technical Notes

My first camera was an old quarter-plate job which I bought from a pawn shop in about 1927 for ten shillings. This served me well until I made the great leap into 35mm photography, which was the move that affected my whole career. Here is a list of my other cameras:

LEICA: old and black, with a fixed 50mm lens of f3.5. I still think that Leicas are unbeatable for quick and quiet work.

LEICA: another second-hand purchase, in about 1930. This also had a 50mm lens.

ROLLEIFLEX: this was a fine 2¼-square camera, again with a standard length lens. I bought it in about 1938 and used it for many years.

PEELING AND VAN NECK: a large Press camera, 9 × 12cm.

CONTAX: another 35mm camera, which I used with a 50mm Sonnar lens of f1.4. You can see the camera below, with me looking like a proper newsman, with a tough expression and turned-up collar!

LEICA: two early model M3 cameras. I fitted a superior Japanese f1.5 lens to one, and a 35mm wide-angle of f3.5 to the other. I also used a 135mm portrait lens of f4.

MAMIYAFLEX: two 2¼-square cameras with a range of (twin) lenses.

HASSELBLAD: I used two early models (of around 1960) in my advertising days, with a full range of lenses.

I have left out two cameras worthy of particular mention: a Box Brownie, which took the pictures on page 154–5 to answer the challenge for *Picture Post*, and a real horror, the Super Ikonta. This silly camera, which you can see in the picture of me in my flying jacket, was slow, awkward, heavy and annoying. I can only think that it was adopted by the army in order to make life difficult for us.

You shouldn't, of course, expect miracles from any camera. When I was faced with the grand scene for the 1957 visit of the Queen to the Paris Opera, I knew that I could only do justice to the occasion by including the whole view, and no lens could do that. I knew that *Picture Post* had joined two or even three shots together before, so I started shooting in a sweep, anti-clockwise, aiming to keep the pictures on a level. I don't know how many I took in all, but they used fifteen in the manner shown for a spectacular result. You can see what it looks like large-scale on pages 172–3.

Lighting is important to any photographer. Beginners are often taught to keep the light coming from behind ('stand with the sun over your left shoulder'), but many of my favourite shots use backlighting. A good trick is to get something to provide a light background, such as the dust I got the man and his donkey to kick up for the picture on page 150. In the photograph shown here, the water spray caught the backlighting of the streetlamps (with a little help from my flash unit) to make a nice picture. It was taken on my Contax.

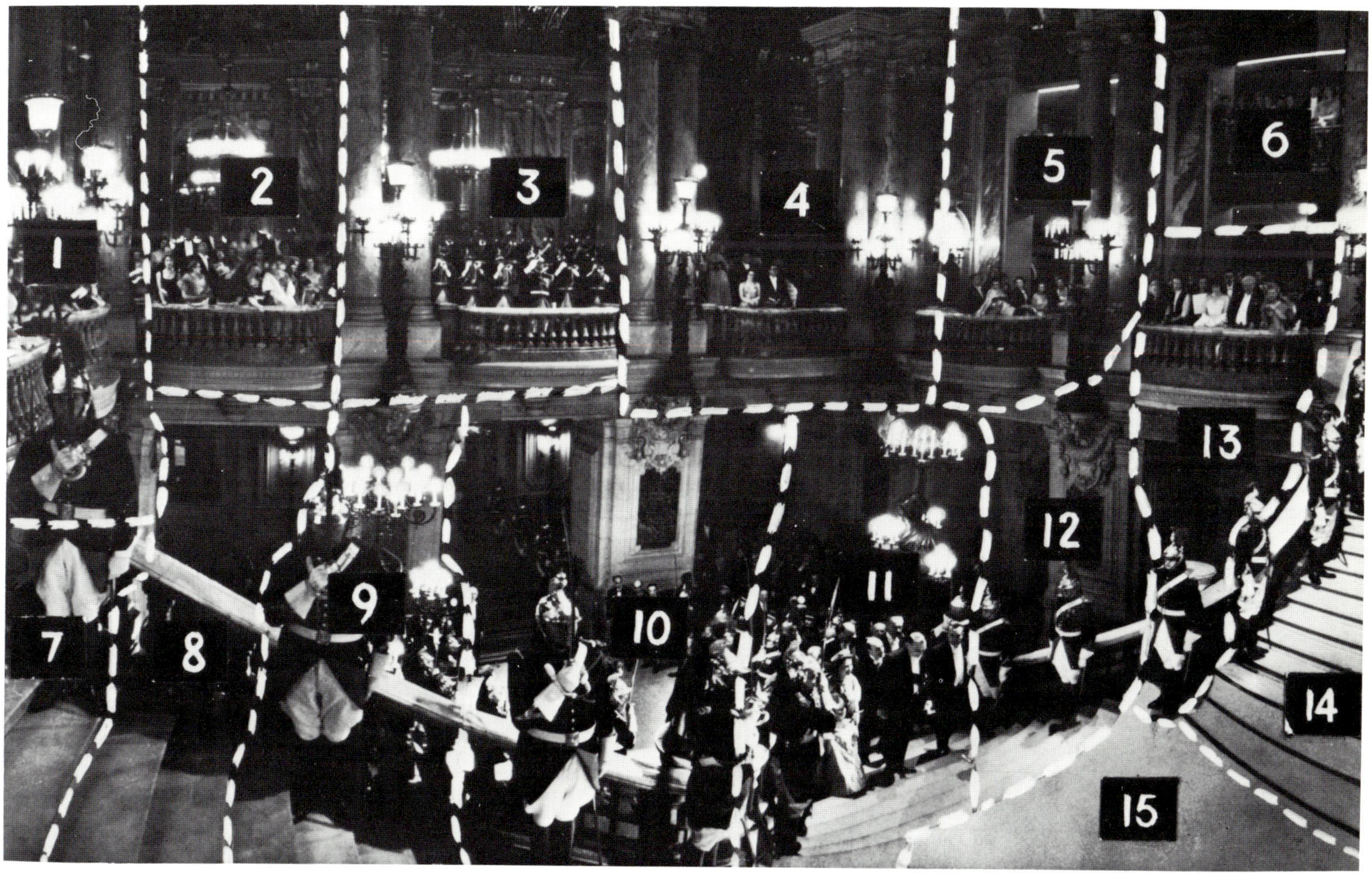
1
2
3
4
5
6
7
8
9
10
11
12
13
14
15

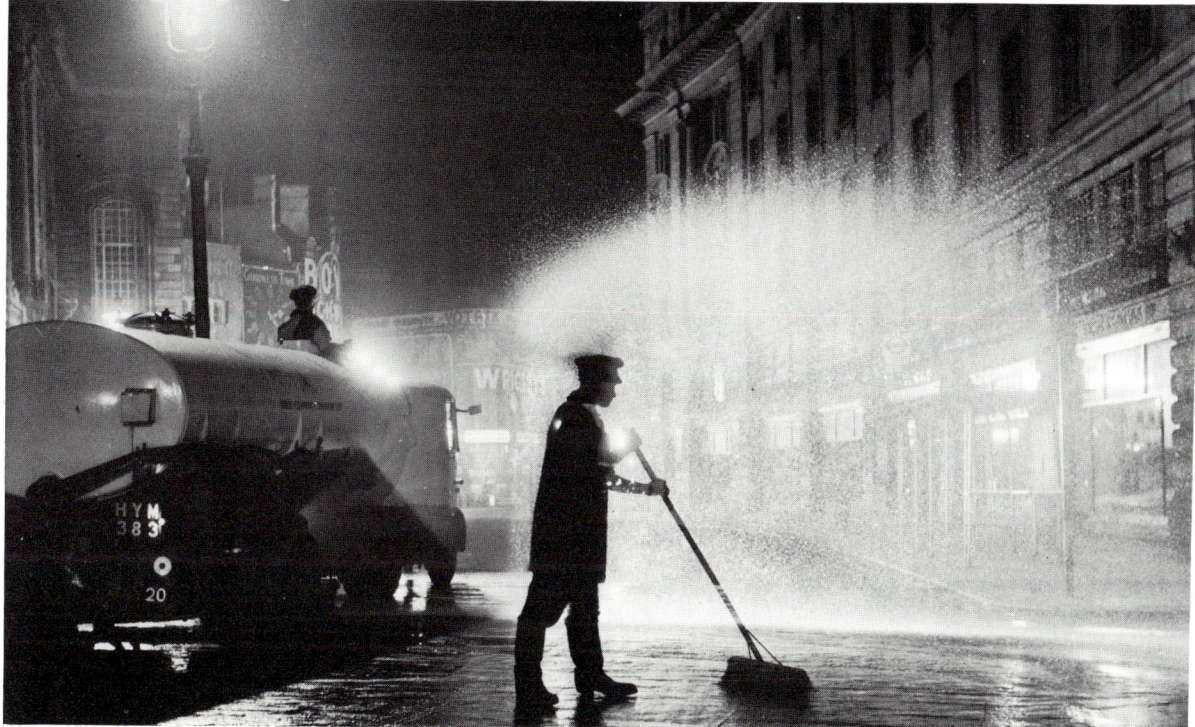

Index

Numbers in italics refer to illustrations